FRESH

FROM THE

FARM

A YEAR OF RECIPES AND STORIES

FARM
STAND →
TOMATOES
SMALL EGGS
PEPPERS

FRESH
FROM THE FARM

FARM

A YEAR OF RECIPES AND STORIES

SUSIE MIDDLETON

The Taunton Press

For Mom, Dad, and Ellie—my family of great cooks and gardeners

The Taunton Press
Inspiration for hands-on living®

The Taunton Press, Inc., 63 South Main Street, PO Box 5506,
Newtown, CT 06470-5506
e-mail: tp@taunton.com

Editor: Carolyn Mandarano
Copy editor: Li Agen
Indexer: Heidi Blough
Art Director: Alison Wilkes
Cover design: Stacy Wakefield
Interior design & layout: Stacy Wakefield
Photo Editor: Erin Giunta
Illustrator: Martha Garstang Hill
Photographers: © Alexandra Grablewski: p. ii, vi (top left), 2, 4 (top left, bottom center), 5 (bottom right), 7, 9, 12, 15 (bottom left, top right, bottom right), 18, 20, 24, 27, 28 (top left, right), 29 (top left), 31, 34, 37, 40, 43, 44, 46, 51, 54, 58, 59, 61, 62 (top right), 67, 68, 70, 71, 72, 73, 77, 78, 79 (top right, bottom right), 85, 86 (top right, bottom left), 88, 92, 95, 96, 101, 102, 103, 106, 107, 111 (top left, top right, bottom right), 113, 114, 117, 118, 120, 122, 123, 126 (right), 129, 133, 136, 138, 141, 143, 146, 149 (top left, bottom right), 153, 156, 157, 161, 163, 164, 165, 168, 172 (top left), 175, 177, 181 (left), 182, 188, 193, 196, 199, 202, 203, 207, 208, 212, 214 (left), 217, 219, 222, 225, 231 (bottom right), 232; © Susie Middleton: p. vi (bottom left, top right, bottom right), 4 (bottom left), 5 (top right), 6, 8, 10, 15 (top left), 17, 21, 23, 25, 26, 28 (bottom left), 30, 32, 33, 35, 38, 39, 45, 48, 49, 52, 53, 56, 60, 62 (top left, bottom left, bottom right), 64, 65, 66 (top left, bottom left, bottom center), 74, 75, 79 (left), 80, 82, 83, 86 (top left, bottom right), 90, 91, 97, 98, 99, 104, 108, 110, 111 (bottom left), 124, 126 (top left, bottom left), 128, 130, 131, 132, 135, 137, 140, 142, 145, 147, 149 (top right, bottom left), 150, 154, 158, 160, 166, 167, 169, 170, 171, 172 (top right, bottom left, bottom right), 174, 176, 178, 179, 180, 181 (top right, bottom right), 185, 186, 187, 189, 192, 195, 200, 205, 210, 214 (top right, bottom right), 215, 216, 220, 221, 224, 227, 229, 231 (top, bottom left), 233, 234, 235, 237, 238; Roy Riley: p. 190
Food Stylist: Mark Pederson
Prop Stylist: Paige Hicks
Cover Photographer: Alexandra Grablewski

The following names/manufacturers appearing in *Fresh from the Farm* are trademarks: Applegate®, Baker's Joy®, Barilla®, Bell & Evans®, Burpee®, Fage®, Total Garden-opoly™, Goya®, Nabisco® FAMOUS™ Chocolate Wafers, Old Bay®, Pepperidge Farm®, Pez®, Pyrex®, Schwinn®, Starbucks®, Tabasco®

Library of Congress Cataloging-in-Publication Data

Middleton, Susie.
  Fresh from the farm : a year of recipes and stories / Susie Middleton ; photographer, Alexandra Grablewski.
    pages cm
  ISBN 978-1-60085-904-5 (hardback)
1. Seasonal cooking. 2. Farm life. 3. Middleton, Suzie--Homes and haunts. I. Title.
  TX714.M533 2014
  641.5'64--dc23
                        2013036727

Printed in the United States of America
10 9 8 7 6 5 4 3 2 1

ACKNOWLEDGMENTS

IT'S ONE THING TO DO what you love cooking, growing, writing, photographing—and quite another thing to have people you admire and respect want to turn what you've created into a book. This so totally rocks my world that I gladly bear the daily burden of gratitude to the folks responsible for what you hold in your hands—chiefly my agent, Sarah Jane Freymann, and my editor at The Taunton Press, Carolyn Mandarano. Together these two embraced my proposal and envisioned something truly exciting. Carolyn took it from there, guiding the project with a sure hand and a strong sense of what was right for this book. I can't thank her enough for her intuition and confidence.

My admiration and thanks go far and wide to each of the talented people who participated in creating *Fresh from the Farm,* starting with my veteran recipe testers and dear friends Jessica Bard and Eliza Peter, who cross-tested every single recipe, from spring to fall, pesto to pizzette.

To photographer Alexandra Grablewski, I owe many, many thanks, not just for traveling out to the Vineyard on a stormy ferry ride to photograph the farm, but also for her genuinely gorgeous food photos that grace these pages. To food stylist Mark Pederson and assistant Tracy Keshani, heaps of gratitude for making my food look beautiful and natural. And to Paige Hicks for awesome props.

To the Taunton design team, led by Art Director Alison Wilkes, thank you for an amazing job of artfully weaving together the elements of this book to make our story come alive. Kudos to designer Stacy Wakefield for her thoughtful work and to Erin Giunta and Sandy Mahlstedt for organizing and editing the photos.

A quick thank you to all my friends and colleagues at *Fine Cooking* magazine and The Taunton Press, especially Maria Taylor for her enduring support. And a special thanks to the Taunton marketing folks, Jay Annis, Audrey Locorotondo, Missy Robinson, and Janel Noblin, for their enthusiastic support of *Fresh from the Farm.* To the best copy editor in the world, Li Agen, I couldn't do a book without you.

Back here at home, the complete list of incredibly supportive friends and farm stand customers (many of them one in the same) is too long to include here. But a special thanks must go to Tom Hickie, Drusilla Hickie, Joannie Jenkinson, Judy Fraser-Pearce, Mary Wirtz, Sarah Saltonstall, M. J. Delekta, Cathy Walthers, Doug Smith, Katherine Long, Kay Goldstein, Bob and Irene Hungerford, Scott Bliss, Angela Beasley Dion, Susan Davy, Don McKillop, Ronnie and Heidi Schultz, and the Athearn family of Morning Glory Farm.

And to our families—Peg and Bob Riley, Kelly Crocker (for sharing Libby so selflessly), Bob and Pauletta Evans, and Eleanor Evans—thank you for all your love and support. And for not calling us crazy.

Fresh from the Farm may bear my byline, but it is as much Roy's and Libby's as it is mine. We share a life second to none, and for that we will always be grateful.

← FARM STAND

TOMATOES
CARROTS
BEANS BEETS
EGGS
BUTTERNUT
SQUASH
FLOWERS
PEPPERS

INTRODUCTION

ONE DAY YOU WAKE up and your fantasy has become reality, and you are more surprised than anyone at what you've managed to pull off. This is how it happened to me: I longed for a simpler life, I quit my big job and my fancy suburb, moved to a rural island, became a freelance writer, sold my high heels and frilly skirts at a consignment shop, and bought a pair of work boots.

I planted a teeny little garden. Then a bigger one. I met a carpenter, fell in love, moved into a creaky old farmhouse on the edge of an endless hay field, and planted an even bigger garden.

Then the carpenter built me a little farm stand from salvaged wood. We stuck it at the end of the dirt driveway and neighbors and friends and visitors came shopping for lovely lettuce and skinny string beans and glossy cherry tomatoes from our market garden. We counted up the quarters and dollar bills, and one day, we broke even—and the season was still high. Oh joy!

And we cooked from our garden every day. We grilled Fairy Tale eggplants and we stir-fried Shuko Pac Choi with lime basil and we baked Red Gold potato gratins with our own Big Daddy onions. We made lobster rolls with fresh peas and minestrone with our carrots and turnips and fennel. We ate well. We were happy. (Still are!)

Then we got some baby chicks and watched them grow rosy red combs and spangly feathers and dance in the grass with squirmy bugs. We fell in love with the Ladies even before they started laying those miracles—eggs warm as dinner buns and smooth as marble, eggs so eggy flavored they taste like Sunday morning itself.

So we got a few more hens. And then a few more (more than a few actually). And built more coops. Doubled the size of the garden, put up a hoop house, grew lettuce all winter, and planted blueberry bushes. Talked our way into four more acres of farm land out back and gave ourselves a real name: Green Island Farm.

That's the short story of how the little farm and the farm stand came to be. The whole story features wild raspberries and wild turkeys, a farm dog and a bunny, hurricanes and blizzards, a rope swing and a fish pond—and one very special little girl. But the vegetables—how we shaped our lives around growing and harvesting them and how we honored them in the kitchen—are the real stars. Here are their stories—and ours.

Eggs in Cooler

LATE SPRING AND EARLY SUMMER

(AKA "WE BRAKE FOR SALAD GREENS")

NERVOUS AS HELL I WAS, that Memorial Day weekend, 2011. We'd moved into the farmhouse in September, planned the garden over the winter, and started turning the soil over in March. Roy set up his table saw in the backyard, made a quick sketch, and pretty soon we had a handsome little farm stand, fashioned from salvaged fir and roofed with old clapboards. Now here it was May 27 and we had the audacity to put the stand out at the end of the driveway.

I had maybe three bunches of cheery Cherry Belle radishes in a pink Pyrex® bowl of ice water, six or eight bags of spring greens—arugula, mustard, and lettuce mix—in a cooler, and four or five pickle jars filled with bunches of herbs up on the shelf. Oh, and ›

› a quartet of lovely little Tom Thumb Bibb lettuces.

We filled out the stand with potted geraniums, two wooden bluebird boxes Roy had made, and a couple of copies of my cookbooks. I hung up a clipboard of recipes and a colorful notice about who we were and what we'd have coming up. And I added a note about how to leave your money in the coffee can. If you happened to stop by—if *anybody* happened to stop by, that is. Gulp.

Like Kevin Costner in *Field of Dreams*, we set the chalkboard sign out by the side of the road... and waited.

Our friend Cathy turned into the driveway first, followed by Katherine, and then Joannie. ›

DEVILED EGGS WITH SPINACH, BASIL & TOASTED PINE NUT PESTO

MAKES 12 DEVILED EGGS

6 hard-cooked eggs (see Cook's Tip), peeled and halved lengthwise

3 tablespoons mayonnaise

1½ teaspoons Spinach, Basil & Toasted Pine Nut Pesto (p. 8), drained of excess olive oil

½ teaspoon fresh lemon juice

¼ teaspoon freshly grated lemon zest

Kosher salt

Freshly ground black pepper

12 tiny fresh basil leaves, for garnish

12 whole toasted pine nuts, for garnish

Even if you don't live with 572 hens and a man who'd be happy eating meat loaf and deviled eggs every day, you should still have a great recipe for deviled eggs in your repertoire. Our favorite version goes green (and tasty) with a little Spinach, Basil & Toasted Pine Nut Pesto (p. 8) and a touch of lemon zest. No fancy piping required, though we do like to garnish with a tiny basil leaf and a pine nut. Wait to garnish until just before serving.

Gently scoop or squeeze out the yolk from each egg half. Arrange the whites on a plate.

In a small bowl, combine the yolks, mayonnaise, pesto, lemon juice, lemon zest, a pinch of salt, and several grinds of fresh pepper and mash until you get a smooth, pale-green filling. (I use a small silicone spatula.) Using a small spoon or mini spatula, spoon or dollop the mixture evenly back into the egg white halves. (I like to let the mixture sort of fall off the spoon, but do whatever works for you!) Garnish each half with a basil leaf and a pine nut.

COOK'S TIP

To cook eggs for salads or to use as deviled eggs, put them in a saucepan wide enough to hold them in one layer and cover them with cold water that comes up an inch over the eggs. Bring the water to a slow boil over medium-high heat; once the water is boiling, immediately remove the pan from the heat. Cover the pan and steep the eggs for 12 minutes. Carefully drain off the hot water and run cold water over the eggs until they are cool to the touch. Refrigerate until completely chilled before peeling. Use an old-fashioned egg slicer or a hollow-edged Santoku-style knife (run under hot water) to slice.

Deviled Eggs with Spinach,
Basil & Toasted Pine Nut Pesto

SPINACH, BASIL &
TOASTED PINE NUT PESTO

MAKES 1⅓ CUPS

1 large clove garlic

1½ cups packed fresh baby
spinach leaves, stemmed (if
necessary), washed, and dried

1½ cups packed fresh
basil leaves

⅓ cup toasted pine nuts

½ cup extra-virgin olive oil;
more if needed

⅓ cup grated Parmigiano-
Reggiano

Kosher salt

Freshly ground black pepper

1 teaspoon fresh lemon juice

Lovely green spinach leaves are my inspiration for
a greener basil pesto. If I'm lucky, my spinach is still
flourishing in the garden when the basil comes on.
Together with toasted pine nuts and lots of Parmigiano,
they make a delicious, versatile sauce, which I use with
pasta, in deviled eggs (p. 6), over grilled veggies, in
vinaigrettes, and even as a burger mix-in (p. 103). Don't
forget to toast the pine nuts before you make the pesto.

In the bowl of a food processor, process the garlic clove
until it is minced. Add the spinach, basil, pine nuts, and
1 tablespoon of the olive oil. Process, stopping to scrape
down the sides as necessary, until finely chopped. Add the
Parmigiano, ¼ teaspoon salt, several grinds of fresh pepper, and the lemon juice and process until well combined. With the motor
running, gradually pour the remaining olive oil through the feed tube and
process until you get a nice smooth pesto. If the pesto is too thick, add a bit
more olive oil, 1 tablespoon at a time, until you get the ideal consistency.

MINI SPINACH AND SHALLOT PUFF QUICHES

MAKES 24 QUICHES

Cooking spray (or butter), for greasing the pans

2 teaspoons unsalted butter

2 teaspoons extra-virgin olive oil

2 large shallots (3 ounces), peeled and thinly sliced (about ¾ cup)

Kosher salt

5 ounces fresh spinach leaves, stemmed, washed, and dried, ripped into smaller pieces (about 4 loosely packed cups)

3 large eggs

⅓ cup half-and-half or heavy cream

1 teaspoon chopped fresh thyme leaves

Big pinch of garam masala (or a combination of cinnamon, coriander, and cumin)

Freshly ground black pepper

2 sheets frozen puff pastry, thawed (I like Pepperidge Farm® brand)

Unbleached all-purpose flour, for rolling

½ cup crumbled fresh goat cheese, feta cheese, or blue cheese

If you keep a box of puff pastry in the freezer, you can make little quiches any time. In spring, try a combination of fresh, local ingredients that includes spinach, thyme, a fresh cheese like goat or feta, and pastured eggs, of course! You'll need two 12-cup (or one 24-cup) mini-muffin tins and a round pastry or cookie cutter for these. A cutter that's about 3 inches across the bottom makes a dough round that fits most mini-muffin tin cups (width and depth can vary). Use all the filling and all of the custard, even if it comes right up to the top edge of the dough.

Heat the oven to 400°F. Lightly spray or grease two 12-cup (or one 24-cup) mini-muffin tins.

In a medium nonstick skillet, heat the butter and olive oil over medium-low heat. Add the shallots and a pinch of salt and cook, stirring, until the shallots are golden brown and shrunken, 6 to 8 minutes. Add the spinach leaves and a pinch of salt, toss with tongs, and take the pan off the heat. Continue tossing the spinach until all of it is wilted. Transfer the mixture to a plate to cool.

In a small bowl, whisk together the eggs, cream, thyme, ¼ teaspoon salt, a big pinch of garam masala, and several grinds of fresh pepper.

On a lightly floured surface, roll out one sheet of puff pastry into a rectangle that measures about 9 x 12 inches (toss extra flour over and under the puff pastry if it is sticky). Using a 3-inch round cookie cutter or pastry cutter, stamp out 12 rounds. Gently press the rounds of pastry into the muffin cups, crimping or pleating a bit if necessary. Roll out the other sheet of puff pastry and cut

continued on p. 10 ›

› Along came Charlie. And our neighbor Katie. Then some people we didn't even know—amazing! They stopped, they bought lettuce, and said they'd be back. More folks came and we were sold out by 2 o'clock. We even sold one of the bluebird boxes.

Oh, dear, I thought. Seems we have a good location here, but need a little more product.

LAND-HO!
Truth is, our location is awesome—for what we do anyway. No bustling downtown intersection or anything high-volume like that—just a nice well-travelled road that's a ›

COOK'S TIP

The mini-quiches can be frozen. Thaw and reheat on a baking sheet at 350°F for 10 to 15 minutes or briefly in a microwave.

out another 12 rounds. (You will have extra scraps of puff pastry; you can freeze them for a later use.) Press those rounds into the remaining cups.

Distribute the spinach and shallot filling evenly among the cups. (This is easiest using your fingers.) Distribute the goat cheese or other cheese evenly among the cups. (They will look very full—that's okay.) Using a tablespoon measure, portion out the egg-cream mixture evenly among the cups. (Each should take about a scant tablespoon.)

Bake until puffed and golden, about 18 minutes. Let cool for a few minutes and serve warm.

GRILLED "SALAD" PIZZETTES WITH BALSAMIC DRIZZLE AND FLAVORED OILS

MAKES 5 TO 6 SMALL PIZZETTES

2 cups (9 ounces) unbleached all-purpose flour

¾ teaspoon kosher salt

⅔ cup very warm water (110°F)

1⅛ teaspoons active-dry yeast

1 tablespoon extra-virgin olive oil, plus more for the mixing bowl, sheet pan, and brushing

2 to 2½ ounces Parmigiano, Brie, aged Gouda, or other cheese, very thinly sliced or grated

4 cups small salad lettuce leaves, young arugula, baby Asian greens, or a mix, washed and dried

2 ounces very thinly sliced prosciutto, ripped into smaller pieces (optional)

Lemon Oil (optional) (recipe on p. 13)

Balsamic Drizzle (recipe on p. 13)

Extra-virgin olive oil or a selection of flavored or infused oils (such as blood orange oil, pumpkin seed oil, truffle oil, etc.)

1 lemon, cut into six wedges

I'm a big fan of grilled pizza—so much so that I've developed this streamlined, free-form approach to weeknight pizzette as an excuse to feature yummy spring salad greens. Pizzettes make a fun party idea, too, when you put out a selection of "drizzling" oils (raid your pantry and see the ideas here) and let everyone top their own. Choose the freshest greens—spicy arugula, a jumble of tender lettuces, or an Asian mix that includes mizuna and tat soi. The grilling is easier than you think and goes quickly, so have all your ingredients and tools at the ready before you start.

In the bowl of a food processor, combine the flour and salt. In a liquid measure, combine the warm water, yeast, and the 1 tablespoon olive oil. Let the liquid sit for 5 minutes. With the processor running, pour the liquid into the dry ingredients just until a dough forms. Scrape the dough into an oiled mixing bowl and cover it with a dishcloth. Let sit for 50 to 60 minutes.

Heat a gas grill to medium high and scrape the grates clean. Arrange tongs, a cutting board, a little bowl of oil and a brush or spoon, some salt, and your cheese near the grill.

Arrange the salad greens, Balsamic Drizzle, lemons, and salt in small bowls on your kitchen counter or serving area. Put out a few extra bowls for tossing greens.

Coat the back of a sheet pan with a little olive oil, and oil your fingers. Pinch off a knob of dough (about a sixth of the dough) and plop it on the back of the pan. Press it out into a roughly shaped disk that's 5 or 6 inches in diameter and ¼ inch thick. Brush the top of the dough with

continued on p. 13 ›

› byway to Up-Island Martha's Vineyard, the more rural half of the Island. Up-Islanders come by on their way down to the grocery store less than a mile away. And Down-Islanders and summer visitors drive past on their way to site-seeing and hiking—visiting the Gay Head Cliffs, prowling the Artisan Festival, or ponying up for tickets to the big Ag Fair in August, held at the Agricultural Society grounds directly across the street from us. These days, some people even get in their cars just to come to our (somewhat bigger) farm stand.

We are here on State Road because of our friend Joannie, who came and dragged me away from our rented garden plot one hot morning at the end of the summer of 2010.

"You've got to see a house and meet some people. Right now," she said.

I toe-kicked the dirt off my boots, hopped in my car, and followed Joannie's limey-green Element back down North Road. All I knew was this: Joannie had spent part of her childhood in this house I was going to see. ›

Grilled "Salad" Pizzette with Balsamic Drizzle and Flavored Oils

a little more oil and sprinkle with salt. Carry the sheet pan to the grill, set it down, and use both hands to pick up the dough and drape it across the hot grates (it will stretch—don't worry about the shape). Cover the grill and cook for about 1½ minutes. Uncover, flip the pizzetta over with tongs (it should be well marked), and brush it with a little more olive oil. Sprinkle with salt and top with a bit of cheese. Cover and cook for 1 minute. Uncover, transfer to a cutting board or plate, and bring to the serving area.

Arrange a few pieces of prosciutto over the cheese, if using. Grab a small handful of greens, sprinkle with salt, and toss with just a tiny bit of Lemon Oil (if desired), olive oil, or infused oil. Arrange the greens on the pizzette, drizzle with a little bit of the Balsamic Drizzle, squeeze a lemon over all, and drizzle again with a tiny bit of oil. Cut into pieces and eat right away—standing up!

Repeat with remaining dough to make a total of 5 or 6 pizzettes, or grill two or more at a time.

LEMON OIL

2 tablespoons extra-virgin olive oil

1 tablespoon freshly grated lemon zest

Combine the oil and lemon zest. Let sit for 15 to 30 minutes before using. Store, covered, in the fridge for a week.

BALSAMIC DRIZZLE

3 tablespoons balsamic vinegar

2 teaspoons light brown sugar

In a small skillet, combine the balsamic vinegar and the brown sugar. Bring to a simmer over medium heat and cook for 1 minute, until slightly syrupy. (It will thicken more when it cools so do not over-reduce or it will be very thick.) Remove from the heat. Let cool. Store at room temperature, covered, for up to a week.

› The house wasn't technically for rent, but she knew the family that owned it and had spoken with them that morning. On the Vineyard, that's all you need to hear to know you should drop everything. Year-round rentals are hard to come by, and the best opportunities come word-of-mouth.

Even before I parked under the shade of the most magnificent maple I'd ever seen, I had my hand on the cell phone to call Roy. I'd already fallen in love. My first glimpse of the little L-shaped farmhouse—clearly as old as the hills—hit me right where it counts. All my life I'd lived in modern houses in a modern (noisy) world. Right ›

› here was simplicity, peace, beauty, and purpose, all in one. It wasn't just a house I saw; it was an opportunity for a new life for our newly formed family—Roy, Libby, and me.

By 2 o'clock, we'd met Tom Hickie, shaken hands, and agreed to move in September 1. Tom was getting on a 3 o'clock ferry and wouldn't be back to the Island for a month. Hence the urgency. More important, we'd met Drusilla, Tom's spunky 92-year-old mother, who owns the property. Her grandfather built the house for his bride in 1890; together with the 2-acre parcel it sits on, the house constitutes the original homestead for the more than 80 acres surrounding it that the family once farmed and still owns.

Drusilla lives across the Mill Brook and just beyond the Square Field, a nice walk we can take any time these days. But that day we drove around, across Scotchman's Bridge Lane, and sat in Drusilla's parlor, hoping for her approval. We passed. ›

COLONEL MUSTARD'S NOT-SO-MYSTERIOUS GREENS, SAUSAGE & TORTELLONI SOUP

SERVES 4 OR 5

1 tablespoon extra-virgin olive oil

8 ounces thinly sliced cured sausage, such as andouille

2 tablespoons unsalted butter

1 cup diced fresh carrots

1 large or 2 medium shallots, thinly sliced (a generous ⅓ cup)

Kosher salt

1 tablespoon minced fresh garlic

4 cups thinly sliced stemmed purple or green mustard greens (about 10 to 12 ounces before stemming, 5 to 6 ounces after stemming)

1 quart low-sodium chicken broth

One 8-ounce package cheese (or cheese and spinach) tortelloni (preferably dried or fresh rather than frozen), cooked

1 heaping tablespoon chopped fresh mint

¼ teaspoon balsamic vinegar

2 to 3 tablespoons freshly grated Parmigiano-Reggiano, for garnish

1 loaf crusty bread, for serving

This easy and hearty weeknight soup is my attempt to lure you into trying mustard greens if you never have (hence the silly title). You could certainly use kale or another green here, but just don't tell me! I've used different filled pastas in this soup, but I prefer Barilla®'s dried tortelloni over anything frozen I've used. The sausage provides a lot of flavor here so be sure to choose one you'd enjoy eating on its own. I like Applegate® chicken andouille.

In a medium Dutch oven, heat the olive oil over medium heat. Add the sausage and cook, stirring, until lightly browned, about 5 minutes. Transfer the sausage to a plate with a slotted spoon.

Add the butter, carrots, shallots, and ¼ teaspoon salt. Reduce the heat to medium low, and cook, covered, stirring occasionally, until the vegetables are softened and lightly browned, 6 to 7 minutes.

Uncover, add the garlic, and stir until fragrant, about 30 seconds. Return the sausage to the pot and add the greens, chicken broth, and ⅛ teaspoon salt. Stir and bring to a simmer. Cook, partially covered, until the greens are tender, 3 to 5 minutes.

Add the cooked tortelloni to the pot, stir, and heat through. Take the pot off the heat and add the mint and the balsamic. Stir and taste for salt. (Depending on your sausage, you may or may not need to add salt.) Distribute the pasta, greens, and sausage evenly among four or five soup bowls. Spoon the broth over the top, garnish with the Parmigiano, and serve right away with crusty bread.

› Thanks to the introduction from Joannie, Tom and Drusilla changed their minds about turning the house into a summer rental and decided we'd be good people to live on the "homestead" year-round. They also said we were welcome to grow as many vegetables as we liked.

NO WAY!

We couldn't believe it. The only thing harder to find on the Vineyard than a year-round rental is affordable farm land. Here we were being offered both in a very reasonable package.

Roy did ask me if I was sure about the house—the steep stairs to the second floor, the one little bathroom off the kitchen, the heating (lack of) dilemma. But he knew—just as I did—that this was it, ›

COOK'S TIP

To toast nuts, spread them in one layer on a sheet pan and bake in a 350°F oven until golden brown, 8 to 12 minutes, depending on the nut. They will smell "toasty" when done.

ROASTED FINGERLING POTATO "COINS" AND ARUGULA SALAD

SERVES 4

½ small red onion, very thinly sliced crosswise into rounds

1 tablespoon plus 2 teaspoons white balsamic vinegar

2 teaspoons sugar

Kosher salt

1 teaspoon pure maple syrup

1 teaspoon low-sodium soy sauce

1 teaspoon raspberry jam

½ teaspoon Dijon mustard

Freshly ground black pepper

1 pound fingerling potatoes, unpeeled, sliced crosswise into "coins" about ⅜ inch thick

4 tablespoons plus 1 teaspoon extra-virgin olive oil

3 ounces arugula (5 to 6 cups), washed and dried

½ teaspoon minced fresh garlic

⅓ cup crumbled good-quality blue cheese

2 tablespoons chopped toasted hazelnuts or almonds, for garnish

Warm veggies and cool greens make me happy. I could eat a salad like this for dinner every night. Roy—not so much. He likes the roasted veggies and even the arugula just fine, but there needs to be a hamburger on the side. (Not a bad idea, really.) I have fun with fingerlings in this salad, slicing them crosswise into "coins" and quick-roasting them on sheet pans in high heat until golden. I scatter them over a bed of wispy young arugula and curlicues of pink quick-pickled onions, add a punchy warm vinaigrette, a little cheese and nuts, and I'm good to go.

Heat the oven to 450°F. Cover a large sheet pan with parchment paper.

In a small nonreactive bowl, combine the onion rings, 2 teaspoons of the vinegar, the sugar, and a pinch of salt. Let sit, tossing occasionally, for 20 to 30 minutes. In another small bowl, whisk together the remaining 1 tablespoon vinegar, the maple syrup, soy sauce, raspberry jam, Dijon, a good pinch of salt, and a few grinds of pepper.

Toss the fingerlings with 2 tablespoons of the olive oil and ½ teaspoon salt. Spread them out in one layer on the parchment paper. Roast until they're tender all the way through and golden brown on the bottom, about 20 minutes, flipping with a spatula once after 10 to 12 minutes.

Meanwhile, distribute the arugula on four plates. In a small skillet, heat the remaining 2 tablespoons plus 1 teaspoon olive oil and the minced garlic over medium-low heat. Stir gently and cook until the garlic begins to sizzle, 4 to 6 minutes (don't let the garlic brown.) Remove the pan from the heat and add the vinegar mixture. Tilt the pan and whisk with a small whisk until mostly emulsified.

Scatter the warm potatoes over the arugula. (I don't pile the potatoes—this is kind of a flat salad, not a moundy one!) Drain the onion rings well and scatter a few across each salad. Sprinkle the cheese around and spoon the warm dressing over the salads. Garnish with the nuts and serve right away.

Spring Celebration Salad with Crab Cakes and Avocado–Chive Dressing

SPRING CELEBRATION SALAD WITH CRAB CAKES AND AVOCADO–CHIVE DRESSING

SERVES 8 AS A STARTER

FOR THE CRAB CAKES

1 pound jumbo lump or backfin lump crabmeat (canned pasteurized is fine, as long as it is lump crabmeat)

3½ tablespoons unsalted butter

1 tablespoon plus 1 teaspoon olive oil

¼ cup thinly sliced scallions, white and light green parts

¼ cup finely diced celery

Kosher salt

1 large egg

¼ cup mayonnaise

1½ teaspoons Dijon mustard

1¼ teaspoons Old Bay® seasoning

1 teaspoon fresh lemon juice

½ teaspoon Worcestershire sauce

Tabasco® or other hot sauce

1¼ cups fine fresh breadcrumbs (I use Pepperidge Farm sandwich bread and pulse in a coffee grinder)

1 tablespoon chopped fresh flat-leaf parsley

continued on p. 21

I literally dance for joy when our pretty lettuces start to take shape in the garden in early May. I get so excited, in fact, that around Mother's Day I plan a special celebration salad featuring our family crab cake recipe. (Hint: It's all about the backfin lump crabmeat!) For this salad, I love a combination of tender looseleaf lettuces like Oakleaf and Salad Bowl mixed with young arugula. If you can't find fresh garden lettuces, though, don't buy bagged salad mixes. Go for whole heads of pretty lettuce and choose the inner leaves. The recipe makes 8 first-course-size crab cakes, but you could make 6 larger or 12 smaller with this same recipe.

MAKE THE CRAB CAKES

Drain the crabmeat, if necessary, and pick through it to check for shells (jumbo lump will not have shells). Put the crab in a medium mixing bowl.

In a small skillet, heat 1½ tablespoons of the butter and 1 teaspoon of the olive oil over medium-low heat. Add the scallions, celery, and a pinch of salt and cook, stirring, until softened, about 5 minutes. Let the mixture cool off the heat for about 5 minutes and then transfer it (scraping the pan) to the bowl of crabmeat.

In a small bowl, whisk together the egg, mayonnaise, Dijon mustard, Old Bay seasoning, lemon juice, Worcestershire sauce, a dash of hot sauce, and a scant ½ teaspoon salt. Pour and scrape that mixture over the crab and mix gently until combined. You will need to break up the lumps somewhat but do not overmix.

continued on p. 21 ›

› the solution we didn't know we'd been looking for—though Joannie obviously did!

Understand this: At the time, Roy and I, along with (then) 8-year-old Libby on weekends, were living in a one-bedroom apartment above an antique general store (I'm not kidding)—and driving back and forth every day, several times a day, to a rented garden plot on a farm where we were taking our first stab at market gardening. All while doing our regular work, too. It was kind of fun; the apartment was cozy and sunny, and for Libby, the endless supply of candy and toys downstairs was awesome. Plus, we had a good view out our second story window of Obama's motorcade driving back and forth from the "Summer White House." One day, Roy hung out the window and (he swears) POTUS looked right at him and gave him a thumbs up.

But by the end of the summer, we knew that this combination of crowded apartment/rented farm plot/traveling-tool-shed-in-the-back-of-the-car ›

FOR THE SALAD

3 cups baby arugula

4 cups tender looseleaf lettuce such as Oakleaf or Salad Bowl, or baby Bibb lettuce, torn into bite-size pieces if necessary

¼ to ⅓ cup fresh flat-leaf parsley leaves

Kosher salt

¼ cup extra-virgin olive oil

1 tablespoon white balsamic vinegar

2 teaspoons fresh lemon juice

½ teaspoon pure maple syrup

¼ teaspoon freshly grated lemon zest

¼ teaspoon Dijon mustard

Freshly ground black pepper

1 to 2 tablespoons sliced fresh chives (cut into ¼-inch pieces)

1 ripe avocado

Sprinkle the fresh breadcrumbs and the parsley over the mixture, and mix them in, again, thoroughly but very gently. It might seem counterintuitive, but try not to turn the mixture into a mash—it should still be somewhat loose. Cover the bowl with plastic wrap and refrigerate for 1 to 3 hours.

Shape the crab mixture into 8 cakes, each about ¾ inch thick.

In a large (12-inch) nonstick frying pan, melt the remaining 2 tablespoons butter with the remaining 1 tablespoon olive oil over medium heat. When the butter is frothy, add the cakes to the pan. Cook until the cakes are a dark golden brown on the underside, about 4 minutes. (Use a thin spatula to check.) Carefully flip the cakes, turn the heat to medium low, and continue cooking until the other side is well browned, another 4 to 5 minutes.

ASSEMBLE THE SALAD

In a medium mixing bowl, combine the arugula, lettuces, and parsley. Sprinkle with a bit of salt.

In a small bowl, combine the olive oil, balsamic vinegar, lemon juice, maple syrup, lemon zest, Dijon mustard, ⅛ teaspoon salt, and several grinds of fresh pepper. Whisk well; stir in half of the chives.

Pit, peel, and chop the avocado into small dice. Put the avocado in a small bowl and add 1 to 2 tablespoons of the vinaigrette to it. Stir gently and set aside.

Drizzle 1 to 2 tablespoons of the vinaigrette over the salad greens. Toss, taste, and add more dressing as necessary.

Mound a portion of the salad mix on each of eight plates. Arrange a crab cake next to or in the center of the salad (without crushing the greens too much). Spoon a portion (about 1 tablespoon) of the avocado on top of each crab cake. Sprinkle any remaining avocado in and around the greens. Drizzle a tiny bit of vinaigrette over and around each crab cake and salad and sprinkle the remaining chives over all. Serve right away.

› wasn't sustainable. We just had no idea what was next.

The universe took care of that for us.

HOUSE-HOLD

Rustic living isn't for everyone, I know. But I am strangely happier in this quirky house than I ever was in one with all the trappings. (This is what happens when you finally listen to your gut and do what you really love, no matter how strange it may seem.)

There is something almost transcendental about living in a house that has barely been altered in more than 100 years. With the exception of indoor plumbing (which arrived late—in the 1940s—and only in the form of a kitchen sink and a tiny ›

› bathroom where the cookstove once lived) and a small mud-room tacked on the back, the house is as it was—three rooms down, three rooms up. No clos-ets, no attic, no basement. To reach the bedrooms under the eaves, we lunge up the excep-tionally steep staircase, thereby eliminating the need to do stretching exercises every day. Going down is even more of a thrill—especially in the middle of the night.

We moved in just as I signed a contract to write my second cookbook—quickly. And the kitchen, though suitably cheery with light from windows on three sides, had only a sink, a refrigerator, a stove, and a chest of drawers in it. No counter space or cabinets. So despite the fact that Roy was busy himself (working 50 feet up in the air repairing the steeple on the historic Chilmark Community Church), he quickly tricked out the kitchen for me, rearranging the appliances and building a center island with storage cabinets underneath and book-shelves on the back. ›

BIBB AND FRESH PEA SALAD WITH HERBED BUTTERMILK DRESSING AND CRISPY BACON

SERVES 4

4 ounces fresh peas, shelled (about ¼ cup)

2 heads Bibb or baby romaine lettuce (preferably cold), largest outer leaves removed, quartered through the stem (to yield 4 wedges each), and gently rinsed and dried

3 to 4 tablespoons Herbed Buttermilk Dressing (facing page), plus more if you like

4 slices cooked bacon, crumbled

Classic. Easy. Pretty. Crisp lettuce, tangy dressing, fresh peas, crunchy bacon. Sold?

Now have fun with the lettuce: Choose the cup-shaped pale inner leaves from heads of Bibb or baby romaine and stack them up loosely. Very pretty. Or take two small heads of Bibb and quarter them, keeping the stem intact to make wedges. Dress lightly, sprinkle peas around, crumble bacon on top. Done. By the way, the versatile buttermilk dressing (facing page) is delicious on cucumbers, too.

Put the peas in a small bowl with a teaspoon of water and cover with a damp paper towel. Microwave on high for 15 to 20 seconds. Uncover and transfer to a paper towel–lined plate to cool. (Alternatively, blanch the peas in boiling water for 30 seconds.) Arrange 2 wedges of lettuce on each of four salad plates, and sprinkle a quarter of the peas over each. Drizzle or spoon a few teaspoons (or more if you like) dressing over each salad and garnish with the crumbled bacon. Serve right away.

HERBED BUTTERMILK DRESSING

MAKES 1 CUP

⅓ cup plus 2 tablespoons mayonnaise

¼ cup sour cream

1 tablespoon cider vinegar

2 teaspoons fresh lime juice

½ scant teaspoon freshly grated lime zest

1½ teaspoons sugar

½ teaspoon minced fresh garlic

¼ teaspoon dry mustard

Pinch of cayenne pepper

Freshly ground black pepper

Kosher salt

¼ cup buttermilk (well shaken first)

1 tablespoon thinly sliced fresh chives

1 tablespoon chopped fresh flat-leaf parsley

1 tablespoon chopped fresh tarragon (or other tender herb, such as dill, mint, or cilantro)

We use this easy and versatile creamy buttermilk dressing in springtime with peas and lovely lettuces and in summer with cucumbers (p. 97) and tomatoes, sometimes in chopped salads. You can use it to create your own farm stand salad. If you don't like tarragon, feel free to replace it with dill, mint, cilantro, chervil, or other tender herb. I like to chill the dressing before using it.

In a mixing bowl, whisk together the mayonnaise, sour cream, vinegar, lime juice, lime zest, sugar, garlic, dry mustard, cayenne, several grinds of fresh pepper, and a pinch of salt. Add the buttermilk and whisk again. Stir in the chives, parsley, and tarragon (or other tender herb). Chill the dressing if not using right away. It will thicken slightly as it sits, but will loosen again upon dressing.

› Roy also worked out a heating solution with Tom, suggesting one of the new smaller propane furnaces might work under the staircase, with vents out to the living room and through the top step to the upstairs bedrooms. It worked, and by late fall, we at least had heat, if not insulation.

By winter we were settled into our new home, spending nights curled up on the living room couch with pencil and graph paper, plotting out our first market garden at the homestead. Wrapped in an extra quilt on windy nights when the drafty windows shook, watching for the occasional four-footed furry creature that might dart across the sloping wooden floorboards, we happily paged through seed catalogues, drew plans, and made lists of supplies we needed. (The furry creatures were dispatched when Libby wasn't around.)

Spinach Cobb Salad with
Bacon, Blue Cheese, Avocado
& Derby Dressing

SPINACH COBB SALAD WITH BACON, BLUE CHEESE, AVOCADO & DERBY DRESSING

SERVES 4 OR 5

2 large ripe avocados

1½ cups halved grape tomatoes (about 8 ounces)

2 ribs celery, finely sliced (about ½ cup)

Kosher salt

1 recipe Derby Dressing (p. 26)

6 ounces baby spinach, stemmed if necessary, washed and dried

3 ounces Bibb lettuce (about 1 small head) or inner leaves of Boston lettuce, washed and dried

¼ cup sliced fresh chives (cut into 1-inch lengths)

Freshly ground black pepper

4 hard-cooked eggs (Cook's Tip, p. 6), peeled and sliced

4 ounces Roquefort or other good-quality blue cheese, crumbled

8 slices cooked bacon, crumbled

Oh joy! I finally learned the patience to grow spinach, and it was worth it. Now I can sneak fresh spinach into my favorite salad, the good old Cobb, born at The Brown Derby restaurant in LA many decades ago. What's not to like about blue cheese, bacon, avocados, and tomatoes? With the hard-boiled eggs, you can call this supper. I like to serve the salad family-style, arranged in one big bowl. But you could also make individual composed salads for a more formal dinner; in that case, dress the ingredients separately before arranging them.

Have ready one large shallow serving bowl (about 13 to 14 inches across and 3 to 4 inches deep is nice).

Peel, pit, and dice the avocados. Put them in a mixing bowl along with the grape tomatoes and celery. Season with a pinch of salt, drizzle with a tablespoon of the Derby Dressing, and toss very gently.

Combine the spinach, Bibb lettuce, and half of the chives in a big mixing bowl. Season lightly with salt and a few grinds of fresh pepper. Drizzle and toss with about 3 tablespoons of the Derby Dressing (taste and add more if you like). Transfer the greens to the serving bowl.

Mound the avocado mixture in the center of the greens. Arrange the egg slices in a circle around the avocado mixture. Sprinkle the blue cheese in a circle around the egg slices. Lastly, sprinkle the bacon around the blue cheese, leaving a few greens peeking out around the edges of the bowl. Drizzle most or all of the remaining dressing over everything and garnish with the remaining chives. Bring to the table with tongs and plates to serve.

HOW NOT TO START SEEDLINGS

The only reason we had anything to sell on Memorial Day weekend was that we had started hundreds of seedlings inside the house, just like we had in the apartment the year before. I don't recommend being quite as enthusiastic about this as we are. No matter how many nifty light-supporting-structures-with-rotating-shelves Roy builds, we always wind up with flats on windowsills and a general odor of fresh soil throughout the house from March to May.

But if you want to grow stuff to eat, you will someday have to do this—start at least some seeds inside. You will go buy T5 fluorescent bulbs and 4-foot shop lights and soil-less starting mix and plastic trays for planting. You will gladly drown in a sea of seed catalogues, and ›

› you will plunk down money for a tome-y gardening book (Roy's bible is Bob Thomson's *The New Victory Garden;* mine is Eliot Coleman's *New Organic Gardener*) and read all the tips: Water from the bottom. Keep seedlings close to the lights! Try using a soil blocker.

What the books will not tell you, though, is that you will forget to water, and you will over-water, and you will under-water. There will be death and heartbreak and stringy seedlings along the way. All before you somehow must transition your precious, fragile specimens to the cold, hard outdoors.

And yet...every morning, you will be down on your hands and knees—or standing on a stool on your tippy toes, depending on your setup—staring at tiny green leaves unfold with absolute awe and amazement. You will be so very proud that you will post pictures of these sprouts on your Facebook page. You should be wary of this feeling, if it grabs hold—you may someday wind up starting seeds in 98-cell flats and building ›

DERBY DRESSING

MAKES ½ CUP

6 tablespoons extra-virgin olive oil

2 tablespoons plus 1 teaspoon red-wine vinegar

1½ teaspoons fresh lemon juice

½ teaspoon freshly grated lemon zest

½ teaspoon minced fresh garlic

½ teaspoon sugar

½ teaspoon Dijon mustard

½ teaspoon Worcestershire sauce

¼ teaspoon kosher salt

Freshly ground black pepper

This easy vinaigrette keeps for several days in the fridge and is a great everyday salad dressing.

Put all the ingredients (including several grinds of fresh pepper) in a liquid measure and whisk vigorously. (Or use a jar with a tight-fitting lid and shake well.)

"PINK AND GREEN" RADISH AND ARUGULA SALAD WITH HONEY, ALMONDS & MINT

› a hoop house (kind of like a green house, only thriftier) to house thousands of seedlings. Just sayin'.

SERVES 4

2 tablespoons toasted sliced almonds

6 or 7 large fresh radishes (4 ounces), tops and tails removed, very thinly sliced

2 teaspoons fresh lemon juice plus ¼ lemon, seeds removed

¼ teaspoon sugar

Kosher salt

4 cups loosely packed baby arugula leaves (about 2½ ounces)

Extra-virgin olive oil

4 teaspoons small fresh mint leaves (or large fresh mint leaves torn into smaller piece)s

1 small wedge Parmigiano-Reggiano (preferably a few inches long for easier shaving)

Honey, for drizzling (a squeeze bottle works well)

4 small edible flowers (like violets or chive blossoms) or short mint sprigs, for garnish (optional)

My favorite colors are pink and green, so I go a little nuts in late April and early May, when the first cheery pink radishes can be pulled from the ground and my arugula is ready to harvest. Pairing them with salty (Parmigiano), nutty (almonds), and sweet (honey and mint) flavors is a natural for a simple-to-make but complexly flavored salad. The radishes get a quick-pickle treatment in lemon juice, sugar, and a bit of salt, so they are really sublime. Dress and compose this salad just before serving.

Crush the almonds with your hands or chop them lightly; set aside.

Put the sliced radishes in a small nonreactive bowl and add the 2 teaspoons lemon juice, the sugar, and a big pinch of kosher salt. Let sit for 5 minutes and toss occasionally.

Put the arugula leaves in a medium bowl and squeeze the lemon quarter lightly over them. Drizzle on about 1 teaspoon olive oil, sprinkle with salt, and toss. Taste and season with more lemon, oil, or salt as necessary.

Arrange a quarter of the arugula in a mound in the center of each of four salad plates. Sprinkle one-quarter of the mint leaves and some of the almonds over the arugula. Drain the liquid from the radishes and arrange (or tuck in) a quarter of the radishes in the center of each mound of arugula. Using a vegetable peeler, shave 5 or 6 thin curls or shards of Parmigiano over each salad. Sprinkle each salad with a little bit more of the crushed almonds (you might not need them all) and drizzle each with a bit of honey. Garnish with the edible flowers or mint sprigs, if you like. Serve right away.

THE LITTLE OLD LADY LETTUCE THIEF

We learned two things in the first few weeks and months of operating the farm stand:
1. People love salad mix. 2. Some people are not self-serve friendly. Let me explain.

Thanks to our new "regular" customers, we discovered that folks are happy to part with a chunk of change if you pick a custom mix of fresh, delicious salad lettuces or other greens, rinse and spin them dry, and put them in a nice little plastic bag. It's the convenience. I understand—I'd pay the cash, too, knowing what it takes to get those beauties from seed to cooler.

I sometimes wish (sigh) that more people would go for the big beautiful single heads of lettuce, glistening from a fresh rinse, all jolly-looking propped up in a tub of ice water. That's ›

› why I think I had a soft spot in my heart for the lettuce thief.

Not long after we opened the farm stand, we began to notice that some of the little heads of Bibb lettuce would go missing, carted away without the requisite compensation left in the coffee can. It seemed to happen most days in early to mid-afternoon, so we started spying out the windows through the curtains. We were kind of shocked when we narrowed down the possible thief to a little old lady in a beat-up station wagon.

When I mentioned this to a friend, she said it's not unusual for old folks to be anxious about money, possibly even talking themselves into the right to ›

CHINESE GRILLED CHICKEN AND BIBB LETTUCE "WRAPS"

SERVES 4

5 tablespoons low-sodium soy sauce

2 tablespoons plus 2 teaspoons fresh lime juice

3 tablespoons chopped fresh cilantro, plus 20 more short sprigs

1 tablespoon plus 1 teaspoon minced fresh ginger

1 tablespoon plus 1 teaspoon minced fresh garlic

1 tablespoon light brown sugar

1 tablespoon peanut oil

¾ teaspoon Asian chili-garlic paste

2 pounds boneless skinless chicken thighs, trimmed

¼ cup thinly sliced scallions (any part)

2 teaspoons oyster sauce

20 to 24 medium or large Bibb or Boston lettuce leaves, washed and dried (from about 3 heads lettuce)

20 fresh mint, basil, or Thai basil leaves

1½ cups cooked white rice, hot or reheated if leftover, or 4 to 5 ounces rice noodles, cooked, rinsed, and drained

2 medium carrots, julienned or coarsely shredded

¼ cup chopped roasted peanuts

You know those late May evenings when the days are getting longer and the air is a bit warmer? That's when our lettuce is thriving and it just feels right to make supper out of those lovely greens. Everyone loves to put together little Asian "tacos," too, and juicy, marinated grilled chicken thighs are the perfect warm component. We use the biggest outer leaves from our Bibb lettuce, pick cilantro and mint from the garden, and set out peanuts, scallions, rice noodles or rice, and dipping sauce. Add cucumbers or fresh chiles, if you like, and double or triple the recipe for a party.

In a large nonreactive bowl, combine 3 tablespoons soy sauce, 2 tablespoons lime juice, the chopped cilantro, 2 teaspoons ginger, 2 teaspoons garlic, 2 teaspoons brown sugar, the peanut oil, and ½ teaspoon chili-garlic paste. Mix well. Add the chicken thighs, toss, and let sit for 30 to 45 minutes, tossing occasionally.

In a small bowl, combine the remaining 2 tablespoons soy sauce, 2 teaspoons lime juice, 2 teaspoons ginger, 2 teaspoons garlic, 1 teaspoon brown sugar, 1 tablespoon of the scallions, the oyster sauce, and 2 teaspoons water. Mix well and put in a little serving bowl. Arrange the lettuce leaves, herb leaves, and cilantro sprigs on a platter. Put the rice or noodles, carrots, peanuts, and the remaining sliced scallions in small serving bowls or on a serving platter.

Heat a gas grill to medium. Arrange the chicken thighs on the grill and cook, covered, until grill marks form on the first side, about 3 minutes. Using tongs, move the pieces

continued on p. 32 ›

Chinese Grilled Chicken
and Bibb Lettuce "Wraps"

› help themselves to something that shouldn't really cost as much as it does (in their opinion).

It was an interesting theory, and certainly we felt that if the little old lady really needed lettuce, well, that was that. But then one day, all the cash in the can, maybe $25, went missing. Probably not the little old lady. (We blamed that one on a stealthy bicycle thief. Not that there's anything wrong with bicyclists!)

So we moved the farm stand down the driveway, closer to the house, and within view of my kitchen window. A much better spot, since the driveway circles around and there are obvious parking spots within range, too. We put up a sign directing people to the farm stand, where it contentedly remained until just recently, when Roy built us a bigger, fancier model. We also attached a locked money box to the stand, and we leave just a few bills in the coffee can for people to make change if they need it. ›

on a slight angle and continue cooking, covered, for 2 minutes to form crosshatch marks. Flip the pieces over and cook for 3 to 4 more minutes, or until the thighs are shrunken and cooked through. Transfer to a cutting board, let rest for a couple of minutes, and cut lengthwise into thin strips. Arrange the chicken on a serving platter and bring all the components to the table for everyone to assemble their "wraps" as desired.

PAN-SEARED FILET MIGNON WITH WILTED CHARD AND CREAMY THYME PAN SAUCE

SERVES 4

½ cup heavy cream

2 large cloves garlic, smashed

2 strips fresh orange peel, about 3 inches long and ¾ inch wide

1½ teaspoons lightly chopped fresh thyme, plus 4 sprigs, for garnish

Kosher salt

Freshly ground black pepper

4 filets mignons of even thickness (about 1 inch thick), 1¼ pounds total

½ tablespoon unsalted butter

2 teaspoons olive oil

10 cups (packed) washed and well-dried stemmed fresh Swiss chard leaves, roughly chopped (10 ounces after stemming, about 1¼ pounds before)

⅓ cup freshly grated Parmigiano-Reggiano

> And the funny thing is, some of our best customers are now little old ladies!

Here's a twist on the classic steak-house special of steak and "creamed" spinach—only I use Swiss chard instead of spinach and make a quick garlic-and-herb-infused cream sauce instead of a thicker white sauce. Beef has a great affinity for chard, so if your budget isn't filet-friendly, try another steak or even hamburgers instead. (Chicken breasts or sea scallops would work, too.) Cook the chard quickly at the end as it tends to shed water as it sits over heat. Don't worry if your sauce thins a bit in the pan—it will still be delicious. Serve with mashed potatoes.

In a small saucepan, combine the heavy cream, smashed garlic, orange peel, and chopped thyme. Watching carefully, bring to a boil over medium-high heat, then immediately reduce to a simmer and cook for 30 to 45 seconds. Remove from the heat and let sit for 5 to 10 minutes. Use a fork to remove the orange peel (and the garlic pieces if you like). Season with a pinch of salt and freshly ground pepper. Set aside.

Season the steaks with salt and freshly ground pepper. In a large (12-inch) nonstick skillet, heat the butter and olive oil over medium-high heat. When the butter has melted and is bubbling, add the steaks. Cook without moving until they're well browned on the bottom, 3 to 4 minutes. Turn over and cook again until browned on the other side, another 3 to 4 minutes. (The steaks will be medium rare. Cook 1 minute longer on each side for medium.) Transfer the steaks to a plate.

Add the chard and a pinch of salt to the skillet. The pan will be very crowded at first, so add the chard in handfuls as the bottom leaves begin to wilt, using tongs to work the newly added chard to the bottom. Continue

continued on p. 34 ›

THE ZEN OF SALAD

Our loyal customers have unwittingly fueled my obsession with leafy green things. I'm not sure why I love greens so much. It's not about nutrition—people often confuse me for a health nut, when in reality I'm just a vegetable lover. And it isn't all about cooking, though greens are so darn versatile that we eat them in some sort of dish—a salad, a stir-fry, a quesadilla, a whatchamacallit—just about every day.

No, there's something else. I think I'm attracted to the way greens look and feel. I'm mesmerized by the kaleidoscope ›

› of colors and textures every time I harvest lettuce leaves to make a salad mix. You might think I'm crazy, but I'd even say that harvesting and prepping salad mixes is therapeutic—it engages me in a way that shuts down my overly chatty inner voice. Something to be grateful for, yes?

We grow over 20 varieties of lettuce now. Some of my favorites are Flashy Green Butter Oaks, Kinemontpas Butter Head, Royal Oakleaf, Speckled Amish, Forellenschluss (aka Trout Speckled), Pirat, Blushed Butter Cos, Buttercrunch Bibb, and Red-Eared Butterheart. The names are killer, huh? I choose a combination of green and red and speckled lettuces for color. And I treat every kind of lettuce—not just loose-leaf varieties—as "cut and come again" lettuces. This means that I only harvest leaves from the outside of the plant, leaving the inner leaves to keep coming and grow bigger.

To jazz up our salad mixes—and for almost instant gratification in the early spring—we also grow Asian greens, which ›

turning with tongs until the leaves are just shy of being completely wilted (about 1½ minutes). Add the cream mixture to the pan and stir as it bubbles and coats the chard. Immediately remove the pan from the heat and stir in half of the Parmigiano.

Arrange a portion of chard on each of four warm serving plates. Put a filet on top of or next to the chard and spoon over any sauce left in the pan. Garnish with the remaining Parmigiano and thyme sprigs. Serve right away.

SPICY THAI SHRIMP AND BABY BOK CHOY STIR-FRY

SERVES 4

2 tablespoons fish sauce

2 tablespoons fresh lime juice

1 tablespoon brown sugar

¾ teaspoon Asian
chili-garlic paste

1 teaspoon cornstarch

1 tablespoon plus 1 teaspoon
minced fresh ginger

1 tablespoon plus 1 teaspoon
minced fresh garlic

2 teaspoons finely chopped
serrano peppers (about 1 large
or 2 small, seeds and ribs
removed; or use 1 teaspoon
with seeds and ribs left in if
you like a little heat)

1¼ pounds large shrimp
(31 to 35 count),
peeled and deveined

2 tablespoons fresh
orange juice

Kosher salt

1 pound baby bok choy
(4 to 6 small heads,
depending on size)

3 tablespoons peanut oil

2 cups pea greens (leaves and
stems from young pea plants)
or 1 cup pea shoots (optional)

2 to 3 tablespoons chopped
fresh Thai Basil (or any
combination of basil,
mint, or cilantro)

Cooked rice, for serving

¼ cup chopped roasted
peanuts (optional)

This crowd-pleaser, bursting with Thai flavors and boasting a bit of heat, is one of my favorite destinations for baby bok choy. It takes a bit of time to prep, but the cooking goes quickly. Have a pot of rice going before you start. You certainly don't have to use Thai basil here, though I love its alluring cinnamon scent. A combo of cilantro and mint or basil works great, too. Pretty pea greens are optional, too, as are pea shoots.

In a small bowl, combine the fish sauce, lime juice, 2 tablespoons water, the brown sugar, chili-garlic paste, and cornstarch. Whisk thoroughly and set aside. In another small bowl, combine 1 tablespoon ginger, 1 tablespoon garlic, and 1½ teaspoons of the serranos and set aside. In a mixing bowl, toss the shrimp with the remaining 1 teaspoon ginger, 1 teaspoon garlic, ½ teaspoon serranos, the orange juice, and ½ teaspoon salt.

Cut each head of baby bok choy in half lengthwise and then crosswise at the "neck" where the leafy part begins. Reserve the leafy tops. Notch the core (with a V-cut) out of the stem ends. Cut the stems lengthwise into pieces about ½ inch wide. Drop all the stems and leafy tops into a big bowl of tepid (almost warm) water, swish around, and let sit for a few minutes. If stubborn dirt clings to the stems, rub it off with your hands. Remove the bok choy from the water and spread on a dishtowel. Let the pieces sit for a few minutes to drip a bit (they do not need to be dry).

In a large (12-inch) nonstick stir-fry pan or skillet, heat 2 tablespoons of the oil over medium-high heat. When the oil is hot (it will loosen up), add the bok choy and ½ teaspoon salt. Using tongs, toss to coat. Turn the heat to high.

continued on p. 36 ›

› mature quickly. Greens like the graceful toothy-leaved mizuna and the emerald green spoon-shaped tat soi, which forms a gorgeous rosette-shaped plant as it grows. And mustard. Green Mustard. Purple Mustard. Pink Mustard. Frilly Golden Mustard. (C'mon, you've got to try mustard; it really is tangy and tasty—and just the thing for a quick weeknight soup, like the one on p. 14.) We begin harvesting the baby leaves in less than 30 days from planting seed, and we add them to salad mixes until they start flowering and get too spicy.

I get so excited about our lettuces and other salad greens that I invent dishes to let them ›

› shine: Grilled pizzettes with frilly greens (p. 11) are fun for a party, and grilling pizza is easier than you think—I promise. And we use the outer leaves of our pretty Bibb lettuce as an excuse to make Roy and Libby's favorite, Chinese Grilled Chicken and Bibb Lettuce "Wraps" (p. 30). Stylish and jaunty, these billowy lettuce cups are the fashionistas of the salad world—and a great "make-your-own," too. And since crab cakes are a family specialty (blue crab backfin lump meat only!), I've created a salad (p. 19) with avocado–chive dressing just for them. You'll see—boring lettuce is a thing of the past.

THE FAB FOUR AND THE SECRET GARDEN

Beyond lettuce and Asian greens, there's The Fab Four: arugula, baby bok choy, Swiss chard, and kale (any kind of kale). These are the greens, out here at least, that are on everyone's radar.

Baby bok choy is a genuine rock star; whenever I write its name up on the chalkboard ›

Cook, tossing with tongs occasionally, until browning begins, 2 to 3 minutes. Lower the heat to medium high and continue cooking and stirring until all the pieces have some browning and the stems are pliable (but not completely limp), 3 to 4 minutes. Transfer the bok choy to a plate. Let the pan cool for a minute.

Add the remaining 1 tablespoon oil to the pan, turn the heat back to high, and return the pan to the heat. When the oil is hot, add the shrimp. (Scrape the bowl to add any bits of garlic and ginger left behind.) Cook, stirring frequently, until the shrimp are just shy of being cooked through (they will have curled up but will not be totally opaque), about 2 minutes. Return the bok choy to the pan, stir, and add the reserved ginger–garlic mixture. Stir until well combined and fragrant, about 30 seconds. Scrape the fish sauce mixture into the pan, stir constantly for 10 to 20 seconds as the sauce thickens slightly, and remove the pan from the heat. Continue stirring to coat the shrimp and vegetables with the sauce. Stir in the pea greens or shoots (if using) and about 2 tablespoons of the herbs. Stir again. Arrange cooked rice on a serving platter or in individual shallow serving bowls. Transfer the shrimp and bok choy mixture to the platter or bowls, arranging over the rice. Garnish with the remaining herbs and peanuts (if using).

Spicy Thai Shrimp and Baby Bok Choy Stir-Fry

› out by the road, I can practically hear the tires screeching. It's also one of my favorite vegetables to cook and eat—a little kiss of high heat brings out its deeply nutty flavor. Sometimes I wish it didn't sell so well so we could keep more for ourselves. If I luck into a few small heads, I slice them lengthwise, turn up the heat under my stir-fry pan, and give them a quick twirl with my tongs. A little lemony finish or a lashing of garlic and ginger—and bada bing bada boom. If I manage to fling my body over an entire pound of it, shielding it from the greedy throngs, we can make Spicy Thai Shrimp and Baby Bok Choy Stir-Fry (p. 35). Double-yum. Killer sauce. Just so you know. ›

SERVES 2 AS A STARTER OR 4 AS A SIDE DISH

1½ pounds fava beans in the pod

¾ pound fresh peas in the pod

Kosher salt

½ package (about 4.5 ounces) fresh angel hair pasta, torn into shorter lengths

4 thin slices pancetta (about 1 ounce; ask the deli counter to slice it thinly for you)

3 tablespoons unsalted butter

½ cup thinly sliced shallots (from about 2 large)

½ teaspoon freshly grated lemon zest, plus ¼ lemon, for squeezing

¼ cup finely grated Parmigiano-Reggiano

2 tablespoons thinly sliced fresh mint

Freshly ground black pepper

FRESH FAVA BEANS AND PEAS WITH SHALLOTS, MINT, PANCETTA & ANGEL HAIR

If you see fava beans at a farm stand, grab them. (They're much fresher than their grocery-store kin.) Grab a few fresh peas, too, and make this lovely little pasta dish for you and your sweetie. (Or use it as a side dish for four, and serve with grilled salmon.) To highlight the veggies, I keep the pasta minimal, and complement the favas and peas with classic flavor partners—bright mint, salty pancetta, and nutty Parmigiano. Favas take some time to prep, but their fabulous flavor is worth it, I promise.

Remove the favas from their pods and shell the peas.

Bring a large pot of water with 2 teaspoons salt to a boil. Prepare an ice bath by adding a generous amount of ice to a medium bowl of water. Add the favas to the boiling water and cook for 2 minutes (if the favas are small) or 3 minutes (if they are large). Remove the favas with a fine-mesh strainer (reserving the water in the pot) and transfer to the ice water. Let sit for a minute or two. Bring the water in the pot back to a boil and add the peas. Cook for 1 minute and use the fine-mesh strainer to transfer the peas to a folded dishtowel or a few layers of paper towels. Keep the pot on the stove.

Remove the favas from the ice water and remove the outer coating of each fava by pinching the stem end of the bean with your thumbnail and popping or slipping the bean out of the skin.

Bring the pot of water back to a boil and add the angel hair. Cook, stirring, for about 45 seconds, or according to the package instructions. Reserve some of the cooking water and transfer the angel hair to a strainer in the sink.

In a large (12-inch) nonstick skillet, arrange the pancetta slices over medium heat. Cook until crisp and browned, about 5 minutes. Transfer to a paper towel–lined plate. When cool, crumble and set aside.

Add 2 tablespoons of the butter to the skillet. When melted, add the sliced shallots and a pinch of salt, and cook, stirring, until the shallots are softened and lightly browned, 4 to 5 minutes. Add the favas and the peas to the pan, season with a pinch of salt, and cook, stirring, just until the veggies are heated through, 1 to 2 minutes. Turn the heat to low. Add the remaining 1 tablespoon butter, the lemon zest, a few tablespoons of the pasta water, the cooked pasta, half of the Parmigiano, half of the mint, a pinch of salt, and several grinds of black pepper. Stir and toss until all the ingredients are mixed together as thoroughly as possible (the veggies will roll around a bit!), adding a little more pasta water if needed to loosen the mixture. Squeeze a small bit of lemon over all. Remove the pan from the heat and transfer to serving bowls. Garnish with the remaining mint, remaining Parmigiano, and pancetta.

COOK'S TIP

Fava beans have to be shelled twice! First remove them from their fuzzy pod as you would any shell bean. Then follow the directions in the recipe (facing page) to blanch the beans, which have an outer coating around them. Blanching and then submerging the beans in ice cold water will allow you to slip the coating off. What remains are two bright green halves of the fava bean, which can now take a quick turn in the sauté pan or be used in soups, dips, crostini toppings, and more.

Lobster Salad Rolls with
Fresh Peas, Lemon & Chives

LOBSTER SALAD ROLLS WITH FRESH PEAS, LEMON & CHIVES

MAKES 4 BODACIOUS ROLLS OR 6 RESPECTABLE ROLLS

FOR THE SALAD

1 pound (or a generous ¾ pound) cooked lobster meat (tail and claws), cut into ½- to ¾-inch dice or pieces

⅓ cup fresh peas (from 6 to 7 ounces fresh English pea pods)

1 large or 2 medium Cherry Belle or other red or pink radishes, cut lengthwise into wedges and very thinly sliced crosswise

¼ cup sliced fresh chives

2 tablespoons finely sliced fresh mint (optional; choose spearmint over peppermint)

Kosher salt

Freshly ground black pepper

¼ cup plus 1 tablespoon mayonnaise

¼ cup crème fraîche

½ teaspoon freshly grated lemon zest

1 teaspoon fresh lemon juice, plus more to taste

FOR THE ROLLS

1 to 1½ tablespoons unsalted butter

4 to 6 top-split frankfurter rolls (preferably) or regular hot dog buns

8 to 12 small arugula leaves or baby Bibb lettuce leaves, washed and dried

Fresh peas love shellfish. And we love lobster rolls. (They're a big deal in New England. Around here, churches have weekly Lobster Roll nights to raise money.) Everyone has their favorite version, but mine is elegant and very fresh since I use a bit of lemon and crème fraîche to lighten the dressing, and I add chives, mint, thinly sliced radishes, and those fabulous fresh peas. One tradition I stick with—the toasted frankfurter bun. Lobster meat isn't cheap, but it's a yummy splurge every once in a while.

MAKE THE SALAD

Put the lobster meat in a large mixing bowl. Put the peas in a small dish with a tablespoon of water, cover with a paper towel, and microwave on high for 10 to 20 seconds, or just until tender. Drain the water and let cool for a few minutes, then add to the lobster meat. Add the sliced radishes and most of the chives and mint (if using). Set aside the remaining herbs for garnish. Sprinkle a scant ¼ teaspoon salt over the lobster mixture and season with several grinds of black pepper.

In a small mixing bowl, whisk together the mayonnaise, crème fraîche, lemon zest, and lemon juice. Using a silicone spatula, pour and scrape the dressing over the lobster mixture and stir gently but thoroughly. (If you have less than a pound of lobster meat, start by adding just three-quarters of the dressing—you don't want to overdress.) Taste and season with more fresh pepper or lemon juice if you like. Refrigerate if not using right away (for up to 6 hours).

continued on p. 42 ›

› These days, in an effort to have plenty of everything, I start seeding flats of baby bok choy, chard, and kale in late winter in the hoop house, and I keep on seeding flats every week or so until I run out of room for the flats—or beds to transplant them into. I wind up with greens all over the farm, and I can drive myself crazy some days running around looking for more bok choy or chard to restock the stand.

When I come up short, I resort to stealing from children.

Looking furtively over my shoulder, I creep into Libby's garden. This is a small plot we set aside for her to grow whatever she wants—and to design as she pleases. There's a wobbly brick path down the middle and a cast-iron iguana lounging around. There's a plant "hospital" marked off by rocks and ›

COOK'S TIP

You can make the lobster salad a few hours ahead, refrigerate it, and toast or grill the buns just before assembling.

› sticks, and at the entrance sits a concrete-and-sea-glass stepping stone we made from a kit that Mimi (Grandmother Riley) gave us.

Flanking the entrance are two bright pink Swiss chard plants; Libby loves the color—and the flavor, believe it or not, especially if maple syrup is involved. (This is a trick I use to lure adults, too. My Swiss chard side dishes— like the one on p. 47 with ham and fresh peas—often feature a sweet-and-sour *thang*, a holdover from my southern days.) Libby's chard plants are more bodacious than mine, because they don't get harvested much. Until I come along and sneak a leaf or two or three. Once I found out how easy this was the first time, I came back one day for a bit of lettuce. (Yeah, this is how trouble starts.)

Honestly, I don't think Libby would mind. I think she'd forgive me with that coy smile of hers—the same one she gives me when she's counting up her cash when we're playing Garden-opoly™, a game she wins repeatedly. Roy and I tried to figure out why we were ›

PREPARE THE ROLLS

When ready to serve, heat half of the butter in a large (12-inch) nonstick skillet over medium heat. When the butter has melted, unfold two of the frankfurter rolls and press them, cut side down, into the pan and fry them in the butter until golden brown on the cut side, 3 to 4 minutes. Repeat with the remaining rolls and butter.

TO SERVE

Arrange a few leaves of arugula or lettuce along the length of each warm roll. Divide the lobster salad equally among the rolls, spooning the salad down the middle. Sprinkle the salad with the remaining herbs and serve the lobster rolls right away, with lots of napkins!

STIR-FRIED BABY BOK CHOY WITH LEMONY SAUCE

SERVES 4

1 tablespoon plus 2 teaspoons
fresh lemon juice

2 teaspoons sugar

½ teaspoon freshly grated
lemon zest

½ teaspoon low-sodium
soy sauce

½ teaspoon cornstarch

1 pound baby bok choy
(4 to 6 heads)

2 tablespoons peanut oil

1 large clove garlic, smashed

Kosher salt

This is your straight-from-the-farm-stand, make-it-tonight baby bok choy side dish. It's great with grilled fish and some friends or just a bowl of brown rice and you. You could practically go straight to the stove, except the cute little heads harbor dirt, so slice and swish in tepid water first. Then crank up the heat and the whole dish will be ready in less than 20 minutes. Feel free to add a bit of fresh ginger or scallions at the end of cooking.

Arrange a serving dish near your stove. Combine the lemon juice, 1 tablespoon water, the sugar, lemon zest, soy sauce, and cornstarch in a small bowl and whisk together well. Set aside.

Cut each head of baby bok choy in half lengthwise. Lay each half, cut side down, on a cutting board and cut the halves lengthwise into pieces about ½ to ¾ inch wide (the stems will hold some pieces together but it's okay if they don't). Don't worry about cutting the green leafy tops too accurately

continued on p. 45 ›

as they will cook quickly, but the stem ends shouldn't be too thick. Drop all the pieces in a big bowl of tepid water, swish around, and let sit for a few minutes.

Lift the bok choy from the water and spread on a dishtowel. Let the pieces sit for a few minutes to drip a bit (they do not need to be dry). In a large (12-inch) nonstick stir-fry pan or skillet, heat the oil over medium heat. When the oil is hot (it will loosen up), add the bok choy, the garlic clove, and ¾ teaspoon salt. Toss the bok choy to mix with the oil and turn the heat to high.

Cook, tossing with tongs only every minute or so at first, but more frequently as browning begins (you want to allow pieces to sit on the bottom and sear and steam a bit before moving them around), until all the pieces have some deep browning on them and most of the stems have lost their opacity (the tops will be wilted), 5 to 7 minutes. (If browning is happening too fast, reduce the heat slightly.)

Remove the pan from the heat, give the lemon sauce a quick stir, and scrape it into the pan. Toss and stir the bok choy with the sauce and transfer to a serving dish. (Remove the garlic clove if you like.) Eat hot, warm, or cool.

› always losing to her, until she mentioned that she memorizes the properties that people land on the most, and only buys those. The girl is all about quiet observation—she'd be a scary poker player for sure.

Plus, Libby loves her time out on the Island with Daddy and Susie. She has a great life with her mom Kelly, brother Matt, and grandparents Judy and Bob over in Falmouth on the mainland (or what we call America over here). But the Friday night ferry ride with Daddy brings her back to what one of my friends calls "The Magic Kingdom," where there's a whole other world waiting.

Libby and Daddy are great *National Geographic*-esque explorers (on our fridge, we have clippings from the *Vineyard Gazette* of bird sightings they've made), and we all love to take ›

Swiss Chard and Fresh Peas with
Ham and Maple–Balsamic Sauce

SWISS CHARD AND FRESH PEAS WITH HAM AND MAPLE–BALSAMIC SAUCE

SERVES 3 OR 4

1 tablespoon pure maple syrup

1½ teaspoons balsamic vinegar

1½ teaspoons fresh lemon juice

¾ cup fresh peas (from about 1 pound peas in the pod)

1 bunch (12 to 14 ounces) Bright Lights or Rainbow Swiss chard

1 tablespoon extra-virgin olive oil

Kosher salt

3 slices thinly sliced honey ham (I like Applegate), cut into narrow ¾-inch pieces

1 tablespoon unsalted butter

2 teaspoons minced fresh ginger

Talk about colorful! This dish is a visual feast, and it tastes pretty swell, too. The sweet and tart combo of maple syrup and balsamic vinegar takes the slightly minerally edge off Swiss chard, and adding ham and fresh peas makes a serendipitous side dish even greens-avoiders will like. My chard is knee-high in the garden by the time the peas are ready to harvest in June, so the two are naturals together.

In a small bowl, whisk together the maple syrup, balsamic vinegar, and lemon juice. Set aside.

Put the peas in a small bowl with a tablespoon of water and microwave, covered, on high for 10 to 20 seconds, or until just tender. Drain.

Pull or cut away the stems from the chard leaves. Rinse and dry the stems, slice them thinly (¼ inch thick) cross-wise, and reserve. Cut or rip the leaves into large (2- to 3-inch) pieces and wash and dry them well.

Heat the olive oil in a large (12-inch) nonstick skillet over medium heat. Add the chard stems and a pinch of salt, and cook, stirring occasionally, until the stems are slightly shrunken, about 5 minutes. (You will hear them crackle as the water begins to evaporate.) Add the ham and ½ tablespoon of the butter and cook, stirring, until both the chard stems and the ham pieces are shrunken and beginning to brown lightly, about another 4 min-utes. Add the fresh ginger, stir, and cook just until fragrant, a few seconds. Add all of the chard leaves and ¼ teaspoon salt. Using tongs, gently toss and fold the chard leaves until just wilted and well mixed with the other ingredients, 1 to 2 minutes. Add the peas and stir well. Scrape the maple mixture into the pan, stir, and remove from the heat. Add the remaining ½ tablespoon butter and toss and stir until it is melted. Taste for salt. Transfer to a serving platter or plates and eat hot or warm.

› advantage of the miles of sea-shore and nature trails out here when we're not on farm duty. There isn't a living creature—from lizards and turtles to piglets and pygmy goats—with which Libby isn't fascinated. She informed me recently that when she grows up she is going to be a veterinarian first, and then the president of the United States.

I guess she'll have to win the world poker tournament some time after that.

PEAS, PLEASE

One June evening around 7:30, a car came down the driveway and stopped halfway around the circle. Normally we don't get customers that late in the day—we take the sign down so that hopefully they know we're closed. But I recognized the car—a very un-Vineyard sedan without scratches or mud on it—and the woman who stepped out of it. She was a regular customer—a reserved, ›

COOK'S TIP

The easiest way to peel fresh ginger is to scrape the skin away with an ordinary tablespoon.

› quiet lady who I later learned was a respected clergy member on the Island. She usually came by in the morning and I would wave to her and occasionally have a brief chat. This night, when I stopped chasing errant chickens and walked over to her, I could see she had a look of desperation on her face.

"I'm sorry to bother you, but do you have any peas?" she said. "They're the only thing my daughter wants to eat right now. We bought some from you the other day and she ate the whole bag."

I could see the skinny teenager sitting in the front seat of the car, and I could tell that this wasn't a casual request. Fortunately, I had picked a ›

GRILL-ROASTED BABY BOK CHOY AND CREMINIS WITH GARLIC-CHILE-LIME OIL AND SPAGHETTI

SERVES 3

12 ounces baby bok choy (about 4 small heads)

2 tablespoons plus 2 teaspoons extra-virgin olive oil

Kosher salt

6 ounces cremini mushrooms, quartered (halved if small)

1½ teaspoons minced fresh garlic

¼ teaspoon crushed red pepper flakes

¼ teaspoon freshly grated lime zest, plus ½ lime, for squeezing

1 teaspoon unsalted butter

2 ounces whole-grain spaghetti, broken in half

A grill basket is just the thing for cooking baby bok choy because the stems get nicely browned but not overcooked. Add earthy cremini mushrooms, a kicky garlic-chile-lime oil, and a bit of whole-grain spaghetti (as more of a condiment to fill out the side dish rather than as a major player), and you've got an intensely flavorful veggie side dish to serve with whatever else you're popping on the grill.

Put a grilling stir-fry basket directly on the grates of a gas grill and heat the grill, covered, on medium.

Trim the stem end of the baby bok choy heads and pull or peel off each individual leaf, cutting away any inner core as necessary. Put all the leaves in a tepid bowl of water and swish. (Rub off any stubborn dirt with your fingers.) Let sit for a few minutes. Lift the leaves out of the water and spin-dry. In a medium bowl, toss the bok choy leaves with 2 teaspoons of the olive oil and a big pinch of salt. In another bowl, toss the mushrooms with 1 tablespoon olive oil and a big pinch of salt.

In a small skillet, combine the remaining 1 tablespoon olive oil, the garlic, and red pepper flakes over medium heat. Bring the oil to a simmer, stirring occasionally, until the garlic is sizzling (about 5 minutes). Continue cooking just long enough to infuse the oil (a minute or so), but don't brown the garlic. Remove from the heat and stir in the lime zest, butter, and a pinch of salt. Stir until the butter melts. Set aside.

In a large saucepan of well-salted boiling water, cook the pasta according to the package instructions, about 10 minutes. Drain and let sit in a colander, tossing occasionally.

Put the mushrooms in the grill basket and cook, covered, stirring occasionally, until shrunken and golden brown on some sides, 6 to 7 minutes. Add the bok choy leaves (they will just fit in the basket), cover, and cook for 1 or 2 minutes to wilt. Uncover and stir with tongs. Continue cooking, covered, stirring frequently, until the bok choy stems are pliable and browned in spots, 6 to 7 minutes more. Transfer the bok choy and mushrooms to a clean bowl. Season the pasta with a big pinch of salt and add it to the vegetables. Drizzle all with the garlic-chile-lime oil and toss well. Gently squeeze the lime half over the veggies and pasta and toss again. Taste and adjust the seasoning if necessary. Serve hot or at room temp.

› small basket of peas late that afternoon and I had them inside. I went in to weigh them up and came back to tell her, with a sheepish comment about the steep price, that the total would be $8. "I don't mind," she said. "If my daughter will eat them, I'm happy."

Fresh shell peas are just that good—like candy. If I ask Libby to help me harvest, she eats most of what she picks. The pods might as well be little green-veggie Pez® dispensers.

It took me awhile to get the hang of growing peas. Or I should say, germinating them. But a great tip from West Coast organic gardener Willi Galloway set me right: Now I pre-sprout the peas by covering them with very damp paper towels and ›

COOK'S TIP

The flower bud on a chive plant is really a cluster of many little purple blossoms. All you have to do is pinch the flower off of the top of the stem with your thumb (breaking all those little tiny green stems), and the lovely little purple blossoms will come tumbling out. The flowers have a predictably oniony flavor and make a colorful addition to salads, pizzas, soups, and more.

MAY DAY RADISH AND PARSLEY SALAD WITH LEMON AND GINGER

SERVES 4

12 ounces trimmed fresh radishes (about 1½ bunches), preferably Cherry Belle or Easter Egg, cut in half lengthwise and then into lengthwise wedges about ¼ inch wide

½ cup whole small (or large torn) fresh flat-leaf parsley leaves

3 to 4 tablespoons sliced fresh chives (cut into ½-inch lengths), plus chive blossoms if available, for garnish (optional)

1 tablespoon peanut oil

2 tablespoons finely chopped crystallized ginger

2 tablespoons fresh orange juice

2 tablespoons fresh lemon juice

1 teaspoon freshly grated lemon zest

Kosher salt

Pretty in pink and green, this bright little salad makes a festive addition to a spring lunch or brunch, especially one starring fish, shrimp, or crab. Crystallized ginger is the secret ingredient in the dressing, giving the spring-harvest trio of radishes, parsley, and chives a perky boost. Super-quick to make, this is the destination for that drop-dead-gorgeous bunch of radishes you find at the farm stand.

Put the radishes, parsley leaves, and chives in a medium bowl.

Whisk together the peanut oil, crystallized ginger, orange juice, lemon juice, lemon zest, and ¼ teaspoon salt. Let sit for a few minutes to let the juices mingle and the ginger soften, then whisk again. Pour and scrape the dressing over the radish-herb mix. Toss and mix well and let sit for 15 to 20 minutes, stirring frequently and tasting occasionally. (The radishes will release some liquid and will absorb some of the flavor of the dressing as they sit. They will stay crisp.)

Serve the salad in little glass bowls along with some of the juices. If you like, garnish with chive blossoms (see Cook's Tip).

*May Day Radish and Parsley
Salad with Lemon and Ginger*

COOK'S TIP

You can use the brown butter-chive recipe on the facing page to flavor fresh fava beans (see blanching and peeling directions on pp. 38–39) as well. The favas will need a minute or two in the skillet with the butter back on the stove to heat them.

SIMPLEST FRESH PEAS WITH BROWN BUTTER AND CHIVES

SERVES 2

1 cup fresh peas (from about 1¼ pounds peas in the pod)

1 tablespoon unsalted butter

2 teaspoons sliced fresh chives

1 bushy sprig fresh thyme

¼ teaspoon freshly grated lemon zest

¼ teaspoon fresh lemon juice

Kosher salt

Freshly ground black pepper

1 chive flower, broken into individual blossoms (optional; see Cook's Tip, p. 50)

If you're lucky enough to come upon a farm stand that has bushels of fresh peas, buy as many as you can eat in one day. You won't make it home without snacking on at least a few, but then you can make a nice little side dish for two out of the pound or so you've got left. (Certainly, if you've got more you can double this recipe.) Take care not to overcook the peas—a short stint in the microwave or a quick dip in boiling water is all they need. Then dress with a flavorful butter.

To microwave, put the peas in a small bowl with a tablespoon of water and cover with a damp paper towel. Microwave on high for 15 to 20 seconds. Uncover and transfer to a paper towel–lined plate. Alternatively, bring a saucepan of water to a boil. Have ready a fine-mesh strainer. Drop the peas in the water and cook for 30 seconds (small peas) to 1 minute (larger peas). Use the strainer to transfer the peas to a paper towel–lined plate or dishtowel to drain.

In a small skillet, melt the butter over medium heat. Continue cooking the butter, swirling the pan occasionally, until the milk solids turn a nutty brown color and smell fragrant, 4 to 7 minutes. (Do not overbrown.) Remove the pan from the heat and carefully add half of the chives, the thyme sprig, lemon zest, lemon juice, a big pinch of salt, and several grinds of pepper. (The butter will sputter a bit.) Stir and let sit for a minute or two to infuse. Add the peas to the skillet and toss until coated. (If you want your peas to be very hot, you can return the skillet to the heat briefly and stir.) Remove the thyme sprig. Serve right away, garnished with the remaining chives and the optional chive blossoms.

› leaving them in a perforated plastic bag in a warmish spot for a few days. Once the little tails appear, I know I can plant them and they will all be up in less than a week. Next, I foil marauding birds by covering the beds with fabric row cover until the plants are a few inches tall.

After that, it's all about the miracle. When the vines grow tall and tangly, they create sort of a tropical pea jungle. Jack had his beanstalk, but I'm telling you, there is something quite magical about loitering on the shady side of a pea trellis on a hot June day.

Finally, we just have to figure out when to pick the pods so that the peas are not too small and not too big. That's why we ›

Green Island Farm Open-Faced Egg Sandwich with Local Bacon, Cheddar & Asian Greens

GREEN ISLAND FARM OPEN-FACED EGG SANDWICH WITH LOCAL BACON, CHEDDAR & ASIAN GREENS

SERVES 4

4 slices bacon, preferably local

Four ¾-inch slices peasant bread (from an oblong loaf) or challah bread (either way, pieces should be around 2½ x 5 inches in diameter)

1 tablespoon plus 2 teaspoons unsalted butter, softened

2 to 2½ ounces aged sharp Cheddar cheese (I like Grafton Tavern Select) or any good local or regional semi-hard cheese, sliced thinly (about 10 to 12 small slices total)

4 fresh, local large eggs, preferably at room temperature

1 tablespoon heavy cream

Kosher salt

Freshly ground black pepper

1 to 2 teaspoons tender herb leaves (such as chives, chervil, cilantro, or parsley) or chive blossoms, plus 4 small tender sprigs or edible flowers for garnish (optional)

12 to 16 mizuna leaves (or other baby greens such as mustard, tat soi, arugula, or kale)

Honey, preferably local, for drizzling

Fleur de sel or sea salt (optional)

I love this sophisticated take on a breakfast sandwich, because it's possible to include so many local ingredients in it. Bacon, bread, cheese, eggs, greens, honey—challenge yourself to see what you can source locally. In spring, we use some of our young Asian greens like mizuna and tat soi, because they're pretty and delicious. These open-faced sandwiches are a bit like giant crostini, so eat them out of hand and eat them right away!

Cook the bacon using your favorite method and drain on paper towels. Snap each piece in half so that you have 8 shorter strips of cooked bacon.

Arrange an oven rack 6 inches from the broiler and heat the broiler to high. Put the bread slices on a baking sheet and toast lightly. Turn the slices over, spread the untoasted sides with about 1 tablespoon of the butter, and put the baking sheet back under the broiler. Broil until the tops are golden brown. Arrange the cheese slices on top of the bread and broil until just beginning to melt.

Meanwhile, in a medium (10-inch) nonstick skillet, heat the remaining 2 teaspoons butter over medium heat. In a bowl, whisk together the eggs, cream, a generous pinch of salt, and a few grinds of pepper. Stir in the herb leaves or chive blossoms. When the butter has melted and is foaming, pour in the egg mixture. Let it sit until the edges start to set and then, using a silicone spatula, gently pull the edges of the egg toward the center, letting uncooked egg

continued on p. 56 ›

› have an active sampling program. Libby's in charge of that.

What we don't eat raw, we cook very briefly, dipping them in boiling water or (gasp!) microwaving them for about 30 seconds (it works). Since a pound of shell peas only yields about a cup of peas, I've devised clever recipes—like Lobster Salad Rolls with Fresh Peas, Lemon & Chives (p. 41) and Bibb and Fresh Pea Salad with Herbed Buttermilk Dressing and Crispy Bacon (p. 22)—that star fresh peas without hogging them. But sometimes it just has to be all about the peas. When we have enough, we can indulge in something like Simplest Fresh Peas with Brown Butter and Chives (p. 53). In fact, I can eat the whole @#*! dish by myself if I want to. So there.

THE ROTOTILLER WRECKED MY RHUBARB—AND SOMEONE ATE THE STRAWBERRIES

I know it isn't right to play favorites, but I have to tell you that my favorite recipe in this chapter ›

run underneath (tilting the pan if necessary). Continue to cook the egg this way, gradually gathering the soft folds of eggs together into a rough circle about 6 to 7 inches around. (This is really just scrambled eggs with a little less scrambling.) When the eggs are mostly set, flip (use the spatula to divide the eggs in half first for easier flipping) and let the bottom side cook and brown up a bit. Transfer the egg to a cutting board and cut into four portions.

Arrange a few mizuna leaves on each of the bread pieces and top with a portion of egg. Top each with 2 pieces of bacon, another leaf or two of mizuna, and the herb sprig or flower (if using). Drizzle all with honey, sprinkle with a little fleur de sel or sea salt if desired, cut each piece in half, and serve right away.

SWISS CHARD AND CARAMELIZED ONIONS QUESADILLAS WITH PEPPER JACK CHEESE

MAKES 4 QUESADILLAS, OR 12 SLICES TOTAL

1 teaspoon sherry vinegar

1 teaspoon honey

1 tablespoon unsalted butter

1 tablespoon plus 4 teaspoons extra-virgin olive oil

2 medium yellow onions (12 ounces), thinly sliced (about 1½ cups)

Kosher salt

1 teaspoon minced fresh garlic

4 cups thinly sliced Swiss chard leaves (from 8 ounces of chard, stemmed)

Four 6-inch (fajita-sized) flour tortillas

2 cups (6 to 7 ounces) coarsely grated Pepper Jack (or Cheddar) cheese

2 tablespoons chopped fresh cilantro (optional)

Sautéed greens make awesome quesadilla fillings, so if you've gotten a big bunch of greens from a farm stand or your CSA and you can't quite figure out how to use them all up, think tortillas for a truly easy and tasty snack, lunch, or light supper. I especially like this combination of earthy Swiss chard and sweet caramelized onions with a little kick from Pepper Jack cheese.

Heat the oven to 200°F if you want to keep each quesadilla warm as you make it. In a small bowl, combine the sherry vinegar and honey.

In a medium (10-inch), heavy nonstick skillet, melt the butter with 1 tablespoon of the olive oil over medium-low heat. Add the onions and ¼ teaspoon kosher salt and cover. Cook, stirring occasionally, until the onions are translucent, 5 to 6 minutes. Uncover and continue cooking until the onions are very limp and a light golden brown, 10 to 12 minutes. (Turn down the heat if the onions are browning too fast.) Add the garlic, stir, and cook until fragrant, about 30 seconds. Add the Swiss chard and a pinch of salt to the pan and toss with tongs until wilted. Remove the pan from the heat and drizzle the vinegar-honey mixture of the top, tossing well. Transfer the chard-onion mixture to a plate to cool a bit and wipe out the pan.

Return the pan to medium heat and add 1 teaspoon olive oil. When the oil is hot, add one tortilla to the pan. Sprinkle a small amount (one-eighth) of the cheese over one-half of the tortilla. Cover that with a quarter of the chard-onion mixture and a sprinkling of cilantro (if using). Top with a bit more (another eighth) of the cheese. Fold the empty half of the tortilla over

continued on p. 58 ›

› is the Gingery Strawberry–Rhubarb Crisp with Brown Sugar Pecan–Topping (p. 60). But I'd be lying if I said we could make more than one or two of these crisps with our own goodies—up until now.

When we moved into the farmhouse, I felt sure there must be a rhubarb plant or two hiding around the property. I had fond memories of visiting my best friend's grandmother at her farmhouse in Maine and marveling at the giant rhubarb plants growing along an old stone wall—they were planted in 1932! So I thought that every farmhouse had at least one rhubarb plant and that rhubarb lived forever. But alas, nothing ever showed up here (not even near the old well—the rumored spot). Plenty of other old ghosts remain on this property, including a magnificent old stone barn foundation and quirky cement fish ponds in the maple grove. (Apparently the family had a pet alligator, too.)

But no rhubarb. So I planted a few plants the first year. They rotted and died. Argh! I planted ›

› more and they expired from heat and drought the next summer. Or so I thought. Until Roy ran the rototiller over them and cut them to pieces. I just shrugged when I saw that. And laughed when I saw them send up shoots anyway a few weeks later! I hope they will live long and prosper, but I've planted more just to be sure that we can make plenty of crisps—and supply the farm stand, too.

Strawberries have also been scarce. Because of the limited space in the original market garden (even though we doubled it the second year), we lived with only a few strawberry plants. They did well, since we meticulously followed Victory Garden man's method of plastic mulching, which eliminates runners and makes the mother plants strong and productive. But between Libby and me, very few of those strawberries would make it out of the garden—or to the farm stand.

How I have longed for a giant strawberry patch—and a stand of asparagus. It seems I'm going to get both in a big way now, ›

onto the full side and press down lightly with the back of a spatula. When the bottom of the tortilla has lightly browned, 45 seconds to 1 minute, turn the quesadilla over and cook until the other side is browned (and the cheese is melty), another 45 seconds to 1 minute.

Transfer the quesadilla to a wooden cutting board and let cool for a minute or two before cutting into wedges. (Alternatively, you can hold the quesadillas in the warm oven.) Let the pan cool for a couple minutes. Return to the heat and repeat with the remaining filling and ingredients.

› since Roy has his sights set on tilling and fencing a huge plot for both. Roy grew up on Cape Cod, where strawberry farms proliferated in the sandy soil, and he sees dollar signs. (I see shortcakes, tarts, and happy customers. And, of course, visions of birds and deer eating all of our strawberries. But that won't happen—will it?)

YOU'VE GOT MAIL—IT'S BABY CHICKS!

There's something even better than juicy strawberries or fresh peas in late spring (I know, how could that be?): Going to the post office to pick up a box of day-old chicks, shipped straight from the hatchery. Gently ›

SERVES 6

FOR THE TOPPING
8 tablespoons unsalted butter, softened, plus more for the baking dish

1 cup unbleached all-purpose flour

¼ cup finely chopped toasted pecans

½ cup light brown sugar

½ cup regular oats

¼ teaspoon kosher salt

⅛ teaspoon ground cinnamon

⅛ teaspoon ground ginger

FOR THE FILLING
2½ cups hulled, quartered strawberries

2½ cups thick-sliced rhubarb stalks (cut ½ inch thick; about 10 ounces)

½ cup plus 2 tablespoons sugar

3 tablespoons unbleached all-purpose flour

2 tablespoons finely chopped crystallized ginger

2 teaspoons pure vanilla extract

1 teaspoon balsamic vinegar

¼ teaspoon kosher salt

FOR SERVING
Vanilla ice cream or frozen yogurt, or heavy cream (optional)

GINGERY STRAWBERRY–RHUBARB CRISP WITH BROWN SUGAR–PECAN TOPPING

I'm sorry, but I'm truly biased about this crisp—the flavor rocks! Sweet and tangy with a most excellent crunchy topping, it gets a flavor jingle from two secret ingredients—crystallized ginger and a touch of balsamic vinegar. Cook the crisp until the topping is plenty golden (about 45 minutes)—enough time to let the fruit juices reduce and thicken a bit, too. This looks pretty in a 10-inch quiche pan, but any 2-quart baking dish will work. Great warm with vanilla ice cream, this crisp is pretty tasty leftover for breakfast, too. I should know.

Heat the oven to 350°F. Rub a shallow 2-quart baking dish or large ceramic quiche dish all over with a little butter. In a medium mixing bowl, combine all the ingredients for the crisp topping and mix together with your fingers until well combined into large "crumbs."

In a large mixing bowl, combine the filling ingredients and mix thoroughly. Arrange the filling mixture in the baking dish and top evenly with the topping mixture. (Depending on the size of your pan, you may have a little leftover topping. Freeze it for another use.)

Bake the crisp until the topping is firm and golden, about 45 minutes. (The juices will have been bubbling around the edges for a bit.) Let cool for 15 to 20 minutes and serve warm, alone or with ice cream, frozen yogurt, or heavy cream.

Gingery Strawberry–
Rhubarb Crisp with
Brown Sugar–Pecan Topping

RHUBARB FOOL WITH WHIPPED GINGER MASCARPONE CREAM

SERVES 6

1 recipe Whipped Ginger Mascarpone Cream (p. 64)

1 recipe Rhubarb Compote (p. 64)

⅓ cup crumbled gingersnap cookies or several cookies, for garnish (optional)

Mint sprigs (optional)

A fool is a classic British dessert that's lately taken a star turn state-side, probably because it's easy and whimsical and luscious. It's basically a fruit compote lightened with something creamy. I lighten my rhubarb compote with a very stable mascarpone whipped cream, a versatile recipe I learned from Vineyard chef Michael Brisson. Make the compote and the cream ahead to give them time to chill. Mix (use a light hand and don't overmix) and eat right away if you like, or assemble and chill for serving later.

Put the cream and the compote side by side in a mixing bowl. Using a silicone spatula, gently cut and fold the compote into the cream just until partially mixed and "stripey" looking. Use the spatula to scoop and dollop the fool into individual small custard cups, glasses, or small glass dessert bowls. Cover loosely with plastic and refrigerate until well chilled, a few hours or overnight. Serve as is or garnished with crumbled gingersnaps and/or mint sprigs.

Alternatively, layer the fool with gingersnap cookies in glasses to make individual trifles. Refrigerate for a few hours before serving. Or make frozen fool "sandwiches" by spooning the fool between two cookies and freezing.

continued on p. 64 ›

› lifting out the fuzzy little puff balls and cradling them in your hands while you offer them a drink of water. Putting them down in a bed of shavings in a warm brooder, built from old barn boards in the corner of Roy's shop. Watching them learn to hop up on the edge of a little piece of wood and jump down with glee. Looking all around the farm for Libby and finding her glued to the brooder, naming each chick—Sugar, Jelly Bean, Oreo, Chippy—and pointing out to us which one is which, based on subtle color differences. Seeing their feathers start to emerge from the tips of their wings in only a few weeks time. Carrying them out, one by one, to their new coop and watching them marvel at the space and open air—and fresh grass.

We love baby chicks so much that we get some every spring. We started with just 8 the first year, then 50 the next spring, and 25 the next. And that's not counting the 500 laying ›

› hens we now have that we purchased as pullets (16-week-old female chickens). So, yeah, we don't really need more baby chicks, but we can't help ourselves. Plus it's fun to have a variety of breeds in your flock (our pullets are all one heavy-laying breed), so we get Buff Orpingtons (fat and friendly—the absolute best backyard hen in my opinion) and Aracaunas (smart, quick, and layers of the famous blue eggs) and other breeds here and there. We've even raised an injured chick inside. Bambi (short for Bambino) not only lived and thrived, but got to hang out on the tummy of our dog Farmer, with a little help from Libby. A little girl, a dog, and a baby chick—just about the cutest thing I ever did see.

WHIPPED GINGER MASCARPONE CREAM

MAKES A GENEROUS 2 CUPS

¾ cup heavy cream

½ cup (about 4 ounces) mascarpone cheese

⅓ cup sugar

1 teaspoon pure vanilla extract

½ teaspoon grated fresh ginger (finely grated on a rasp-style grater)

You can make this ahead and hold it in the fridge for up to 8 hours. In addition to using this in the Rhubarb Fool (p. 63), you can layer it with berries or roasted plums or peaches for an easy dessert parfait. Use it in shortcakes, too. I also use this cream in the Molasses Crinkles with Honey–Vanilla Roasted Pears dessert (p. 233). When making the cream for that recipe, I substitute 2 tablespoons honey for the ⅓ cup sugar. Sometimes I up the amount of fresh ginger a bit, too.

Combine the heavy cream, mascarpone, and sugar in a cold mixing bowl. Whip (with the whisk attachment) on medium speed until the mixture is thick and stiff (it will hold firm peaks), 2½ to 4 minutes. Add the vanilla extract and ginger and whisk again just until combined.

RHUBARB COMPOTE

MAKES 1⅓ CUPS

12 ounces rhubarb stalks (trimmed if necessary), cut into ½-inch pieces (about 3 cups)

⅔ cup sugar

3 tablespoons orange juice

If you don't want to make the fool, you can certainly make this easy compote to top ice cream or pound cake or to layer with Greek yogurt and granola in a breakfast parfait. It will keep in the fridge for a week or more (and can be frozen, too) so it's a good way to preserve rhubarb.

In a medium saucepan, combine the rhubarb, sugar, and orange juice. Bring to a simmer over medium-high heat. Reduce the heat as necessary to maintain a gentle, not vigorous, simmer, and continue cooking until the mixture has reduced and thickened but before the rhubarb has completely broken up, about 12 minutes. (The mixture will pull away from the sides and separate a bit when a spoon drags through it, but will still be fairly loose. It will thicken up as it cools.) Transfer to a bowl and refrigerate to chill completely.

HIGH SUMMER

(AKA "TOMATOES AND
GREEN BEANS AND
SQUASH—OH MY!")

I MAY HAVE BEEN NERVOUS the first day, the first season, the first year. But by the time July 4th rolls around now, my adrenaline is pumping. I jump into my jeans at sunrise and join Roy (earliest riser ever) in the dance of daily chores that doesn't end until we shoo the chickens into their coops at sunset. We've settled into a rhythm that works, though it isn't always completely graceful. There's a lot of "discussion" over things like who watered when and how much, and who's going to pick that last row of green beans after supper. But we sleep well, falling into bed exhausted every night.

For me, the morning is all about getting the farm stand set up—which is a total kick for a girl who really liked to play house (and store!) as a kid. I like arranging things—especially vegetables. ›

› I have a collection of shallow wicker baskets that I fill with green beans and zucchini and beefsteak tomatoes. Stacks of little green cardboard pint containers stand at the ready, waiting to be filled with our signature colorful cherry tomatoes, French fingerling potatoes, and striped Fairy Tale eggplants.

And when the zinnias and cosmos start blooming profusely, I'm out in the cutting garden with scissors and rubber bands just as soon as the dew is dry. I did not inherit the fancy-flower-arrangement gene, so I know I must slip the stems into my waiting fingers as soon as I cut them, bunching them up as best I can. I strip the lower ›

SERVES 4 TO 6;
MAKES 12 BRUSCHETTA

12 slices ciabatta (sliced about ¾ inch thick)

2 tablespoons extra-virgin olive oil, plus more for the bread

Kosher salt

3 to 3½ cups cored, diced, ripe, juicy beefsteak tomatoes (about 1½ pounds tomatoes)

¼ cup thinly sliced fresh basil leaves

2½ teaspoons minced fresh garlic

¼ teaspoon balsamic vinegar

CLASSIC BEEFSTEAK BRUSCHETTA

I keep my bruschetta simple—straight-up tomatoes, garlic, basil, and olive oil. There's really no reason to mess with this powerhouse combination. When you have truly juicy, ripe, flavorful beefsteak tomatoes, nothing's better. (Please don't make bruschetta with grocery-store tomatoes!) Bruschetta makes the simplest, most delicious lunch you can throw together, straight from the garden on a hot August day. But it's also a killer way to welcome friends over for a summer supper.

Heat a gas grill to medium or a broiler to high. Brush both sides of the bread slices generously with olive oil and sprinkle with salt. Put the slices directly on the grill grate or put on a baking sheet a few inches under the broiler element. Cook until golden brown on the first side, 1 to 2 minutes. Flip and cook for 1 to 2 minutes more until the other side is golden.

In a small mixing bowl, combine the tomatoes, the 2 tablespoons olive oil, basil, garlic, balsamic vinegar, and ¼ teaspoon salt. Stir well and let sit for a few minutes, stirring occasionally. (The tomatoes will let off a lot of juices.) Taste and season with more salt, if desired.

Arrange the toasted bread slices on a platter or on serving plates and spoon the tomato mixture over them. Let sit for a few minutes so that the bread soaks up a bit of the juices.

TOMATO PARTY SANDWICHES ON FRESH CORN BISCUITS WITH BASIL MAYO

MAKES 14 TO 16 SANDWICHES

1 large egg yolk

1 tablespoon heavy cream

1 cup fresh corn kernels, from about 2 medium or 3 small ears

2 cups unbleached all-purpose flour, plus more for the surface

1 tablespoon double-acting baking powder

½ teaspoon table salt

6 tablespoons unsalted butter, cut into pieces and chilled

½ cup grated sharp Cheddar cheese

¾ cup cold milk

Sea salt, coarse or flaky

1 recipe Basil Mayonnaise (p. 71)

8 small tomatoes (about 2½ inches in diameter), preferably 4 red or purple and 4 orange or yellow, sliced ¼ inch thick, very lightly salted, and arranged on paper towels to drain slightly

32 large basil leaves, preferably a mix of purple and green or Green Ruffles; more sprigs for garnish, if desired

Everyone has a favorite take on a tomato sandwich and mine just happens to be on a biscuit—a biscuit spiked with fresh corn and a bit of cheese, no less. I make a quick basil mayonnaise and layer slices of small juicy ripe tomatoes with colorful leaves of fresh basil for a "sandwich" bursting with flavor. These are great for a cocktail party, but just as nice for a light lunch, too. You'll need a 2-inch biscuit cutter for this recipe.

MAKE THE BISCUITS

Heat the oven to 450°F. Line a heavy-duty rimmed baking sheet with parchment paper. Whisk together the egg yolk and heavy cream and set the egg wash aside.

Put the corn in a small dish with a tablespoon or two of water and microwave on high for 40 seconds or submerge them for a few seconds in boiling water (use a handheld strainer). Drain and pat dry.

In a medium bowl, stir together the flour, baking powder, and table salt. Add the chilled butter pieces and the Cheddar. Using a pastry cutter (or two table knives), blend the butter into the flour until the mixture resembles coarse breadcrumbs. Make a well in the center of the mixture and pour in the milk. Mix with a wooden spoon just until the dry ingredients are moistened and the dough comes away from the side of the bowl (the dough will be a sticky). Quickly mix in the corn kernels.

Transfer the dough to a floured surface. Flour your hands and fold the dough onto itself five or six times. (Don't be afraid to flour the surface or

continued on p. 71 ›

› leaves, trim the stems, and scooch the flowers into Mason jars and coffee cans. When I step back and look at all the colors blinking in the sunlight, I am pretty much giddy with joy. Sure, it's kind of amateur hour where the flowers are concerned, but I don't care. And I don't charge much for them. Roy, on the other hand, takes great pride in the elegant gladiolus he grows. Gruff Builder Boy meets Pretty Flowers. Amusing for sure. Who knew?

Inevitably the first customers arrive before I have the farm stand completely set up. That's okay. You can tell they have their summer schedules to stick by, too. A day at South Beach in the roaring surf awaits. A swing by the Chilmark Flea Market and ›

COOK'S TIP

Choose tomatoes the same diameter as your biscuit cutter or, if necessary, quarter slices of large tomatoes.

Tomato Party Sandwiches on
Fresh Corn Biscuits with Basil Mayo

the dough as needed.) Pat it into a square shape and sprinkle it with flour. Roll it out to a thickness of about ¾ inch. With a lightly floured 2-inch biscuit cutter, cut out biscuit rounds (do not twist the cutter). You should have 12 to 14 biscuits. (You can put pieces together and reroll the dough once.) Place the rounds on the baking sheet. Brush the tops with the egg wash and sprinkle with sea salt. Bake until the biscuits are puffed and lightly browned, 14 to 15 minutes. (The bottoms will be golden.) Let the biscuits cool on the pan.

ASSEMBLE THE SANDWICHES

Split the corn biscuits in half and spread each half with basil mayonnaise. Arrange one red tomato slice on the bottom half and top with one leaf of green basil. Layer another tomato slice (of a different color if you have it) on top, followed by a leaf of purple basil (if you have it). Finish with the top half of the biscuit. Arrange the sandwiches on a platter for serving, garnished with sprigs of basil, if you like.

BASIL MAYONNAISE

MAKES ABOUT 1¼ CUPS

1 cup lightly packed fresh basil

1 cup mayonnaise

2 teaspoons fresh lemon juice

Freshly ground black pepper

Scant ¼ teaspoon freshly grated lemon zest

I like to make this quick-and-easy flavored mayo in a small or mini-food processor, but if you don't have one, you can hand-mince the basil and stir all the ingredients together.

In the bowl of a small food processor, combine the basil, ¼ cup of the mayonnaise, the lemon juice, and several grinds of black pepper. Process until the basil is finely chopped. Add the remaining mayonnaise and lemon zest and process again.

Store tightly covered in the fridge for up to 3 days.

› a lobster roll up in the fishing village of Menemsha are on the list. Maybe a ride on the Flying Horses Carousel and an ice cream cone at Ben and Bill's later on. But the stop at the farm stand is important, too. It's part of what being on Martha's Vineyard in the summertime is all about.

I understand those expectations—my own ripe memories of farm stand visits as a child drive me to try and match the memories-in-the-making that go hand-in-hand with a ride on the ferry from Woods Hole, Massachusetts, to this island in the middle of the Atlantic. Certainly, everyone who boards that boat has a different picture ›

> of their perfect idyll. But more than likely, a juicy tomato, a bunch of freshly picked flowers, or an ear of sweet corn will slip into that reverie at some point along the way.

I only have to close my eyes to remember hanging my head out the station wagon window as we neared the farm stand in Lewes, Delaware, every summer afternoon when I was a kid. I can smell the melon-perfumed air, feel the gravel bite my bare feet as I run to ogle the giant peaches, brushing my fingers over their fuzzy cheeks. I can see the dust cloud following the old red Ford truck as it rattles in from the field piled high with freshly picked ears of Silver ›

MAKES 1⅔ CUPS

½ cup lightly packed cilantro (leaves and any upper stems—just lop the top off a bunch)

½ teaspoon kosher salt, plus more to taste

½ teaspoon sugar, plus more to taste

1 large clove garlic, peeled

1 small serrano pepper, roughly chopped

2 cups cored, seeded, and roughly chopped very ripe plum tomatoes (about 14 to 15 ounces or 4 to 6 large plum tomatoes)

2 teaspoons olive oil

2 teaspoons fresh lime juice, plus more to taste

2 to 4 tablespoons thinly sliced scallions (white and as much of the green part as you like) (optional)

LAZY SUMMER DAY SALSA WITH SERRANOS, CILANTRO & LIME

This super-fast, super-easy food-processor salsa (hence the "lazy"—very little chopping!) is so tasty that it will put the kibosh on the store-bought stuff once and for all. It's just as perfect with chips as it is with grilled fish or steak fajitas (p. 109). It's a loose style of salsa, one like what you might see on the table at a Mexican restaurant. Be sure to use very ripe plum tomatoes. (If you get them at the grocery, let them sit on the counter until they are very ripe.)

Put the cilantro, salt, sugar, garlic, and serrano in the bowl of a food processor. Process until finely chopped. Add the tomatoes and pulse six to eight times again until very finely chopped. (Don't overprocess. The salsa should have a very loose consistency but should still have visible small chunks of veggies.) Scrape down the sides of the bowl and add the olive oil and lime juice. Pulse once or twice until combined. Taste for seasonings, adding more salt, sugar, or lime juice if desired, and process briefly again if necessary.

Transfer the salsa to a bowl and stir in as many scallions as you like (or none at all). Serve right away or store in the fridge, well covered, for several days.

GRILLED CORN AND ROASTED TOMATO SALSA

MAKES 3 CUPS

10 Quick-Roasted Tomato halves (p. 84)

3 medium ears fresh corn, shucked and grilled (see the method below)

1 medium red bell pepper, grill-roasted, peeled, and seeded (see the method on p. 119)

1 medium red onion (about 7 ounces), peeled, sliced, and grilled (see the method on p. 209)

1 serrano pepper, roasted (see the method on p. 74) (optional)

1 tablespoon extra-virgin olive oil

½ to 1 teaspoon balsamic vinegar

½ to 1 teaspoon fresh lemon or lime juice

½ to 1 teaspoon minced fresh garlic

¼ to ½ teaspoon ground cumin

Kosher salt

2 to 3 tablespoons chopped fresh basil or a combination of basil, mint, cilantro, or parsley

As much as I love my quick, fresh salsa (facing page), there are times when I crave the deep flavors of a salsa that features grilled and roasted veggies. Making a batch of roasted tomatoes (p. 84) usually kick-starts this craving. I'm also a big fan of grilled corn; combining the two makes a substantial salsa that's almost more like a side dish. It does take a bit of time to cook everything, but it can all be done ahead, so it's perfect for an entertaining menu that stars grilled meat.

Cut the roasted tomato halves into medium dice and put them (and any residual juices) in a mixing bowl. You should have about ¾ cup. Cut the kernels off the corn cobs. You should have about 1½ cups. Add the kernels to the mixing bowl. Cut the roasted bell pepper into small dice and add to the bowl with any residual juice. Chop the grilled onion and add it to the bowl. Remove the peel (and the seeds if you like) from the roasted serrano (if using), chop the flesh very finely, and add it to the bowl. Add the olive oil, ½ teaspoon balsamic vinegar, ½ teaspoon lemon or lime juice, ½ teaspoon garlic, ¼ teaspoon cumin, and ¼ teaspoon salt to the bowl and toss and mix gently but thoroughly with a silicone spatula. Add 2 tablespoons of the herbs and toss again. Taste and add more of any of the seasonings or herbs, stir well, and taste again. Serve at room temperature or store covered in the fridge for up to 2 days.

TO GRILL THE CORN

Heat a gas grill to medium. Shuck the corn and remove all the silk. Put the corn in a shallow dish and toss it with a few tablespoons of water, a little

continued on p. 74 ›

› Queen corn. There are lima beans and cantaloupes and big crisp heads of iceberg lettuce, too. My dad is talking with Mr. Knapp, the farmer, and saying hello to old Hazel, a friend of my grandmother's. I've got an ice-cold Nehi grape soda to sip on, too. I think I carried that pleasant memory, hidden inside me, through the crazy-busy years of my early adulthood, always wondering how to reconnect to it. Well, you know what they say—be careful what you wish for!

DUMB LUCK AND GREEN BEANS

Summer leaves the station and we are heading full-tilt for the Fair in August. Kind of a cool goal. Of course every day we get the satisfaction of seeing customers buy our vegetables ›

COOK'S TIP

If you don't have a grill, you can still make this. Broil the corn and peppers and sear the onions in a hot cast-iron pan.

olive oil, and salt. Toss the corn directly on the grate, cover the grill, and cook until browned in spots on the underside, 2 to 3 minutes. Uncover, rotate the cobs about 90 degrees, cover, and cook again for 2 to 3 minutes. Repeat until the cobs are nicely browned in spots all over. Transfer to a plate to cool.

TO ROAST THE SERRANOS

Put the hot peppers in a dry cast-iron skillet and place directly on heated grill grates. Toss frequently until blistered. Remove and cover with foil to steam. If you don't have a cast-iron skillet, put the peppers on a grill screen over the grates. Always be cautious about breathing steam or smoke from roasting hot peppers—steer clear of direct fumes!

TANGY GARDEN GAZPACHO WITH SUN GOLD SALSA AND GRILLED CROUTONS

SERVES 4 TO 6

Eight ¾-inch slices from a French baguette

2¼ to 2½ pounds beefsteak tomatoes

1 large clove garlic

½ teaspoon minced serrano peppers (seeds and ribs included)

⅓ cup chopped fresh cilantro stems and leaves, plus 1 teaspoon chopped leaves

Kosher salt

4 tablespoons olive oil; more for the salsa, croutons, and drizzling

1 small cucumber (about 8 ounces), peeled, seeded, and thickly sliced

1 small red bell pepper, grill-roasted, peeled, seeded (see the method on p. 119), and roughly chopped (to yield about ½ cup)

1½ teaspoons balsamic vinegar

16 Sun Gold or other orange cherry tomatoes, cut into quarters

1 to 2 tablespoons thinly sliced scallions (green part only)

I can't help myself. I know gazpacho is supposed to be a cold soup made from raw vegetables, but every time I make it, I wind up sneaking in a little something roasty-toasty. In this case, just one little roasted pepper counters the tomatoes' acidity with depth and sweetness. Cool cucumbers, a resounding punch of garlic, spicy serranos, and an herby base of cilantro build a boldly flavorful soup, which also manages to be quite elegant since it is puréed. Serve it in a shallow bowl and show off the salsa-and-crouton topping.

Remove (and discard) the crusts from 4 of the baguette slices and rip the bread into pieces. You should have about ½ cup bread pieces.

Core the beefsteak tomatoes and cut them in half cross-wise (through the equator). Over a small bowl, gently poke out most of the seeds and pulp using your fingers. (Don't throw away the seeds and pulp—put them in a fine-mesh strainer and capture the tomato liquid that gathers. You can use that liquid later to thin the soup if you like.) Roughly chop the tomato halves and measure out 3 packed cups for the soup (some liquid will come with the chopped tomatoes). Save any extra for salads.

Put the garlic, serranos, ⅓ cup cilantro stems and leaves, ¼ teaspoon salt, and 1 tablespoon of the olive oil in a blender. Blend on high, stopping to scrape the blender from time to time, until well chopped. Add the chopped tomatoes, cucumbers, roasted peppers, balsamic vinegar, the remaining 3 tablespoons olive oil, ¼ teaspoon salt, and the ½ cup of the ripped baguette pieces. Blend on high for 2 full minutes until very smooth and a tad frothy. Taste and add

continued on p. 76 ›

› and eggs, and hearing their appreciation. But we always have our eyes on the prize, too. Or prizes. We've won blue and red ribbons for most of our veggies since the very first year we entered the Fair. Am I bragging? Hell, yes. You've got to. There's enough heartbreak in farming to fill a whole hoop house and then some. Some of those baby chicks don't make it, you know. And entire crops of kale get eaten by cabbage worms. The irrigation "system" leaks, tangles, breaks. Weeds grow and grow. Hurricanes hobble hoop houses. That sort of thing.

We always win a ribbon for our green beans, because they are the best beans ever, ›

› anywhere. You know I am just having a little fun here, but honestly, this is very close to the truth. Those farm stand customers who show up early in the morning? They're looking for the green beans, which sell out by the middle of the afternoon.

I wish I could tell you this is due to our incredible growing prowess, but it's mostly about the bean variety, which we found by accident. There's a whole component of market gardening-turned-farming that thrives on trial and error. Which reminds me that I've been meaning to offer you this disclaimer: You should question every word of gardening/farming advice I give in this book and back it up with at least two dozen Internet searches. It's not like I'm saying that we've been making it up as we go along. Well, actually, that is exactly what I'm saying. (Don't worry, I swear by my cooking advice.)

We stumbled upon Beananza in the Burpee® catalogue the very first year we grew vegetables. These days we don't order much from Burpee (expensive!); ›

more salt if desired. If the soup seems a bit thick, add some of the reserved tomato liquid (start with about ¼ cup) and blend again. Chill in the refrigerator until very cold, at least 2 hours.

In a small bowl, combine the Sun Gold tomatoes, scallions, the remaining 1 teaspoon chopped cilantro, a pinch of salt, and 1 teaspoon olive oil. Toss the salsa well.

Heat a gas grill on medium or a broiler on high. Brush the remaining bread slices generously with olive oil and sprinkle with kosher salt. Grill or broil until nicely toasted on both sides, about 1 minute per side. Coarsely chop each baguette slice into small pieces. (They do not have to be uniform; crumbly is good.)

Ladle the cold gazpacho into shallow bowls and garnish each portion with a generous sprinkling of croutons and a nice scattering of Sun Gold salsa. (You may not use all of the croutons.) Drizzle a small bit of olive oil over all, too, if you like.

COOK'S TIP

Since beefsteak tomatoes come in so many shapes and sizes, it's hard to predict what they'll yield after coring and seeding. Be sure you cut up enough to get a final volume of 3 cups chopped tomatoes to use in the soup, but don't be tempted to use more than 3 cups, or the soup proportions will be out of whack (and your blender will complain, too). Use any extra in salads.

Tangy Garden Gazpacho with
Sun Gold Salsa and Grilled Croutons

› most of our seeds come from a co-op in Maine called FedCo. But unlike a lot of seed catalogue promises that turn out to be so much hot air, the description of Beananza was spot on. Not only is this slender-tender bean delicious, but it's also very prolific. Most bush beans peter out after a few weeks, but these plants produce continuously until the first frost. They're a real find, so we snatch up a big order of them every January.

You'd think I'd be dancing around, singing "Oh happy day—continuous production!" But you realize what this means, don't you? Someone has to pick the friggin' green beans every single day. Every plant. ›

GRILLED ANTIPASTO OF GREEN AND YELLOW ZUCCHINI WITH BLACK OLIVE–LEMON VINAIGRETTE

SERVES 6

6 tablespoons extra-virgin olive oil

2 tablespoons chopped pitted Kalamata olives

1 tablespoon white balsamic vinegar

1 tablespoon chopped fresh oregano

1 teaspoon (packed) finely grated lemon zest

½ teaspoon honey

Kosher salt

1½ pounds green and yellow zucchini (about 3 medium-large), ends trimmed, sliced on the diagonal into ⅜-inch slices

3 to 4 ounces fresh goat cheese, crumbled

¼ cup fresh flat-leaf parsley leaves

2 tablespoons toasted pine nuts

A little goat cheese surprise lies in wait beneath the grilled squash in this dish. I call it an antipasto, but it's really kind of a warm salad. And I let Greek flavors (oregano, lemon, olives) influence the vinaigrette, so maybe it's more of a mezze! I like to serve this on a platter, family-style, but you could also pair it with grilled fish on a dinner plate. If you see deep yellow zucchini (I like Sunbeam variety), include it in the mix with the green. But skip (paler yellow) summer squash, which sheds a lot of moisture when cooked.

Heat a gas grill to medium high. Scrape the grill grates clean.

To make the dressing, combine 3 tablespoons of the olive oil with the olives, balsamic vinegar, oregano, lemon zest, honey, and ⅛ teaspoon salt. Whisk well and set aside.

Toss the squash slices with the remaining 3 tablespoons olive oil and ½ teaspoon salt.

Arrange the squash slices directly on the grill grate and close the lid. (The grill will be crowded.) Cook, checking the slices after 2 minutes, until the bottom of each slice is nicely browned in places, 3 to 4 minutes. (After 2 minutes, you can turn the slices on an angle to make crosshatch marks if you like.) Carefully turn each slice over as it browns, close the lid again, and cook until the other side is lightly browned, 2 to 4 minutes. Transfer all of the squash slices to a baking sheet or a few plates. Don't stack or they'll overcook.

Choose a platter or plates and sprinkle the goat cheese over it (or them). Arrange the warm squash slices, slightly overlapping, over the goat cheese as you like. (Try pinwheel-style for small plates.) Whisk the dressing and spoon over all. Scatter the parsley and pine nuts over. Serve warm.

ROASTED TOMATO RUSTIC TART

MAKES ONE 8-INCH TART

FOR THE DOUGH
1 cup (4½ ounces) unbleached all-purpose flour, plus more for dusting the surface

2 teaspoons sugar

¼ teaspoon table salt

1 stick (½ cup) cold unsalted butter, cut into cubes (keep cold if working ahead)

2 tablespoons plus 1 teaspoon ice water

FOR THE ASSEMBLY AND FILLING
1 large egg yolk

2 tablespoons heavy cream

⅓ cup coarsely grated Parmigiano-Reggiano

15 to 16 Quick-Roasted Tomato Halves (p. 84)

1 teaspoon thyme leaves

Hands down, this is my favorite savory tart of the many I've made over the years. I'd like to be buried with a slice of it (no, not a slice—the whole thing!). Seriously, I know I'm constantly praising the virtues of Quick-Roasted Tomatoes (p. 84), but I think they've found nirvana nestled into this buttery crust. Yes, there's a bit of cooking to do, but with planning, this gorgeous tart comes together seamlessly. Make the dough a day ahead; remember to take it out of the fridge 30 minutes before assembling.

MAKE THE DOUGH

In the bowl of a food processor, combine the flour, sugar, and salt. Pulse briefly to combine. Add the cubes of butter and pulse about 20 times, or until the butter particles are quite small. With the motor running, add the ice water. Process until the dough is beginning to come together (but will still be loose—if you pinch some together it should form a clump.) Don't over process. Turn the loose dough out into a mixing bowl and knead it briefly to finish bringing it together. Shape the dough into a disk about ¾ inch thick, wrap in plastic, and refrigerate for at least 45 minutes and up to 2 days.

TO ASSEMBLE AND COOK THE TART

Remove the dough disk from the refrigerator and let it sit at room temperature for 30 to 40 minutes. Heat the oven to 400°F. Line a heavy-duty rimmed baking sheet with parchment paper.

In a small bowl, whisk together the egg yolk and heavy cream and set aside.

Sprinkle a light dusting of flour on a rolling surface. Roll the dough out into a round about 11 to 12 inches in diameter, sprinkling flour underneath as necessary to keep from it sticking. Transfer the dough to the parchment-lined sheet.

continued on p. 82 ›

› Every row. Every day. Crouching, kneeling, crouch-kneeling—whatever your favorite technique, you're in it for the long haul. If you don't pick every day, the beans get oversized quickly. This is why a lot of small farms don't even grow green beans, or they ask their CSA members to pick their own—too labor intensive. And for teeny farms like us, hiring someone else to pick our green beans (while we do other things) doesn't make sense—the little bit of profit you make on them would evaporate.

Hmmm. This dilemma really puzzled me after our first summer here. I never had enough green beans, and I hated the disappointed look on a customer's face when she'd hop out of her car, rustle up a brown paper bag, and then stare down into a basket with one withered-up weenie bean left hanging around. (Picture me, of course, inside again, peering through the curtains—too embarrassed to go out and apologize!) What to do. I wanted to plant more but it didn't make a whole lot of economic sense. ›

COOK'S TIP

I like the brilliantly simple flavor of roasted tomatoes, Parmigiano, and buttery crust, but if you want to "tart" the tart up a bit, you can sprinkle a couple of tablespoons of crumbled feta and/or finely chopped olives or capers over the Parmigiano before layering on the tomatoes.

Sprinkle about 3 tablespoons of the Parmigiano over the middle of the dough (in a rough circle, leaving a 2-inch border). Arrange the roasted tomato halves over the cheese, starting in the center and slightly overlapping the tomatoes as you go, being sure to leave the 2-inch border of dough uncovered. (Tip: Arrange the tomatoes on a plate first to figure out how they will work on the dough.) Sprinkle all but a few of the thyme leaves and all but 2 teaspoons of the remaining Parmigiano over the tomatoes.

Pleat and fold the edge of the dough up and over the tomato filling. Brush the dough (including under the folds) with the egg mixture. (You won't use it all.) Sprinkle the remaining thyme leaves and the remaining 2 teaspoons of Parmigiano over the dough edge.

Bake until the crust is deeply golden and the bottom is crisp and brown (check with a spatula), about 40 minutes. Let cool slightly on the baking sheet then transfer to a cutting board. Slice into 8 pieces and eat warm or at room temperature. Store, covered with foil, at room temperature for a day, or wrap well and freeze. Reheat slices on a baking sheet for 10 minutes in a 350°F oven.

ROASTED EGGPLANT, ROASTED TOMATO, FRESH MOZZARELLA & BASIL "STACKS"

SERVES 6 TO 8

1 medium globe eggplant (about 1 pound; preferably one with a narrower, rather than wider girth)

3 tablespoons extra-virgin olive oil

Kosher salt

6 to 8 Quick-Roasted Tomato halves (p. 84) or smaller Slow-Roasted Tomato halves (p. 213), gently reheated if you like

5 to 6 ounces fresh mozzarella, cut into ¼-inch-thick slices (if using a large ball, slice in half or quarters first to get slices that will fit in the stacks; you will need 6 to 8 large slices or 12 to 16 smaller slices)

Garlic Oil (p. 87)

Balsamic Drizzle (p. 13)

16 to 24 fresh basil leaves

4 to 6 cups baby salad greens, washed and dried (optional)

This is a roasted veggie marriage made in heaven. The smoky richness of roasted eggplant paired with the sweet-tart flavor of roasted tomatoes and cooled off by creamy mozzarella and bracing basil is what I consider the perfect taste of late summer. Eat these with a knife and fork. The salad greens are optional, but along with the Balsamic Drizzle and Garlic Oil, they make for a lovely first course for a special summer dinner.

Heat the oven to 450°F. Line a heavy-duty rimmed sheet pan with parchment paper. Trim the ends of the eggplant. Score the eggplant skin by dragging a fork down it lengthwise, repeating all over until the whole eggplant is scored. Cut the eggplant into ½-inch slices (you should have between 12 and 16).

Arrange the slices in one layer on the sheet pan and brush both sides of each slice with plenty of olive oil. Season the tops with a little salt. Roast, carefully turning over halfway through cooking if desired, until the eggplant is tender and nicely browned, 24 to 26 minutes. (Cooking times vary depending on the maturity of the eggplant. If you don't flip, the undersides will be most brown, which is fine.)

Before you arrange the stacks, look at your roasted eggplant slices and pair off sets of two that are similarly sized to each other. Decide whether you will arrange all of the stacks on a platter or whether you will plate them individually on salad plates, surrounded by a few salad greens. Arrange half of the eggplant slices on the plates or platter to form the first layer of the stack. Put one roasted tomato half on top of each eggplant slice. Top each

continued on p. 84 ›

› Solution: I raised the price a dollar per pound the next summer. I knew the beans were worth it; in fact, I knew they were far better than anything you could get at the grocery store for almost as much money. I tried not to feel bad about this, held my head high, and planted more beans. The extra dollar made enough difference to justify the time we invest in them. So we planted more beans the third year. And now, yes, we are slaves to green beans.

GREEN BEANS FOR DINNER, AGAIN?

This whole green bean thing is ironic, considering I swore I'd never eat beans again after growing up in my family. My mother, in her pre-Julia Child days, relied heavily on boiled-green-beans-as-easy-side-dish for family dinners. I think we ate them three or four nights a week. Always plain. ›

› And my father grew pole beans (Kentucky Wonder) in his little vegetable garden at our beach cottage in Delaware. One summer, my mother got sick and my father had to be with her at the hospital back in Washington. He left my big sister and I alone in the beach cottage, and what was supposed to be one week turned into two. We ran out of grocery money at some point. But not green beans. So we ate them every night. (To be fair, my father had instructed my grandmother to check on us, but she was busy playing bridge and going to cocktail parties. Her name was Honey, but it could have been Auntie Mame.) That August pretty much finished me for green beans. Or so I thought.

A funny thing happened many years later when I got a job at *Fine Cooking* magazine. My boss asked me to write about green beans, to create delicious recipes using them. I started to experiment with ›

tomato with one or more slices of mozzarella to cover the tomato. Sprinkle the mozzarella with a little kosher salt and then drizzle with a tiny bit of Garlic Oil and a little bit of Balsamic Drizzle. Top with 2 or 3 basil leaves and another slice of roasted eggplant. Arrange a portion of salad greens next to or around the stack if you are using them and drizzle Garlic Oil and Balsamic Drizzle lightly over both the stack and the greens. Garnish the top of the stack with another small basil leaf. Serve right away.

QUICK-ROASTED TOMATOES

MAKES 24 TOMATO HALVES

⅓ cup plus 1 tablespoon extra-virgin olive oil

1 tablespoon balsamic vinegar

2 teaspoons honey

2 to 3 teaspoons lightly chopped fresh thyme

Kosher salt

12 small meaty sandwich tomatoes (about 4 to 5 ounces each) or 12 plum tomatoes

I developed this technique for my first cookbook, *Fast, Fresh & Green*, in order to get that great slow-roasted tomato flavor a bit more quickly. I got great results with seeded plum tomatoes and high heat. So this summer, I decided to try the quick-roast method with my Early Girl (small sandwich) tomatoes. Success—hip hip hooray! (I still use the slow-roast method, p. 213, for big beefsteaks.) The caramelized flavor is awesome, making these tomatoes not just a great nibble alone, but a versatile recipe ingredient, too: Think burger toppings (p. 103), tarts (p. 81), sides (Cook's Tips on p. 87), salsas (p. 73), starters (p. 83), and more.

Heat the oven to 425°F. Line a large heavy-duty rimmed sheet pan with aluminum foil and then with a piece of parchment paper. (Covering the pan with foil first makes cleanup a whole lot easier.) Brush 1 tablespoon of the olive oil over the parchment.

In a glass measure, combine the remaining ⅓ cup olive oil, the balsamic vinegar, honey, thyme, and a pinch of salt. Whisk well. If you're using sandwich tomatoes, slice each tomato in half through the equator. If you're using plum tomatoes, slice the tomatoes in half from stem to blossom end. Gently poke the seeds out of each half and arrange the tomato halves, cut side up, on the parchment. Season very lightly with salt.

Pour the olive oil/balsamic mixture gently into and around the rims of each tomato half, distributing as evenly as possible.

continued on p. 87 ›

Roasted Eggplant, Roasted Tomato, Fresh Mozzarella & Basil "Stacks"

Roast the tomatoes until they are brown on the edges and somewhat collapsed, 55 to 65 minutes. Let them cool for at least a few minutes on the sheet pan. Tip any excess oil out of the tomatoes if you like. (That oil is delicious on bread!) Serve warm or at room temperature. Store in a covered container in the refrigerator for a week or in the freezer for 2 to 3 months.

GARLIC OIL

4 tablespoons extra-virgin olive oil

2 large cloves garlic, sliced crosswise

Combine the olive oil and garlic in a small skillet over medium heat. Cook, swirling the pan occasionally, until the garlic is sizzling and just turning a light golden brown, about 2 minutes. Remove the pan from the heat and let sit for 5 to 10 minutes before using (don't remove the garlic slices). Store covered for up to 2 days in the fridge.

COOK'S TIP

Here's a great idea for serving quick-roasted tomatoes as a side dish. Tip the roasted tomatoes a bit (if necessary) to drain any excess oil. Arrange in a small baking dish. For each tomato half, combine 1 tablespoon grated Parmigiano, 1 tablespoon fresh breadcrumbs, a pinch of salt, a few thyme leaves if you have them, and ½ teaspoon olive oil. (Multiply this as many times as you like for the number of tomato halves you want to serve—2 is a good amount per person for a side dish.) Put the baking dish in a moderate oven (350° to 400°F) and bake for 7 to 10 minutes, or until heated through. Turn on the broiler and set the dish under it for a couple of minutes, or until the crumb topping is browned and crispy.

› stir-fries and sautés and braises and roasts. Yum. Now here were some reasons to like green beans. I was primed; once I started to grow them, like turned to love.

These days, the very simplest and most delicious thing we do with a handful of green beans— especially on a busy summer night when we need to eat quickly—is to toss them in a hot sauté pan with a smashed garlic clove, a sliver of ginger, or a little serrano pepper cut in half (or all three), turn up the heat, cover loosely, and stir often. Browned and cooked through in only a couple minutes, they're the bee's knees.

I'm also fond of dicing green beans into cute little pieces. The beans then become a super-fast cooking ingredient—they star in our fried rice (p. 100) and in my yummy fresh corn sautés (p. 132), too. ›

Colorful Cherokee Purple and Sun Gold Tomato–Basil Salad

COLORFUL CHEROKEE PURPLE AND SUN GOLD TOMATO–BASIL SALAD

SERVES 6

½ medium red onion, very thinly sliced (about ¾ cup)

2 tablespoons fresh lime juice

Kosher salt

2 tablespoons pure maple syrup

2 tablespoons best-quality extra-virgin olive oil

2 teaspoons minced fresh ginger

1½ pounds stemmed and cored Cherokee Purple tomatoes or other dark-fleshed ripe tomatoes, cut into wedges or 1-inch pieces, or 1½ pounds Black Cherry tomatoes, halved (or a combination)

12 ounces (about 1 scant pint) Sun Gold cherry tomatoes or other small yellow or orange tomatoes, halved

¾ cup loosely packed small or medium whole green and/or purple basil leaves (about 50 to 60 leaves)

Edible flowers, such as borage or gem marigolds or pinks (optional)

Color in the garden (and on the farm stand) really excites me, and I can't help carrying it onto the plate. And everyone needs a good tomato salad in their repertoire—and a way to showcase special tomatoes, too. This salad does all that. I use our juicy Cherokee Purples, our Black Cherries, and our tangy Sun Golds to set up a fun color contrast. But with plenty of basil and a sprightly lime-ginger dressing, you could make this refreshing salad with any ripe summer tomatoes. Just cut everything about the same size.

In a small bowl, combine the onions, 2 teaspoons of the lime juice, and a pinch of salt. Toss well and let sit for 10 to 15 minutes. Drain.

In another small bowl, combine the remaining lime juice and the maple syrup. Add the olive oil, ginger, and ¼ teaspoon salt. Whisk the dressing well.

In a larger mixing bowl, combine the tomatoes, onions, and most of the basil (reserve some leaves for garnish). Season with a big pinch of salt and drizzle with all the dressing. Toss gently but thoroughly and let sit for 5 to 10 minutes, stirring occasionally. Transfer to a pretty serving bowl and garnish with the remaining basil leaves and edible flowers (if using).

› For a real treat, we build a veggie paella (p. 105) around our best green beans. And when the beans do get a little overgrown, I don't fret. I give the "honkers," as I call the hugest ones, to the chickens. And I take the rest and slowly cook them in olive oil with lots of aromatics like mushrooms, onions, and bacon and, voilà, they melt into tenderness. I do this with our pole green beans, too (p. 202). That's right, every summer I nab just a small corner of the garden to throw up a simple bamboo and twine trellis and plant a few Kentucky Wonder seeds, in honor of my dad.

COOK'S TIP

Because my Cherokee Purple tomatoes grow in such funky shapes, I never know how much one will yield after stemming or coring. A lot of heirloom tomatoes are like this. That's why I've called for a trimmed weight in the ingredients list to keep the ingredients in proportion. You may need 4 or 5 tomatoes or you may need a bit more.

THE BEST CORN IS GROWING NEXT DOOR

People ask me all the time what my favorite vegetable is. I have a hard time answering that because I can't settle on just one. I wouldn't want to live in a world without juicy beefsteak tomatoes, but then again, a big pan of roasted carrots and onions and potatoes and garlic and sweet potatoes and...well, I really do love vegetables. But when I am practicing my sound bites for radio spots (!), my answer is, "Why, sweet corn, of course!"

This is probably just pure nostalgia—that Silver Queen corn we ate in Delaware was really something. But at the same time, since I have a ›

GREEK ISLANDS GRILLED BREAD, TOMATO & CUCUMBER SALAD

SERVES 8

3 tablespoons extra-virgin olive oil, plus more for brushing the bread

1 tablespoon plus 1 teaspoon good-quality sherry vinegar

1½ teaspoons minced fresh garlic

Kosher salt

Six 1-inch-thick slices ciabatta or other airy artisan bread

2 to 2¼ pounds ripe, juicy tomatoes (a combo of all different size and color heirlooms is lovely)

1 medium cucumber

¼ pound feta cheese, cut into small cubes

24 small Manzanilla (Spanish green olives) or Kalamata olives, smashed and pitted

¼ cup thinly sliced scallions (white and light green parts)

Freshly ground black pepper

½ cup small whole fresh herb leaves (basil, oregano, and mint) and tiny herb blossoms if available

It may be a stretch to imagine Martha's Vineyard as a sunny Greek Island, but sometimes I pretend anyway when I make this classic Mediterranean salad. Juicy tomatoes and cucumbers, crusty bread, and a garlicky, herby, feta cheese-y dressing makes a stunning and delicious summer dish, perfect for the beach, no matter what island (or, uh, sand spit) you're on. I prefer to grill the bread here, but broiling works just fine, too. To turn this into a main dish, add chopped grilled shrimp.

In a small bowl, combine the 3 tablespoons olive oil, the sherry vinegar, garlic, and a pinch of salt. Set aside.

Heat a gas grill to medium or a broiler to high. Brush the bread generously with olive oil on both sides and sprinkle with salt. Put the slices directly on the grill grate or a few inches under the broiler element and cook until light golden brown on the first side, about 1 minute. Flip and cook for 1 minute more until the other side is golden. Transfer the bread to a cutting board and cut into ¾-inch cubes.

Cut the tomatoes into pieces all about the same size. (A rough guideline: Cut large tomatoes into 1-inch pieces; medium tomatoes into wedges; small tomatoes into quarters; very small tomatoes in half.) Peel the cucumber, trim the ends, and cut it in half lengthwise. Scoop the seeds out with a spoon. Cut each piece in half again lengthwise (so that you have four long pieces); cut the pieces crosswise into ½-inch slices.

In a large mixing bowl, combine the tomatoes, cucumbers, feta, olives, scallions, ¼ teaspoon salt, a few grinds of black pepper, and half of the herbs. Add the bread pieces and toss gently to combine. Drizzle the olive

› serious sweet tooth, it makes sense I'd pick something like corn. Plus, I go totally nuts in the kitchen with corn off the cob—I've developed literally dozens of recipes with corn over the years—my favorites are sautés with other veggies, like the Corn-off-the-Cob and Yellow Bean Sauté with Bacon and Herbs on p. 132. But I also love to grill corn and build a salsa-y side dish around it, too (p. 73). Actually, in the summer and fall, there isn't much I don't add corn to—potato salad, pasta salad, grain dishes, vinaigrettes, scrambled-egg tostados (p. 137).

If you're like me and want to improvise with fresh, sweet corn kernels (blanched or raw), just be picky about where you get your corn. Buy it from a farm stand or at least a store that is selling locally grown corn. Avoid the corn in the grocery store that's been shipped from hundreds of miles away and is withered and browned. (Much of that corn is of the newer super-super-sweet variety, which has tough-skinned kernels and has lost some of its inherent corn flavor.) ›

oil–vinegar mixture over the salad and toss gently but thoroughly. Taste for salt and pepper. Let sit for 5 to 15 minutes to let the bread absorb some of the tomato juices, tossing once or twice. Turn out into a pretty shallow serving bowl and garnish with the remaining herbs.

ROY'S ALMOST-CLASSIC POTATO SALAD WITH FARM EGGS, CELERY & CRÈME FRÂICHE

SERVES 4 TO 6

2 pounds Yukon Gold potatoes, peeled and cut into ¾-inch pieces

Kosher salt

½ cup mayonnaise

½ cup crème frâiche or sour cream

1 tablespoon plus 1 teaspoon cider vinegar

1 tablespoon fresh lemon juice

1 teaspoon freshly grated lemon zest

¾ teaspoon ground coriander

Freshly ground black pepper

3 hard-cooked eggs (Cook's Tip, p. 6), peeled and sliced

2 long or 3 short ribs celery, halved lengthwise and thinly sliced (¾ cup)

½ small red onion, thinly sliced (a scant ½ cup)

2 to 3 tablespoons chopped fresh flat-leaf parsley

2 tablespoons sliced fresh chives

Roy likes a traditional American potato salad, so I developed this recipe for him. (He gives it two thumbs up. He said he'd give it three if he had an extra hand.) Two musts for him—the celery and the hard-cooked eggs. But he did let me lighten the mayo dressing with crème frâiche and add brightness with lemon, cider vinegar, parsley, chives, and a little ground coriander. Still, in the end, the potatoes are the star. Roy says to make this ahead; he likes it even better the next day.

Put the potatoes and 2 teaspoons salt in a large saucepan and cover with plenty of water. Bring to a boil, reduce to a simmer, and cook until just tender, 10 to 12 minutes. Drain carefully in a colander, rinse briefly with cool water, and spread on a clean dishtowel to cool to room temperature.

In a large mixing bowl, whisk together the mayonnaise, crème frâiche, cider vinegar, lemon juice, lemon zest, ground coriander, a pinch of salt, and several grinds of black pepper. Add the cooled potatoes, eggs, celery, onions, most of the parsley, and most of the chives. Sprinkle ½ teaspoon salt over all. With a silicone spatula, mix everything together until well combined, breaking the eggs apart as you mix. Transfer to a serving bowl and garnish with remaining parsley and chives. Serve right away or refrigerate for up to 24 hours.

› I have to confess that I am a little intimidated by growing corn, probably because I don't want mediocre corn—I want the best corn. I know that corn needs lots of room for proper pollination, which may be why our one feeble attempt to grow decent corn here did not yield anything I'd want to sell at the farm stand. We might try again someday, but in the meantime, we lucked out: The best corn on the Island is grown in a field right next to us—so close, in fact, that I can see it out my office window.

Morning Glory Farm, founded and run by the Athearn family, is actually located down in Edgartown, but they lease some land from our landlords, too. ›

> **COOK'S TIP**
>
> If you can't find crème frâiche, sour cream is a perfectly good substitute here, especially if you loosen it just a bit with a little cream or half-and-half.

› They are the most successful farmers on the Island (with the most fabulous farm stand of all!)—and genuinely helpful to new farmers like us. So it has been nice to bump into them out back.

At the end of last summer, Roy spoke with Simon Athearn about selling a little of their corn at our farm stand, and we then gave it a test-spin with a half-bushel a week. Roy would walk down and meet the pickers in the field and then carry the burlap bag back up to our picnic table, where we'd empty it out and inhale that fresh green smell as if it were chocolate chip cookies. Bliss. We're hoping to make an arrangement like this again this year, starting a little earlier in the summer. Morning Glory Farm corn is probably the ›

COOK'S TIP

There's a salad within a salad here. The black beans, veggies, and dressing ingredients can be tossed together and served on their own if you're not up for quinoa.

SERVES 8

Kosher salt

1¼ teaspoons ground cumin

1¼ teaspoons ground coriander

½ teaspoon ground cinnamon

4 tablespoons olive oil

1½ cups red quinoa, rinsed well if not pre-rinsed

One 15½-oz. can black beans, drained and rinsed

1 medium zucchini (about 7 ounces), trimmed and cut into small dice (1⅓ cups)

1 cup halved grape or cherry tomatoes

1 cup fresh corn kernels (from about 2 ears), microwaved or blanched for a few seconds

1 small (or ½ large) red bell pepper, seeded and cut into small dice (½ cup)

⅓ cup sliced scallions (white and light green parts)

¼ cup chopped fresh cilantro, plus sprigs for garnish

¼ cup fresh orange juice

1 tablespoon plus 2 teaspoons fresh lime juice

2 teaspoons minced fresh garlic

2 teaspoons honey, preferably local

¼ teaspoon Asian chili-garlic paste

½ to ⅔ cup toasted pine nuts

SOUTHWESTERN QUINOA SALAD WITH BLACK BEANS AND FARM STAND VEGGIES

Since I'm a sucker for color, once I discovered there was such a thing as red quinoa I had to have it. The brick-adobe red immediately made me think of the Southwest, so along came the spices, the black beans, and farm stand veggies like corn and zucchini to make up this tasty salad for picnics and potlucks. Since it takes a while to cool down, get the quinoa cooking before prepping the rest of your ingredients.

Combine 1 teaspoon salt, the cumin, coriander, and cinnamon in a small bowl.

In a 3-quart saucepan, heat 1 tablespoon of the olive oil over medium-low heat. Add the salt-spice mixture, stir well, and cook for 30 seconds. Add the quinoa, stir again, and add 2 cups water. Bring to a boil, reduce to a low simmer, cover, and cook until the quinoa has absorbed all the water and the germ has separated from the seed (it will look like a ring), 20 to 22 minutes. (If there is a little water left, bring back to a simmer and cook for 3 to 4 minutes more to boil off the water.) Remove the pot from the heat and stir once. Put a folded paper towel over the quinoa and cover with the pot lid again for 5 minutes. Uncover, discard the paper towel, and transfer the quinoa to a large, shallow mixing bowl or a large baking sheet (where it will cool more quickly). Let cool to room temperature, stirring occasionally.

Meanwhile, in a medium mixing bowl, combine the black beans, zucchini, tomatoes, corn, peppers, scallions, chopped cilantro, orange juice, the remaining 3 tablespoons olive oil, lime juice, garlic, honey, chili-garlic paste,

continued on p. 97 ›

Southwestern Quinoa Salad with
Black Beans and Farm Stand Veggies

and ½ teaspoon salt. Stir well and let sit while the quinoa cools, stirring occasionally.

Combine the black bean salad with the cooled quinoa and mix thoroughly. Taste and season as necessary. (It will continue to build flavor as it sits.)

Serve, garnished with the pine nuts and cilantro sprigs (if using) at room temperature or chilled, or refrigerate to serve at a cookout or potluck later. It can be made up to a day ahead.

COOL CUCUMBER SALAD WITH CREAMY BUTTERMILK DRESSING

SERVES 4

2 medium cucumbers (about 1 pound total), chilled

¼ cup Herbed Buttermilk Dressing (p. 23), chilled

1 tablespoon chopped fresh flat-leaf parsley or other tender herb

1 to 2 tablespoons Greek yogurt (not nonfat; I like FAGE Total; optional)

Farm-fresh cucumbers need only a few tablespoons of creamy dressing to become an instant versatile side dish. Use the delicious buttermilk dressing on p. 23 for this, and thicken it up just a bit with Greek yogurt if you like. Also, try substituting cilantro for the tarragon if you're making the dressing just for this salad. Serve with grilled lamb or tandoori chicken and warm naan bread. The recipe doubles or triples easily, too.

Trim and peel the cucumber. Cut it in half lengthwise and use a spoon to scrape out the seeds. Turn each half cut side down on the cutting board and slice it across into ⅛-inch-thick half-moons. Put the cucumber slices in a big bowl, add the dressing and most of the herbs, and toss well. Taste and add a few teaspoons and up to 2 tablespoons Greek yogurt if you like. Put in a serving bowl and garnish with the remaining herbs. Refrigerate if not eating right away. It will hold for an hour or two but will release some juices to the bottom of the bowl.

› most sought-after vegetable on Martha's Vineyard in August, so Roy and I would much rather sell their corn than our own!

LOOKING FOR BASIL IN ALL THE WRONG PLACES

There are all kinds of websites and books devoted to "companion" planting. They lure me in because I'm intrigued by the science, but then I get confused and overwhelmed by all the pairing options: Beets love cabbage! Dill stunts carrots! Horseradish protects potatoes! And on more than one occasion I've regretted trying to mix crops in one bed. ›

› For starters, crops often have different watering requirements, and if you've got drip irrigation, you risk overwatering something to keep the other thing happy. Plus, if you turn your beds over as much as I do, you run into problems when one thing is done producing but the other thing scattered amongst it still has a couple weeks to go.

Instead of thinking about the perfect pairings, these days, I mostly stick to one kind of vegetable per row, and then, for pest management, I plant copious amounts of nasturtiums everywhere. I don't have to worry about them, because they get along with everyone. Pretty and entirely edible, nasturtiums attract the good bugs and repel the bad ones. And as they grow, they can tumble one way or ›

ROASTED RATATOUILLE PASTA "SALAD" WITH FRESH MOZZARELLA

SERVES 6

8 to 10 ounces (1 dry pint) medium cherry or grape tomatoes, halved

8 ounces eggplant (about ½ globe eggplant, but use any kind), skin scored, cut into ¾-inch dice

1 large or 2 small red or yellow bell peppers (8 to 9 ounces), cut into ¾-inch dice

1 medium zucchini (about 6 to 7 ounces), cut into ½-inch dice

1 small red onion (about 4 to 5 ounces), cut into ¾-inch dice

1 tablespoon fresh thyme leaves

⅓ cup plus 1 tablespoon extra-virgin olive oil

Kosher salt

2 teaspoons white balsamic vinegar

2 teaspoons honey

1½ teaspoons chopped fresh garlic

1 teaspoon black olive tapenade

½ teaspoon freshly grated lemon zest

Freshly ground black pepper

8 ounces celentani or other curly dried pasta

I never serve cold, or refrigerated, pasta salads—I think they lack flavor and texture. But a warm or room-temperature pasta salad—yum. This combo of roasted summer vegetables, fresh mozzarella, and a zingy dressing makes a lovely vegetarian supper or a perfect side dish to pair with grilled kabobs. For the best flavor, toss the warm (just-cooked) pasta with the dressing right away, and mix in the fresh-out-of-the-oven roasted veggies and the herbs for a pretty and flavorful summer pasta.

Heat the oven to 400°F. In a large mixing bowl, combine the tomatoes, eggplant, peppers, zucchini, onions, thyme leaves, ⅓ cup of the olive oil, and 1 teaspoon salt. Toss thoroughly. Transfer the vegetables (and any oil and herbs left in the dish) to two 9- x 13-inch baking dishes and spread them out in one layer. Roast, stirring with a silicone spatula or flipping carefully with a metal spatula once or twice, until the veggies have shrunken and caramelized but are still a bit moist, 40 to 50 minutes.

In a large, wide mixing bowl, combine the remaining 1 tablespoon olive oil, the balsamic vinegar, honey, garlic, tapenade, lemon zest, ¼ teaspoon salt, and several grinds of black pepper. Whisk well and set the bowl aside.

Bring a large pot of salted water to a boil. Add the pasta and cook until al dente, about 11 minutes or according to the package instructions. Drain the pasta in a colander and shake off excess water, but do not rinse. Transfer the warm pasta to the large mixing bowl with the dressing. Sprinkle with ¼ teaspoon salt and toss with the dressing.

**6 ounces fresh mozzarella,
cut into ½-inch dice**

**2 tablespoons chopped fresh
flat-leaf parsley**

**2 tablespoons finely sliced
fresh basil**

Add the roasted vegetables and the fresh mozzarella
and toss again. Add most of the parsley and basil and
toss. Taste and season with more salt and black pepper if
desired. Transfer to a serving dish and garnish with the
remaining herbs. Serve right away.

› another, good naturedly getting out of the way of more important crops, like beans or carrots. (The leaves and flowers both wind up in summer salad mixes when other greens are in short supply.) I also tag the ends of beds with marigolds, cosmos, and borage, because these are all solidly in the anti-pest, pro-good-bug department.

In our first garden, I made my biggest companion-planting mistake with basil. I carefully transplanted four kinds of basil seedlings—sweet basil, Thai basil, lime basil, and lemon basil—into our tomato beds. Roy had designed a zigzag trellis system for the tomatoes that year, so there were natural ›

COOK'S TIP

Here's the best way to time the cooking of both the rice and the pork for the recipe here (after prepping all your ingredients and getting the pork into the marinade): Heat the grill, go back inside and cook the fried rice, and then grill the pork, which takes just a few minutes. The rice can rest while the pork cooks.

PAN-PACIFIC GRILLED PORK TENDERLOIN MEDALLIONS WITH FRIED RICE AND TOASTED COCONUT

SERVES 4

FOR THE PORK
¼ cup chopped fresh cilantro, plus 4 small sprigs for garnish

2 tablespoons peanut oil

2 tablespoons low-sodium soy sauce

1 tablespoon plus 1 teaspoon fresh lime juice

1 tablespoon minced fresh garlic

2 teaspoons chopped serrano peppers

2 teaspoons light brown sugar

1 teaspoon chili powder

½ teaspoon ground cumin

½ teaspoon ground coriander

Kosher salt

1½ pounds pork tenderloin, silverskin removed, cut crosswise into ¾-inch-thick medallions (you should have 16 pieces)

FOR THE FRIED RICE
1 teaspoon low-sodium soy sauce

1 teaspoon pure maple syrup

1 tablespoon plus 1 teaspoon minced fresh garlic

1 tablespoon minced fresh ginger

1 teaspoon sliced serrano peppers

continued on p. 103

A zesty, spicy, limey marinade for slices of pork, combined with a sprightly fried rice and a garnish of toasted coconut make this meal-in-one not only tasty but texturally pleasing, too. Set aside a little time for the prep (you could do most of it early in the day) and know that the cooking will go quickly when the time comes. (Just don't marinate the pork for longer than suggested; the lime juice will alter the texture of the pork after awhile.) You'll need cooked (and chilled) white rice to make the fried rice.

MARINATE THE PORK

In a medium shallow mixing bowl, whisk together the cilantro, peanut oil, soy sauce, lime juice, garlic, serranos, brown sugar, chili powder, cumin, coriander, and ¼ teaspoon kosher salt. Add the pork medallions and toss well. Set aside to marinate at room temperature for 30 to 45 minutes.

Heat a gas grill on medium.

MAKE THE RICE

In a small bowl, combine the soy sauce, maple syrup, and 1 teaspoon water. Whisk well. In another small bowl, combine the garlic, ginger, serranos, and scallions.

In a large (12-inch) nonstick stir-fry pan (or skillet), heat the peanut oil over medium-high heat. When the oil is hot (it will loosen up), add the bell peppers, onions, eggplant, and ½ teaspoon salt. Turn the heat to high, and cook, stirring, until the veggies are crisp-tender, slightly shrunken, and lightly browned, 3 to 4 minutes.

continued on p. 103 ›

Pan-Pacific Grilled Pork Tenderloin Medallions
with Fried Rice and Toasted Coconut

¼ cup sliced fresh scallions
(white and light green parts)

2 tablespoons peanut oil

⅔ cup small-diced green, red,
and/or yellow bell peppers

⅔ cup small-diced
yellow or red onions

½ cup small-diced eggplant

⅔ cup fresh corn kernels (from
about 2 small ears)

3 cups cold cooked white rice

⅓ cup toasted shredded
unsweetened coconut

Add the corn and cook for 30 seconds to 1 minute (be careful—the corn will start popping out of the pan!). Add the ginger-garlic mix and stir-fry briefly, just until fragrant, about 30 seconds. Add the rice and a pinch of salt and cook, stirring and breaking up the rice with a spoon, until the rice is heated through, all broken apart, and slightly "toasted" (you will hear it crackle and there will be a little browning), 2 minutes. Add the soy-maple mixture and stir until incorporated. Remove the pan from the heat and let the rice sit for a few minutes. Stir in most of the toasted coconut.

COOK THE PORK AND FINISH THE DISH

Scrape the grill grates and oil them lightly. (I use paper towels held by tongs.) Using tongs, transfer the pork medallions with any marinade clinging to them to the grill grates. Cover the grill and cook for 2 to 2½ minutes. Uncover and use tongs to flip the medallions over. (There may be a bit of resistance, but they will come off—do not be tempted to cook longer on the first side or they will overcook.) Cook for 1 to 1½ minutes more and remove from the grill. The pork will be slightly pink inside and tender, not stiff.

Arrange some of the rice on each of four plates. Arrange the pork medallions over the rice and garnish with the cilantro sprigs and the remaining toasted coconut. Serve right away.

ISLAND PESTO BURGERS WITH ROASTED TOMATOES, ARUGULA & GRILLED ONIONS

MAKES 4 BURGERS

1 pound grass-fed ground beef
(or good-quality ground chuck)

2 tablespoons Spinach, Basil &
Toasted Pine Nut Pesto (p. 8)

Kosher salt

continued on p. 104

We call these "Island" Burgers, because we try to use grass-fed beef from cattle raised on the Island for our burgers. Sometimes the meat can be leaner than you're used to, so a dollop of pesto mixed in moistens

continued on p. 104 ›

› nooks to tuck the basil into. So proud of myself, I then stood by and watched the tomatoes engulf the basil. By August we had a tomato forest; in fact we actually had tomato tunnels instead of paths (that was a good year for tomatoes!), and we had to crawl on our hands and knees down the paths to harvest the tomatoes. Only then would I occasionally encounter a stubborn sprig of lemon basil, still reaching for the sunlight. Most of the rest was lost to the tomato forest.

I didn't get basil right the next year either. I stuck my seedlings in a small bed that never got enough water and that entertained a raucous party of Japanese beetles every night when the sun went down. ›

Freshly ground black pepper

4 Quick-Roasted Tomatoes
(p. 84) or Slow-Roasted
Beefsteak Tomatoes (p. 213)

8 to 12 arugula leaves
or other garden greens,
washed and dried

4 to 8 rings Simple
Grilled Pinwheel Onions
(p. 209; optional)

4 hamburger buns

the burger and adds great flavor, too. We layer our Island pesto burgers with roasted tomatoes, arugula or other garden greens, and sometimes a ring or two of Simple Grilled Pinwheel Onions. A side of Grill-Roasted Fingerlings with Rosemary and Sea Salt (p. 121) would be perfect here.

Heat a gas grill to medium (or medium low if your grill runs very hot). Put the ground beef in a bowl and add the pesto. Gently mix together (the pesto does not have to be fully incorporated—streaks are fine!). Shape the meat into four patties no more than ¾ inch thick. Season the burgers with salt and pepper.

Use a flat spatula to move the patties to the grill. (The pesto will make the burgers a tad sticky and a little bit harder to handle.) Cook for 3 to 4 minutes (you may have a few flare-ups) and carefully flip the burgers over with the spatula. Cook for 3 to 4 minutes more and transfer to a plate.

Toast the hamburger buns by putting the halves facedown on the grill grates. Cover the grill and cook for barely a minute or until nicely marked.

Assemble the burgers with the tomatoes, arugula, and onions (if using) on the toasted buns and serve right away.

SUMMER VEGGIE-PALOOZA PAELLA

SERVES 4

1 pinch (about 18 to 20 threads) best-quality fresh Spanish saffron

3½ cups low-sodium chicken broth

Kosher salt

½ medium (4-ounce) yellow onion, peeled

1 medium (5-ounce) tomato

5 tablespoons extra-virgin olive oil, plus more if needed

12 to 15 whole small or medium cloves garlic, peeled, plus 2 teaspoons minced garlic

4 ounces medium green beans, trimmed and cut in half crosswise if long

4 ounces eggplant (any kind), unpeeled, cut lengthwise in half or quarters and then crosswise about ⅜ inch thick (half-moon or quarter-moon-shaped slices)

½ large red bell pepper (about 3 ounces), stemmed, seeded, and cut into wide strips (about 1½ to 2 inches wide)

2 ounces small Swiss chard leaves, stemmed (or medium leaves stemmed and ripped into smaller pieces)

½ teaspoon smoked Spanish paprika

1½ cups medium-grain Spanish rice (I use Calasparra)

continued on p. 107

My good friend Sarah Jay gave me a great gift: She taught me to make paella—really authentic Spanish paella. It is truly one of the most fun dishes to cook, though I admit it's not something you do every night. I've adapted Sarah's method to work in a skillet, but if you have a paella pan, by all means use it. Plan ahead and find or order saffron and Spanish medium-grain rice (Calasparra, Bomba, or Valencia). In a pinch sushi rice can stand in, but do not use long-grain rice. (Goya® also markets paella rice in the grocery store.) Prep and make the flavor base ahead if you like, and dinner will come together in under an hour. Be sure to serve (and eat) the paella as Sarah and all Spaniards would—plunked down right in the middle of the table with serving forks and lemon wedges.

Crush the saffron threads lightly in a small mortar and pestle. (If you don't have a mortar and pestle, you can skip this step—just use about 5 more saffron threads). Put the saffron in a small bowl (or keep it in the mortar and pestle if using) and pour 1 tablespoon very hot water over the saffron. Let steep for 10 minutes.

Put the chicken broth and ¼ teaspoon salt in a medium saucepan and bring to a boil over high heat. Reduce the heat to a simmer, add the saffron liquid, stir well, and remove from the heat.

Grate the onion on the largest holes of a box grater over a plate. (Discard the onion ends.) Cut the tomato in half and grate on the largest holes of a box grater onto a rimmed plate or shallow bowl to get a loose purée. (Discard the skin.)

Heat 3 tablespoons of the olive oil in a large (12-inch) nonstick skillet over medium-high heat. Add the garlic

continued on p. 107 ›

› Enough. You wouldn't believe the effort I made to get basil right last year, and I did. I treated it as a real crop, gave it its own big bed, kept it covered with row cover to protect it from bugs and drying out, and watered it frequently. Wouldn't you know the stuff was so gorgeous that we had enough to both supply the farm stand and take some up to the general store a few mornings a week—for a while.

I started to get phone calls from the store, saying, could you give us six more bunches of that basil tomorrow? Yikes. I'd harvested too much too fast, whittling down my plants so that I couldn't supply them with as much as they wanted. Worse, I found out that by not delivering the basil, I was disappointing Lord and Lady Foster, the distinguished British couple who had bought Blue Heron Farm, the property up the road where the Obama family used to stay. Apparently Lady Foster was using our fragrant basil in flower arrangements for her guests. Oh well. ›

Summer Veggie-
Palooza Paella

¾ cup fresh corn kernels (from about 1½ ears corn)

2 tablespoons chopped fresh flat-leaf parsley or cilantro

½ lemon, cut into 4 wedges

cloves, green beans, eggplant, bell peppers, and ¾ teaspoon salt and cook, stirring frequently, until all the veggies are nicely browned and the bell pepper is very blistered, 6 to 10 minutes. As the individual veggies brown, remove them with tongs. Put the garlic and bell peppers on one plate, and the green beans and eggplant on another. Cover the garlic and peppers with foil. When cool, peel the skin from the peppers. Add the Swiss chard leaves to the hot skillet (add a touch more olive oil if necessary) and cook, stirring, until just wilted, about 1 minute. Remove the pan from the heat and transfer the chard to the plate with the beans and eggplant.

Return the pan to medium-low heat and add the remaining 2 tablespoons olive oil. When the oil is hot, add the grated onion and a pinch of salt and cook, stirring, until softened, 2 to 4 minutes. Add the grated tomato (including all the juices) and another pinch of salt and cook, stirring, until the mixture has reduced and thickened and is a dark brick-red color, another 8 to 10 minutes. Add the minced garlic and the smoked paprika and stir until well combined and fragrant, about 30 seconds. Remove the pan from the heat. (This mixture is your flavor base, called a *sofrito*. You can make the paella recipe up until this point a few hours ahead; leave the *sofrito* in the pan, loosely covered.)

Return the chicken broth to the heat and bring to a gentle simmer. Return the skillet with the *sofrito* to medium-low heat. When the *sofrito* is hot, add all of the rice and cook, stirring until well combined, for 2 minutes. Spread out the rice in the pan, add 3 cups of the chicken broth (reserve ½ cup), and arrange the green beans, chard, peppers, eggplant, and garlic cloves (in that order) over the rice in a decorative pattern. (Chard leaves can be hoggish so tuck or fold them as necessary to allow room for everything else!) Sprinkle on the fresh corn. (Do not stir from this point on.)

If the broth is not already simmering, bring it to a simmer. Cook, moving the skillet around over the burner as necessary to be sure that all areas are simmering evenly, until the liquid reaches the level of the rice, 8 to 10 minutes. If the broth reduces to this point very quickly (in 6 minutes or less), add the remaining ½ cup chicken broth at this point. Reduce the

continued on p. 108 ›

› I will get basil completely figured out one of these days. I have big plans to try growing it in our new hoop house. In the meantime, I'm staying loyal to the four varieties I've grown every year and am even adding a new, improved Purple Ruffles this year (it's supposed to stay purple as it grows).

Fresh herbs are my biggest ally in summer cooking, and basil is the boss. Take the boss and give it a top hat (like the overtones of lemon, lime, or anise-scented Thai basil), and you've got a celebrity—the ability to turn a tomato salad (p. 89) or a squash stir-fry (p. 134) into a headliner. ›

Labels on the image: parsley, borage, pineapple sage, rosemary, garlic chives

PACKED BY
...MÃO — PORTUGAL

COOK'S TIP

The trickiest part about cooking paella is maintaining just the right simmer so that the rice cooks through before the liquid runs out. So keep an eye on the heat and don't be afraid to turn it up or down. Also keep a little broth in reserve, as you can always add more to finish cooking. If you have a not-so-great electric stove like I do (or small burners), move the pan around on the burner so that simmering happens evenly. If you have a high-powered gas stove, keep an eye on the heat—a gentle flame and simmer will do. Don't worry if the top layer of rice is still a bit crunchy when the pan comes off the heat—it will soften up as the rice rests, covered.

heat to medium low and simmer very gently (continuing to move the pan around as necessary) until all of the liquid has been absorbed, 8 to 10 minutes more. (Use a mini spatula or spoon to peek at the liquid level.) Taste a grain of rice *under* the top layer—it should be just al dente. If not, and if you have not added the extra ½ cup chicken broth, you can add that now and continue cooking until the liquid is absorbed.

Raise the heat to medium high and move the skillet around over the burner as you begin to hear crackling. (You are toasting the bottom layer of rice to create the delicious *socarrat*—a golden layer of crisp rice—so move the pan radically; otherwise the very middle will get overly brown.) Cook for 2 to 4 minutes, moving the pan every 20 or 30 seconds so that a different portion of the rice is directly over the heat.

Remove the pan from the heat and cover loosely with foil or a kitchen towel. Let sit for 8 to 10 minutes. Bring the skillet to the table, garnish with the fresh herbs and lemon wedges, and invite everyone to dig in, working from the perimeter of the pan to the middle, squeezing lemon on their own section if they like.

FIESTA FAJITAS WITH GRILL-ROASTED STEAK, PEPPERS & ONIONS

SERVES 4

¼ cup canola or peanut oil

3 tablespoons low-sodium soy sauce

2 tablespoons fresh lime juice

2 tablespoons fresh orange or canned pineapple juice

2 tablespoons chopped fresh cilantro

1 tablespoon plus 1 teaspoon Worcestershire sauce

1 tablespoon minced fresh garlic

1 tablespoon brown sugar

1 serrano, finely chopped

1½ pounds sirloin tip steak or skirt steak (or ¾ pound steak and ¾ pound boneless butterflied chicken breasts), no more than 1 inch thick

2 large or 3 small bell or other sweet peppers, any color (12 to 14 ounces total), sliced ½ inch thick

2 medium yellow onions (10 to 11 ounces total), sliced ½ inch thick

Kosher salt

1 recipe Double Cilantro Guacamole (p. 110)

1 recipe Lazy Summer Day Salsa with Serranos, Cilantro & Lime (p. 72)

8 fajita-size (8-inch) flour tortillas

½ cup sour cream (optional)

Meltingly tender and charry at the same time, grill-roasted peppers and onions are perfect for fajitas. I use a grill basket or a cast-iron skillet plunked right on the grill to get this result. My favorite steaks for fajitas are sirloin tip (called tri-tip on the West Coast) and skirt steak—very flavorful but sometimes hard to find. Top sirloin is a good alternative. Or use butterflied boneless chicken breasts (I often do half-and-half). Double Cilantro Guacamole (p. 110), and fresh salsa (p. 72) make these fajitas a fiesta!

In a wide mixing bowl, combine 3 tablespoons of the oil, the soy sauce, lime juice, orange or pineapple juice, cilantro, Worcestershire sauce, garlic, brown sugar, and serranos. Mix well, add the steak, and toss to coat. Press the steak down into one layer so some of the marinade pools on top of it. (If using chicken too, transfer half the marinade to a separate bowl and add the chicken to that.) Let sit for an hour at room temperature or up to 4 hours in the fridge, flipping occasionally.

In another bowl, toss the sliced peppers and onions with the remaining oil and ½ teaspoon kosher salt.

Put the guacamole, salsa, and sour cream (if using) in serving bowls.

Put a round grill basket or a medium (10-inch) cast-iron skillet directly on the grill grates and heat the grill to medium high. When the grill and the basket or skillet are hot, add the peppers and onions, stir, cover the grill, and cook, stirring every couple minutes, until the veggies are tender and lightly charred, about 15 minutes. Transfer to a serving bowl.

continued on p. 110 ›

› Don't be afraid to use whole tiny leaves of basil or to mix basil with other tender herbs like mint or parsley or cilantro. (Whole leaves actually hold up better than sliced; basil bruises easily when cut.) And be brave: Use just a little more than you think you need.

BATHTUB BERRY BRAMBLES AND THE BEST ICE CREAM EVER

A juicy junk pile is a farmhouse essential. Lucky for us, the backyard junk pile we inherited featured not only a cast-iron bathtub but a porcelain sink, old windows with bubble glass, and the brick remains of a crumbled chimney. Rich. Turtle lived the better part of one summer in that bathtub. (Turtle was a Painted Slider who Roy rescued from the middle of a busy road, claiming that Libby might like her, though I knew he was sweet on her.) Turtle eventually returned to the wild (Mill Pond) and Roy (mostly) eradicated the junk pile piece by piece. But left behind were the real treasures—berry brambles. ›

› Actually the prickly brambles were everywhere around the edges of the property, but we didn't realize at first just how many there were—or what they were—since they were tangled up with wild roses, scrub oak, pine seedlings, and locust saplings. When we first saw the blossoms, I had to talk myself down from the possibility of edible berries right in our own backyard. "Oh," I thought, "That would just be too awesome." Remember Robert McClosky's classic children's book, *Blueberries for Sal?* Loved it. And loved picking beach plums with my Dad at the end of every summer in Delaware. Maybe everyone has a berry-picking memory from child-hood (or something like it). But I   ›

Remove the steak (and chicken if using) from the marinade and season with salt. Put the meat directly on the grill grate and cook for 2 minutes. Using tongs, carefully move the meat 90 degrees and continue cooking for 2 more minutes. Flip the meat over and cook for 2 to 4 minutes more, or until the steak gives only slightly when poked and the chicken is firm. (Chicken or very thin skirt steak will cook a bit more quickly. Cook thicker steaks 1 to 2 minutes longer on the second side for medium.) Transfer to a cutting board, loosely cover with foil, and let rest for 5 minutes.

Heat the tortillas by toasting each one individually on the hot grill, about 10 seconds per side, or by using your preferred method.

Slice the meat thinly and leave on the cutting board. Bring the tortillas, veggies, salsa, guacamole, sour cream (if using), and cutting board directly to the table (preferably outside!). Let everyone assemble their own fajitas by wrapping a portion of meat, veggies, and condiments in a tortilla.

DOUBLE CILANTRO GUACAMOLE

MAKES 1½ CUPS

1 large clove garlic

1 serrano pepper

Kosher salt

2 medium-size ripe avocados

⅛ teaspoon ground coriander

Big pinch of ground cumin

2 teaspoons fresh lime juice, plus more if needed

¼ cup chopped fresh cilantro, plus more if needed

I like my guacamole bright, fresh, and a little bit chunky. I don't add tomatoes, onions, or sour cream, and I don't pulverize the avocado. I do think of guacamole as the perfect destination for the cilantro that sprouts all over our garden. I call this "double cilantro" because I add a little ground coriander (the seed of the cilantro plant), too. Taste fresh cilantro before you use it—grocery-store cilantro can be completely devoid of flavor at certain times of the year.

On a cutting board, roughly chop the garlic and the serrano. Sprinkle them with a big pinch of salt and continue to chop until the garlic and serrano are very finely minced. Transfer to a mixing bowl.

Cut the avocados in half, remove the pit and peel, and cut them into rough ¾-inch dice or pieces. Add them to the mixing bowl. Sprinkle a

continued on p. 112 ›

› personally feel like we adults need activities like berry-picking, rope-swinging, tree-climbing, and star-gazing (all things I've done since moving to Martha's Vineyard) as much as kids do, especially in today's crazy, high-volume world.

Around the 4th of July, the secret was revealed. Clusters of little red berries appeared. They looked like raspberries, but definitely weren't. Then the middle berry in the cluster turned dark blue, and then black. We picked. We tasted. We thrilled. They were black raspberries and they were delicious. Thus began our "friendly" competition with the birds, who seemed to know the exact moment when the blueish berries would turn a deep delicious black. Roy got in the habit of taking a little bowl out with him very early in the morning and picking whatever ripe berries he could.

At first we only got a handful or two of berries, but it was just enough to mash up with warm maple syrup and drape ›

generous ¼ teaspoon salt, the coriander, cumin, and lime juice over the avocado. Using the back of a fork, gently mash and stir the avocado just until everything is well combined but the mixture is still just a bit chunky. Add the cilantro, stir again, and taste. Add more salt, lime juice, or cilantro if needed.

ROASTED PARMESAN-CRUSTED COD WITH BABY POTATOES, BELL PEPPERS, ONIONS & THYME

SERVES 4

8 ounces small fingerling or baby red potatoes (smallest size you can find), cut in half lengthwise

½ medium bell pepper, cut into 1-inch pieces

1 small or medium onion, cut into 1-inch pieces

10 to 12 pitted Kalamata olives, cut in half

3 tablespoons plus 2 teaspoons extra-virgin olive oil

1 tablespoon plus 1 teaspoon coarsely chopped fresh thyme leaves

2 teaspoons balsamic vinegar

1 teaspoon honey

Kosher salt

Big pinch of crushed red pepper flakes

6 ounces firm-ripe cherry tomatoes (about 20), cut in half

¾ cup fresh breadcrumbs (from 1 English muffin; a little extra is fine)

When we've been working hard on the farm all day, this is a go-to recipe, because everything goes into one pan—and comes out dinner. (To save time, prep the veggies first, get them roasting, then prep the fish.) This is my favorite way to roast cod (or other firm white fish), because it combines a yummy crumb topping with a mayo-mustard coating that keeps it super moist. We add our own freshly dug potatoes, peppers, onions, cherry tomatoes, and thyme, and we get a great marriage of garden and sea, Island-style.

Heat the oven to 425°F. Combine the potatoes, peppers, onions, olives, 3 tablespoons olive oil, 1 tablespoon thyme, the balsamic vinegar, honey, ¾ teaspoon salt, and crushed red pepper in a mixing bowl and toss well. Spread in one layer in a 9- x 13-inch baking pan. Roast for 25 minutes. Reserve the bowl that the veggies were in and add the cherry tomatoes, 1 teaspoon oil, ½ teaspoon thyme, and a pinch of salt. Toss well.

In a small bowl, combine the breadcrumbs, Parmigiano, the remaining 1 teaspoon olive oil, the remaining ½ teaspoon thyme, and a big pinch of salt. In another small

¼ cup coarsely grated Parmigiano-Reggiano

2 tablespoons mayonnaise

1 teaspoon Dijon mustard

1½ pounds cod (or other firm white fish fillet like striped bass or halibut), cut into a few pieces to fit more easily into the pan

bowl, stir together the mayonnaise and mustard. Lay the fish on a plastic cutting board and season with salt. Spread the mayo-mustard mixture over the top of the fish and along the sides.

Add the cherry tomatoes to the pan of roasted vegetables and stir to combine. Push the veggies to the edges of the pan to make room for the fish. Nestle the fish amongst the veggies; then pat the breadcrumb mixture over the fish pieces. Return the pan to the oven and roast for 20 to 22 minutes, until the potatoes are tender and the crust on the fish is golden. Cut the fish into serving pieces with a metal spatula and arrange on four plates. Spoon the veggies, along with the pan juices, around the fish. Serve right away.

COOK'S TIP

I like to use an English muffin, whizzed in the food processor or coffee grinder, to make fresh breadcrumbs. But you can use any coarse fresh breadcrumb for the best texture.

TOMATO, CORN, LEEK & POTATO GRATIN

SERVES 6

2 tablespoons unsalted butter, plus more for the pan

1 cup fresh breadcrumbs

1 cup grated Parmigiano-Reggiano

5 tablespoons extra-virgin olive oil

1 tablespoon roughly chopped fresh thyme leaves

Kosher salt

2½ cups sliced leeks (white and pale green parts; about 4 leeks), washed but not dried

1½ cups fresh corn kernels (from about 3 ears)

Freshly ground black pepper

1½ teaspoons minced fresh garlic

1 pound small red potatoes (about 4 to 5), unpeeled, sliced ¼ inch thick (cut in half first if potatoes are larger)

1½ pounds small ripe tomatoes (about 6), cored and sliced ¼ inch thick

Whenever this gratin shows up on the dinner table, it's the star. It's so satisfying that you won't even miss the meat. (Grilled chicken or steak wouldn't mind sharing the plate, however.) It takes a bit of time to prep, but once you get it in the oven, you know a delicious dinner is coming and you can relax.

Heat the oven to 375°F. Butter a 2-quart shallow gratin or baking dish (preferably oval).

In a small bowl, combine the breadcrumbs, 3 tablespoons of the Parmigiano, 1 tablespoon of the olive oil, ½ teaspoon of the thyme leaves, and a pinch of salt. Mix well and set aside.

Heat 1 tablespoon of the butter and 1 tablespoon of the olive oil in a medium (10-inch) nonstick skillet over medium-low heat. Add the leeks (with any water clinging to them) and ¼ teaspoon salt. Cook, covered, stirring occasionally, until the leeks are limp (they will be shedding water), about 5 minutes. Uncover, turn the heat to medium, and continue cooking until the water has evaporated and the leeks are starting to brown lightly, 6 to 8 minutes. Add the remaining 1 tablespoon butter, the corn kernels, another ¼ teaspoon salt, and a few grinds of pepper. Continue cooking until the corn has lost its raw look (it will be shrunken and glistening) and some of the leeks are lightly browned, 3 to 5 minutes. Stir in the garlic and 1 teaspoon of the thyme leaves and cook until fragrant, about 30 seconds. Remove the pan from the heat and let cool slightly.

Transfer the leek and corn mixture to the baking dish, spreading it evenly over the bottom. Let cool slightly.

In a medium saucepan, cover the potato slices with well-salted water and bring to a boil. Reduce the heat to a gentle boil and cook for 5 minutes,

continued on p. 116 ›

› across our Farmhouse French Toast (p. 139) on Sunday mornings. But one weekend in July, I managed to hoard two cups of berries—just enough to make . . . ice cream! Oh, my, my, my. You know, a food reporter interviewed me at the end of the year to ask me about food trends (why me I don't know) and asked me what my favorite dish of the year was. Well, I doubt very much that black raspberry ice cream was the hot trend—but it was tangy-sweet-sublime and practically perfect in my view. Without a doubt, the best thing I'd made or eaten all year. (Later I combined store-bought blackberries and raspberries to make a truly worthy substitution for the ice cream pie recipe on p. 147.)

Little by little we've uncovered more black raspberry brambles —and even a few raspberries. We found one wild blueberry in the shade of a cedar—and several dozen blueberry bushes in the fields behind us. We planted a half dozen of our own cultivated blueberry bushes the second summer and hope to plant more. ›

› We're not yet berry barons, but at least we get to bliss out on our own berries for a few weeks each summer. And since Roy and I actually went blueberry picking on one of our first dates, now we can pretend we are going on a date and pick berries without having to go anywhere. Yeah, well, it's the little things, you know.

A PICNIC TABLE CHANGES EVERYTHING

July is birthday month here: Libby and I are three days apart. And it just so happens that we both had big decade birthdays the second summer at the farm house. Roy, not being the formal type, started casually mentioning a possible party to friends he would run into. I pointed out to him that you can't just invite friends to a party and not have a party. "Oh, I have it all figured out," he told me. Knowing him, I knew he would pull it off, but I was fixated on one thing: a party table.

We don't have a dining room or a dining room table. Or didn't. We now have a lovely old pine ›

or until the potatoes are just barely tender but still a bit firm. Drain the potatoes and gently rinse them with cold water until they are cool. Pat dry or transfer to a layer of dishtowels to dry.

Starting at one end of the gratin dish, lay a row of slightly overlapping tomato slices across the (narrow) width of the dish. Prop the tomatoes against the dish at a 60-degree angle. Cover the row of tomatoes with a generous sprinkling of Parmigiano. Next, arrange a row of potato slices over the tomatoes, so that the potato slices overlap the tomato slices by about two-thirds. Sprinkle the potato slices with a tiny bit of salt and with Parmigiano. Repeat with alternating rows of tomatoes and potatoes, sprinkling each with cheese, until the gratin is full. (You might have extra veggies. If it looks like you're going to have a lot of extras, gently push the rows back toward the end of the dish you started at and squeeze in a few extra rows.)

Sprinkle any remaining thyme over all and season with pepper. Drizzle all over with the remaining 3 tablespoons olive oil. Sprinkle the breadcrumb mixture evenly over the top of the gratin. Cook until the gratin is well browned all over and the juices have bubbled for a while and reduced considerably, 55 to 60 minutes. Let cool for at least 15 minutes before serving.

Tomato, Corn, Leek
& Potato Gratin

› table in the room downstairs that functions as my office. But we still eat on a little drop-leaf oak table on one side of the kitchen. When Libby's here, the leaf swings up, and Farmer neatly tucks underneath (the closer to Roy the better). It works. But entertaining is tricky. And we started out life at the farm house with no outdoor furniture either (but for a wobbly iron bistro table my sister passed along).

I wanted a picnic table.

For Roy, paying money for a picnic table was about the most ridiculous thing he could imagine. Easy to build. Better still, he wanted to build a really nice ›

SPICY STIR-FRIED GREEN BEANS

SERVES 4

1 tablespoon low-sodium soy sauce

2 teaspoons brown sugar

1 tablespoon sherry or rice wine

⅛ teaspoon Asian chili-garlic paste

2 tablespoons peanut oil

1 pound slim green beans, trimmed

1 serrano pepper, cut in half lengthwise

Kosher salt

1 bunch scallions (white and light green parts), cut into 1-inch pieces (about ⅓ to ½ cup)

1 tablespoon minced fresh ginger

2 teaspoons minced fresh garlic

1 tablespoon chopped fresh cilantro

Stir-frying brings out the nutty sweetness in green beans, and yummy Chinese-restaurant-style seasonings are popular with everyone. I use my favorite 12-inch nonstick stir-fry pan, so I stick with medium-high heat. But if you're using a wok, you can crank up the heat to high (as long as you have an exhaust fan!); the beans will cook more quickly, so keep an eye on them and stir frequently, but they'll taste extra-delicious.

In a small bowl, whisk together the soy sauce, brown sugar, sherry or rice wine, chili-garlic paste, and 1 tablespoon water. Set aside.

In a large (12-inch) stir-fry pan or skillet, heat the peanut oil over medium-high heat. (Turn on your exhaust fan if you have one.) Add the green beans, serrano, and ½ teaspoon salt to the pan. Cook, stirring and tossing frequently with tongs, until the beans are well browned in many places (some will be blackened in spots—that's a good thing!) and no longer stiff, 12 to 14 minutes. (Do not undercook!)

Add the scallions and cook, stirring, until the scallions soften a bit, about 1 minute. Add the ginger and garlic and cook, stirring, until fragrant, about 30 seconds. Remove the pan from the heat, quickly add the soy sauce mixture, and stir briskly for 30 seconds to 1 minute as the sauce bubbles and coats the beans. Immediately transfer the beans and sauce to a serving platter or plates. Remove the serrano halves, sprinkle with the cilantro, and serve right away.

MARINATED GRILL-ROASTED BELL PEPPERS

MAKES ABOUT 2 CUPS

1 pound red bell peppers (about 4 small)

1 tablespoon extra-virgin olive oil

2 teaspoons balsamic vinegar

2 teaspoons orange juice

¼ teaspoon freshly grated ginger (use a rasp-style grater and include any juice)

1 large clove garlic, thinly sliced crosswise

Kosher salt

15 to 20 small fresh basil leaves

My technique for roasting whole peppers is unfussy and much more efficient than using the broiler. I pop them in a covered gas grill while the grill is heating, turn them a couple times, and remove them when they're blistered and mostly blackened. If you're new to roasting peppers, you'll be amazed at the flavor transformation—total sweetness awaits! Marinate them and you've got another secret-ingredient staple for delicious summer meals. Top crostini or pizza or use in salsas (p. 73) or sauces (p. 215).

Heat a gas grill on high. (There's no need to preheat.) Put the peppers directly on the grill grate, lower the lid, and cook, turning every 2 to 3 minutes, until the peppers are well blistered and the skin is mostly blackened, about 10 minutes. (Don't try to get all of the skin completely blackened—there will be patches of red.) Transfer the peppers to a nonreactive bowl and cover tightly with plastic wrap. Let the peppers sit for at least 15 minutes, or longer if you like (they are easiest to handle at room temperature).

Set a strainer inside of a bowl and peel and seed the peppers over it. (Remove the blackened skin, split open the peppers, and gently remove the seeds and stem with your fingers.) The bowl will collect any of the delicious juices dripping down. Do not rinse the peppers under running water—a few clinging seeds will be fine! Separate the peppers into lobes with your fingers, or cut them into long pieces.

To the bowl of juices, add the olive oil, balsamic vinegar, orange juice, ginger, garlic slices, and a pinch of salt. Arrange the peppers and basil leaves in a glass or ceramic storage container (in layers if the dish is small). Pour the juice-oil-vinegar mixture over all. Cover and refrigerate until ready to eat, or use them in other recipes. They will keep this way for a week.

› outdoor table for us. But the day of the party got closer and closer, Roy was busy-busy, and I was worried-worried. My best friend, Eliza, and her husband, Chip, arrived on Thursday, and finally, down the driveway bouncing in Roy's big truck came the picnic table on Friday morning. He'd given in and bought one.

Saturday, party day, was blue-sky beautiful, and between the new picnic table, the wobbly bistro table, a couple of benches, and many assorted funky old chairs, everyone had a place to sit. And yummy food to eat. (You don't think I let Roy do that, do you?) My very favorite Quick-Roasted Tomatoes (p. 84). A Tomato, Corn, Leek & Potato Gratin (p. 115). Grill-Roasted Bell Peppers (left) and grilled bread. Grilled chicken and shrimp. Roy's Almost-Classic Potato Salad (p. 93). Fresh greens. Peanut Noodles with Cucumbers (p. 131). My friend Cathy's awesome peach salad.

And a big birthday cake for me and Libby. Roy, Eliza, and Chip had spent the morning ›

Grill-Roasted Fingerlings with Rosemary, Lemon, Sea Salt & Fresh Corn Vinaigrette

GRILL-ROASTED FINGERLINGS WITH ROSEMARY, LEMON, SEA SALT & FRESH CORN VINAIGRETTE

SERVES 4

1 pound fingerling potatoes, cut in half lengthwise and again crosswise if longer than a couple inches

3 large shallots (about 4 ounces), peeled and cut into ½-inch-thick wedges lengthwise

½ lemon (cut in half lengthwise), thinly sliced into half-moons

3 tablespoons extra-virgin olive oil

1 tablespoon roughly chopped fresh rosemary

1 teaspoon coarse sea salt, plus more to finish

Freshly ground black pepper

4 handfuls arugula, mizuna, baby mustard, or other assertive salad greens, washed and dried (optional)

½ cup Fresh Corn Vinaigrette (p. 122)

I grill potatoes a few different ways, but this is the method I love when I'm looking for hands-off cooking. I wrap the potatoes and some aromatics in a foil package and put it inside a covered grill. The potatoes steam (thanks to the foil package) and get some yummy caramelization, too, from sitting on the grill grates (even through the foil). Serve them straight out of the package or dress with a fresh corn vinaigrette. If you double the recipe, make two separate foil packages for the best results.

Heat a gas grill on medium heat (or medium low if your grill runs hot—an internal temp of 350° to 400°F is good), or light a charcoal fire and let the coals burn down to medium-low heat. Combine the potatoes, shallots, lemon slices, olive oil, rosemary, sea salt, and a few grinds of fresh pepper in a bowl and mix well.

Measure out three sheets of (regular) aluminum foil, each about 20 inches long. Overlap two pieces in a cross pattern. Mound the potato mixture in the middle of the cross and spread it out evenly into a square of even thickness. Fold each piece of foil in and over the potatoes to wrap the package, then wrap the third piece of foil around the package for a good seal.

Put the package directly on the grill grate and cover the grill. Cook for 20 minutes (you'll hear sizzling). Flip over and cook for 20 to 25 minutes more. Remove the package from the grill and open it carefully with tongs. (It will release hot steam.) The potatoes should be nicely browned in places

continued on p. 122 ›

› stringing up birthday decorations from tree to tree in the yard, and Roy's mom arrived with silly hats and flags and all kinds of fun stuff. We had a hula-hoop competition, which Eliza might have won, except for Libby's uncanny ability to hula-hoop nonstop while barely moving.

I was sad when the weekend wound down and everyone left, but the picnic table somehow filled the void. There it was, next to the rope swing under the shade of the maple, right along the path we'd worn from the house to the garden. It was weird, but it felt like it had always been there. It transformed the backyard into a living room and a dining room.

Soon we were eating dinner out on it every night. In the mornings, I'd cover the table with harvest baskets and mason jars and cucumbers and eggplants and scissors and rubber bands and whatnot, arranging everything for the farm stand. In the afternoons, Roy would come home from work, plunk down on the table with a root beer in ›

and will be tender when pierced with a fork or paring knife. If they aren't tender yet, rewrap and cook for 10 minutes longer.

Arrange the greens (if using) on a small platter or four plates and portion the potatoes and shallots over the greens (keep the lemons in or remove them, as you please). (You may have to peel a few shallots off the foil—if some are very charred, just discard them.) Sprinkle a little more sea salt over the potatoes and spoon over a few tablespoons or as much as you like of the Fresh Corn Vinaigrette. Serve right away.

› hand, and tell me about his job. I amused myself by decorating the table with a rotating display of odd snips of flowers, too short or straggly for bouquets. I picked the first brilliant blossom that bloomed on the America rose Roy bought me for my birthday and arranged it with white cosmos and sprays of dill and garlic chive blossoms.

Eating outside on a warm summer evening is transforming in itself. But swinging your legs over the bench of a picnic table, eating straight out of the skillet (a slice of Very Berry Vanilla Clafoutis on p. 144 or a piece of Libby's Lemon Blueberry Buckle on p. 151), and watching the remains of a brilliant fuchsia ›

FRESH CORN VINAIGRETTE

MAKES ¾ CUP

½ cup fresh raw corn kernels, from about 1 ear

¼ cup extra-virgin olive oil

1 tablespoon sherry vinegar

2 teaspoons fresh lemon or lime juice

2 teaspoons pure maple syrup

Kosher salt

Freshly ground black pepper

1 tablespoon sliced fresh chives, cut about ¼ inch long

I created this fun dressing to top off the Grill-Roasted Fingerlings (p. 121), but it would be equally good spooned into a fish taco, over sliced tomatoes, or tossed with some grilled shrimp.

Put half of the corn kernels in a medium bowl and use a fork to mash them to release some of their milk. (Depending on the freshness and/or tenderness of the corn, you might have to mash vigorously or only lightly.) Add the olive oil, sherry vinegar, lemon or lime juice, maple syrup, ¼ teaspoon kosher salt, and several grinds of black pepper. Whisk well. Stir in the remaining corn kernels and the chives. Store any leftover vinaigrette in the fridge and use within a couple days.

GRILLED FAIRY TALE EGGPLANT "FANS" WITH CHIMICHURRI SAUCE

SERVES 3 OR 4

1 pound Fairy Tale eggplant
(about 10 to 14)

3 to 4 tablespoons olive oil

Kosher salt

1 recipe Parsley and Mint
Chimichurri Sauce
(facing page)

Folks are surprised when I tell them you can cook a little
Fairy Tale eggplant pretty much any way you can cook
a regular eggplant (roast, sauté, bake, grill). But there
is one thing I do with these striped minis that's a little
different. I "fan" them—slice them lengthwise while
keeping the stem intact—and let them soften, spread
out, and brown up on the grill. Rustic and delicious,
they're even better with a pleasantly assertive rendition of Argentine
chimichurri sauce (facing page) drizzled over the rich flesh.

Heat a gas grill to medium. Cut each eggplant lengthwise, starting at just below the stem to leave the stem intact, at about ¼-inch intervals so you have two or three cuts for 3 or 4 slices. Brush the eggplant (both the slices and skin) generously with olive oil and sprinkle all over with salt. Arrange the eggplant on the grill grate, perpendicular to the grates. (The eggplant will be stiff at this point and the slices still hanging together.) Cover and cook for 2 to 3 minutes. Uncover, and using tongs, turn the eggplant over and spread the slices out a bit (they will be floppier now). Cook for another 2 minutes, flip, and spread out again. Continue cooking and flipping until the flesh is tender and cooked through and the skin is browned, 1 to 3 minutes more. Transfer to a rustic serving platter (I like to use a wooden board) and serve with the sauce in a little bowl on the side.

PARSLEY AND MINT CHIMICHURRI SAUCE

MAKES ¾ CUP

1 large clove garlic

⅔ cup (packed) fresh flat-leaf parsley leaves

⅓ cup (packed) fresh mint leaves

⅓ cup plus 1 tablespoon extra-virgin olive oil

1 tablespoon plus 1 teaspoon white-wine vinegar

1 tablespoon orange juice

1½ teaspoons black olive tapenade

⅛ teaspoon ground cumin

Kosher salt

Freshly ground black pepper

This easy and tasty green sauce takes advantage of abundant garden herbs and offers a bold counterpoint to everything from grilled eggplant (facing page) to grilled bread and grilled steak.

Put the garlic in the bowl of a food processor (a small one works great) and process until finely chopped. Add the parsley and mint and process until coarsely chopped. Add the olive oil, vinegar, orange juice, tapenade, cumin, scant ½ teaspoon salt, and several grinds of black pepper. Process until everything is well chopped and combined and the sauce looks slightly creamy and a paler green color. (The herbs will still be slightly coarse.) Let sit for 20 to 30 minutes before serving to let the flavors bloom. If working ahead, store in the fridge, well covered, for up to a day or two. Bring to room temperature, stir well, and transfer to a decorative dish for serving.

› sunset bounce off the edge of a golden hayfield is the kind of simple pleasure that can turn a whole day around. All for the price of a picnic table.

MEET MR. POTATO HEAD'S NEMESIS

For little girls and big boys and middle-aged women who pretend not to eat a lot of starchy stuff but secretly inhale french fries when no one's looking, there's probably nothing more fun than growing potatoes. Frankly, I was dumbfounded at how dang easy this whole potato thing is the first year we planted them. Well, I should clarify that they're especially easy for me, because Roy plants them and tends them, usually with Libby's help. (However, I do weed the potato beds since no one else seems to care about this.)

There is a bit of a technique to creating the rows so that extra dirt is hanging around to "hill up" over the young potato plants as they grow. But other than that, you basically stick ›

PERKY'S FRIED POTATOES

SERVES 4

1¼ pounds all-purpose (medium-starch) potatoes, peeled

Kosher salt

3 tablespoons unsalted butter

Freshly ground black pepper

Perky is my mom's name. We tried to honor my mom by naming our prettiest hen after her, but Perky the chicken turned out to be a ne'er do well who pecks everyone else's eggs. Fortunately, my mom is much better behaved, and a great cook to boot. Her fried potatoes seem simple at first glance, but actually get their complex flavor from three tricks: Starting with all-purpose (medium-starch) potatoes; boiling them first; then very slowly frying them in butter without disturbing them much. They get a dark and crispy crust while keeping a light and fluffy texture inside.

Cut the potatoes into 1-inch pieces (no need for precision here). Put in a large saucepan with 2 teaspoons salt and cover with 2 inches of water. Bring to a boil, reduce to a simmer, and cook until *just barely* tender (err on the firm side), 12 to 13 minutes. Drain gently.

In a large (12-inch) nonstick skillet, heat the butter over medium-low heat. Add the potatoes, season with 1 teaspoon salt, and toss gently with a spatula to coat with the butter. Cook, without stirring or flipping, until the bottoms are a dark golden brown, about 10 minutes (lift up one edge with the tip of the spatula to check). Flip and cook until golden on the other side, 4 to 5 minutes. Flip one last time and cook for 3 to 4 minutes. Season with freshly ground pepper. Serve warm.

COOK'S TIP

The all-purpose potatoes we grow are called Kennebec. They are medium- to large-sized white-fleshed, brown-skinned potatoes and have great keeping quality. If you're looking for all-purpose potatoes in the grocery, they will be labeled as such or may be called "California Whites" or chef potatoes. They will be sold in a bag, not loose.

› a piece of potato in the ground and two months later dig up a dozen or more potatoes. Miraculous!

It's best to order certified potato seed so that you have less chance of disease and better yields. We gang up with other Islanders to order potatoes in bulk to save on shipping. Then long about April 15, a couple of big sacks arrive on our back doorstep. We go in the kitchen, get a sharp knife and a cutting board, and chunk up the potatoes so that each piece has one or two good eyes on it. We set the pieces about 10 inches apart in shallow trenches and cover them with soil. In no time, shoots and leaves are cracking the earth and soon the plants are as big and bushy as hedgehogs. (Oh, yes, and we do water them, too.)

Eventually the plants produce surprisingly comely flowers, and not long after the flowers fade (and sometimes before, when we're cheating), we stick a fork in the ground and lever the root ball up. We never know just how many or what size the potatoes will be, so the surprise is the ›

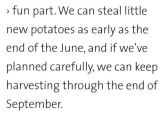

› fun part. We can steal little new potatoes as early as the end of the June, and if we've planned carefully, we can keep harvesting through the end of September.

I am not actually allowed to dig up the potatoes myself—unless Roy gives me the okay. If left unchaperoned, I will dig up one plant, then another, then another. Because they are Very Popular at the farm stand. "I'd like to eat some of those potatoes, you know." Roy says. "Don't sell them all."

So after a few years of potato rationing, we finally (you guessed it) have tilled up an extra field, separate from the market garden, just for potatoes. Plenty to go around; ›

MAKES 12 PANCAKES

3 tablespoons unsalted butter, plus more for frying

1 tablespoon olive oil, plus more for frying

1½ cups small-diced zucchini or pattypan squash (1 medium-small zucchini, or about 7 ounces)

Kosher salt

1¼ cups fresh corn kernels (from 2 to 3 ears)

½ cup sliced fresh scallions (white and light green parts)

½ to 1 teaspoon minced fresh serrano peppers

Freshly ground black pepper

2 tablespoons chopped fresh flat-leaf parsley

2 tablespoons sliced fresh chives

½ cup plus 1 tablespoon unbleached all-purpose flour

½ cup cornmeal

2 teaspoons sugar

½ teaspoon baking powder

½ teaspoon baking soda

1 large egg, beaten

⅔ cup whole milk

2 tablespoons plain thick Greek yogurt or sour cream, plus more for serving

Honey, preferably local, for serving

ZUCCHINI AND CORN PANCAKES WITH GREEK YOGURT AND HONEY

Crispy and golden around the edges, fluffy and chock-full of veggies on the inside, these savory pancakes are my summer-veggie comfort fare. I sauté the veggies first for the best texture, then add herbs and a bit of cornmeal to a fairly traditional pancake batter. I like to serve them with a dollop of Greek yogurt and a drizzle of honey, but they'd also be nice under a saucy tomato ragoût or sliced grilled lamb. The batter will hold if you want to make it a bit ahead and cook to order.

In a medium (10-inch) heavy, nonstick, ovenproof skillet, heat ½ tablespoon of the butter with the olive oil over medium-high heat. Add the zucchini and ⅛ teaspoon salt and cook, stirring only occasionally, until the zucchini are shrunken a bit and starting to brown lightly, about 3 minutes. Add another ½ tablespoon butter, the corn, scallions, serranos, and ½ teaspoon salt. Cook, stirring occasionally, until the corn kernels are glistening and some are slightly shrunken, 2 to 3 more minutes. Remove the pan from the heat, season the veggies with black pepper, and transfer to a mixing bowl. Let cool to room temperature, stirring occasionally (20 to 25 minutes). Stir in the parsley and chives.

In a medium mixing bowl, whisk together the flour, cornmeal, sugar, baking powder, baking soda, and ½ teaspoon salt.

Melt the remaining 2 tablespoons butter (in the microwave or on the stovetop) and let cool slightly. In a small bowl, whisk together the egg, milk, yogurt, and the melted butter. Make a well in the center of the dry ingredients

continued on p. 130 ›

Zucchini and Corn Pancakes
with Greek Yogurt and Honey

and pour in the liquid mixture, whisking until just combined. Combine the batter with the vegetable herb mixture and stir well. Let the batter sit for 5 minutes or up to 30 minutes.

In a large (12-inch) nonstick skillet, heat about ½ tablespoon butter and 1 tablespoon olive oil over medium heat. When the butter has melted and is bubbling, use a ¼-cup measure to scoop batter into the pan, forming 3 to 4 pancakes. Cook for about 2 minutes, until the pancakes are golden brown on the bottom (you will see a lot of bubbles on top), then flip. Cook for 1 minute more. (The bottom will brown more quickly.) Transfer to a paper towel–lined plate and keep warm in a low (200°F) oven, if desired. Repeat with the remaining batter, adding butter and oil as necessary, and turning the heat down as necessary.

Serve warm with dollops of Greek yogurt and a generous drizzle of honey.

QUICK AND SPICY GINGER-PEANUT NOODLES WITH CUCUMBERS AND TAT SOI

SERVES 4 TO 6

¼ cup toasted sesame oil

¼ cup low-sodium soy sauce

¼ cup smooth peanut butter

2 tablespoons pure maple syrup

2 tablespoons minced fresh ginger

1 tablespoon rice vinegar

1 tablespoon fresh lemon juice

2 teaspoons minced fresh garlic

1 teaspoon Asian chili-garlic paste

Kosher salt

½ pound whole-grain or whole-wheat thin spaghetti or angel hair

3 to 4 cups tat soi leaves (or other baby Asian greens, such as mizuna or mustard), washed and dried

1 medium cucumber, peeled, halved, seeded, and cut crosswise thinly (about 1⅓ cups)

A nice cucumber from the garden or the farm stand is the best excuse for me to make my favorite peanut noodles. You can make the easy peanut sauce ahead, though don't dress the noodles until close to serving time. Choose your favorite whole-grain spaghetti (I like Barilla); whole grain pastas vary greatly in flavor and texture, so try a few to see what you like. Experiment with baby Asian greens, too; my favorite is the spoon-shaped tat soi. You may have leftover sauce; try it on grilled shrimp or chicken brochettes.

In a food processor, combine the sesame oil, soy sauce, peanut butter, maple syrup, fresh ginger, rice vinegar, lemon juice, garlic, and chili-garlic paste. Process until well mixed and smooth, scraping down the sides once or twice. It will be emulsified but fairly liquidy. Refrigerate the dressing if not using right away.

Cook the pasta in a large pot of salted water, following the package directions. Drain—but don't rinse—the pasta and let it sit in the strainer, tossing occasionally, until it's no longer hot and wet, 15 to 20 minutes. It should be bouncy and a bit sticky.

Put the pasta in a mixing bowl and season with ¼ teaspoon salt. Add most of the greens and all of the cucumbers. Drizzle with about 7 to 8 tablespoons of the dressing and mix well. Taste and add more dressing if necessary. Serve at room temperature, garnished with the remaining greens.

› no fighting. This is a good thing, since Roy is half Irish and half Scottish (with a whisper of Abenaki Indian) so he likes his potatoes something fierce.

Honestly, so do I. I was just kidding about the french fries. When I venture out into the world to teach cooking classes, I always include a potato recipe or two because I've developed a bunch of great techniques for cooking them over the years. In the summer, I love grilling potatoes, and the foil pouch method I use for Grill-Roasted Fingerlings with Rosemary, Lemon, Sea Salt & Fresh Corn Vinaigrette (p. 121) is a great way to get delicious results. We always grow French Fingerlings ›

› and Red Gold Potatoes, but we like a keeper like Kennebec, too, which makes the best fried potatoes, (p. 127).

There are of course, Potato Enemies. And while we've never encountered anything as sinister as Potato Blight, we do have the lovely striped villainess known as the Colorado potato beetle. Fortunately, we also have a child (a girl child at that) who doesn't mind squishing bugs— the best way to deal with these egg-laying, leaf-munching pesties.

NOW ISN'T THAT CUTE?
If I had any sense at all, I'd simply grow teeny tiny vegetables and put them in pint containers and have an entire farm stand filled with minis. Everybody loves minis, right? Boutique vegetables! Micro greens! Baby bells! Yadi yadi ya. ›

CORN-OFF-THE-COB AND YELLOW BEAN SAUTÉ WITH BACON AND HERBS

SERVES 4

2 strips bacon (about 2 ounces)

1 tablespoon unsalted butter

1 cup small-diced yellow onions (about 1 small onion)

Kosher salt

1 tablespoon extra-virgin olive oil

1½ cups small-diced yellow wax beans or green beans (about 8 ounces)

1½ cups fresh corn kernels (from 3 ears)

1 teaspoon minced fresh garlic

Freshly ground black pepper

¼ lemon

1 tablespoon mixed chopped fresh mint and chives

My corn-off-the-cob sautés are always a hit with Libby and Roy, and a sure bet for entertaining, too. I made this version one night when we got a "gift" of a handful of yellow beans (which means they were still on the farm stand at the end of the day), but I've made it with peppers, squash, mushrooms—all kinds of veggies. If you have leftovers for some reason, add them to an omelet, frittata, or taco the next day.

Cook the bacon in a large (12-inch) nonstick skillet over medium-low heat until crisp, 6 to 8 minutes. Transfer the bacon to paper towels and drain off all but 1 tablespoon of fat in the pan. Add the butter to the skillet and turn the heat to medium. When the butter has melted, add the onions and ½ teaspoon salt. Cook, stirring occasionally, until the onions have softened and are just starting to brown, 5 to 7 minutes.

Add the olive oil, yellow beans, and ¼ teaspoon salt. Cook, stirring occasionally, until the beans are somewhat shrunken and both the beans and onions are lightly browned, 5 to 7 minutes more. Add the corn kernels and ¼ teaspoon salt. Cook, stirring frequently, until the corn is glistening, slightly shrunken, and slightly darker in color, 3 to 4 minutes. Add the garlic and cook, stirring and scraping the bottom of the pan, until fragrant and well mixed, about 1 minute. Crumble the bacon and add two-thirds of it to the pan. Stir until heated through and remove the pan from the heat.

Season the sauté with a few generous grinds of pepper and a light squeeze of the lemon. Stir in most of the herbs. Let sit for another couple of minutes if you have time. Stir again, scraping the bottom of the pan, and season to taste with more salt, pepper, or lemon juice. Garnish the sauté with the remaining herbs and bacon.

Corn-off-the-Cob and Yellow Bean
Sauté with Bacon and Herbs

› I happen to be one of those people who suffers from cute vegetable lust, so I indulge myself a bit and grow Fairy Tale eggplant and pattypan squash. I harvest the little stripey Fairy Tales at 4 or 5 inches long and I nab the little yellow Sunburst pattypans at no more than an inch and a half across. They're not just cute; in my opinion, they have both a better texture and sweeter flavor than some of their bigger kin. Little pattypans are particularly dense-fleshed at that size, and they make the perfect quick and pretty stir-fry (at right) or grilled veg—simply quarter them lengthwise. Nip off the stems of Fairy Tales and cut them lengthwise into slices or fans, or crosswise into coins. The creamy white flesh loves garlic, basil, lemon, or anything with soy sauce or sesame.

No one can argue with the cutest, mini-est summer vegetable of all—cherry tomatoes. I am afraid we have taken advantage of this vegetable's universal appeal and totally exploited it. In fact, cherry tomatoes are a ›

PATTYPAN STIR-FRY WITH FAR EAST FLAVORS

SERVES 4

1 pound small yellow pattypan squash, or slim zucchini

1 tablespoon plus 1 teaspoon peanut or canola oil

2 shallots (2 to 2½ ounces total), peeled and sliced into thin rings

Kosher salt

2 teaspoons minced fresh garlic

½ small serrano pepper, thinly sliced

¼ teaspoon garam masala (or a combination of cinnamon, coriander, and cumin)

⅓ cup well-mixed coconut milk

1 teaspoon finely grated lime zest

1 to 2 tablespoons finely sliced basil, preferably Thai basil

1 to 2 tablespoons finely sliced fresh mint

We pick our Sunburst, or pattypan, squash very small (1 to 2 inches across) and sell them by the pint. They're awfully cute at that size, and the flesh is extra-firm, too—perfect for stir-frying. I quarter them or cut them into wedges. You also could use bigger pattypans cut into ½-inch wedges or zucchini cut into half-moons. I love pattypan squash with this Indian-East Asian passel of flavors, but if you want to go super-simple for a weeknight, just stir-fry the pattypans with some garlic and scallions.

If your pattypan squash is very small (1 to 2 inches wide), slice it vertically into quarters. If the pattypans are on the large size, slice each one in half horizontally (through the equator) first and then cut ½-inch-wide wedges through the axis.

In a large (12-inch) nonstick stir-fry pan or skillet, heat 2 teaspoons of the oil over medium-high heat. When the oil is hot (it will shimmer), add the shallots and a big pinch of salt, and cook, stirring, until the shallots are golden brown and crisp in places, 2 to 3 minutes. Transfer the shallots to a plate.

Add the remaining 2 teaspoons of peanut oil and the squash to the pan. Season the squash with another big pinch of salt, turn the heat to high, and cook, stirring, until the squash is deeply browned on most sides and shrunken, 6 to 8 minutes. Return the shallots to the pan, add the garlic, serranos, garam masala, and ¼ teaspoon salt, and cook, stirring constantly, until the garlic and spices are incorporated and fragrant, 30 seconds to 1 minute.

Remove the pan from the stove, add the coconut milk, lime zest, half of the basil, and half of the mint. Stir well, scraping the pan, then transfer the vegetables and sauce to a serving bowl and garnish with the remaining herbs.

BREAKFAST TOSTADAS WITH SCRAMBLED EGGS, SWEET CORN, CILANTRO & FRESH SALSA

MAKES 6 TOSTADAS

1 cup fresh corn kernels (from 2 ears)

8 to 9 large eggs

Milk or cream

Kosher salt

Freshly ground black pepper

1 cup shredded extra-sharp Cheddar

½ cup refried beans

2 to 3 tablespoons chopped fresh cilantro

½ to ⅔ cup Lazy Summer Day Salsa with Serranos, Cilantro & Lime (p. 72) or other fresh salsa

3 tablespoons unsalted butter

Extra-virgin olive oil

6 small (5½-inch) corn tortillas

Nothing beats egg and tortilla combos, and the one we like best has fresh corn kernels, fresh cilantro, and our own fresh salsa layered on top of a crisped-up tortilla. We sneak in a few refried beans, but overall this is a breakfast (or supper) treat that feels light and looks pretty, too. We heat the corn tortillas in a cast-iron pan in a little bit of oil so that they get just a bit crunchy. Made to order, these are a summer farmhouse kitchen classic.

Put the corn kernels in a small microwavable bowl with a few teaspoons of water. Cover with a damp paper towel and microwave for 30 seconds. Beat the eggs with a splash of milk or cream, a couple of pinches of salt, and several grinds of black pepper. Arrange two skillets—one small nonstick for the eggs, the other heavier (such as cast iron)—on your stovetop. Arrange the beaten eggs, corn, cheese, refried beans, cilantro, and salsa in bowls near your stove.

Heat 1 to 2 teaspoons butter in the small skillet over medium heat. Add a portion (about one-sixth) of the eggs to the pan and scramble until just cooked through (they should still look glossy.) Meanwhile, heat 1 to 2 teaspoons of oil in the heavier skillet over medium heat. When the oil is hot, add one tortilla and cook until lightly browned and a little bit puffy or bubbly, 1 to 2 minutes. Flip and cook the other side for a minute.

Transfer the tortilla to a warm plate and smear a few small spoonfuls of refried beans (2 to 3 teaspoons) over it. Sprinkle a couple of teaspoons of cheese over the beans. Arrange the scrambled eggs on top of the cheese and beans and sprinkle 2 tablespoons of cheese and a portion of the corn over them. Top with a generous sprinkling of cilantro and 1 tablespoon or a little more of fresh salsa. Serve the tostada right away. Repeat with the remaining eggs and tortillas and serve hot.

› very big deal for us—our number-one selling product after eggs. If you think about it, this isn't so very surprising. If you've ever grown cherry tomatoes, you know that they're very prolific. Not only are we out in the garden every evening picking hundreds of Sun Golds, Sweet 100s, and Black Cherries, but we are doing that every night through October since the plants just keep growing and growing in our warm fall weather.

Cherry tomato plants tend to suffer less from diseases and pests, too. "Droppers" and "splitters" are the only real annoyance. These are the tomatoes that ripen and fall to the ground or crack down the middle after ›

*Farmhouse French Toast
with Backyard Berry Syrup*

FARMHOUSE FRENCH TOAST WITH BACKYARD BERRY SYRUP

SERVES 4 TO 5

1 teaspoon ground cinnamon

3 tablespoons sugar

6 large eggs, at room temperature if possible

1¼ cups half-and-half

¾ cup plus 1 tablespoon pure maple syrup

2 teaspoons pure vanilla extract

1 teaspoon kosher salt

⅛ teaspoon ground nutmeg

Eight or nine ¾-inch-thick slices Challah bread (from a 1-pound loaf, slightly stale is fine)

3 tablespoons unsalted butter

1 cup fresh ripe summer berries (including diced strawberries, whole raspberries or black raspberries, and blueberries or small blackberries)

Sunday mornings after our chores are done and the farm stand is open, we pick berries out back, crack some of the ladies' eggs, and make our signature French toast with berry syrup. We soak Challah bread (for the best texture) in a tasty custard and cook it to order; then we lightly mash black raspberries, blueberries, and strawberries with warm maple syrup in a skillet. We sprinkle the warm French toast with cinnamon sugar, drizzle with the berry syrup, and all is right with the world.

In a small bowl, combine the cinnamon and 1 tablespoon of the sugar. Set aside.

In a large, shallow mixing bowl, whisk together the eggs and the remaining sugar until well combined. Add the half-and-half, 1 tablespoon of the maple syrup, the vanilla, salt, and nutmeg. Whisk again until well combined.

Submerge two or three slices of the bread (whatever will fit into the bowl and into your skillet in one batch) in the egg custard to soak for about 5 minutes. Meanwhile, heat 1 tablespoon butter in a large (12-inch) nonstick skillet over medium heat. When the pan is hot and the butter is foaming, add the coated bread slices to the skillet. Cook without moving until the bottom is a mottled golden brown, 4 to 5 minutes. Carefully turn the bread pieces over and cook on the other side until golden brown, 3 to 4 minutes. Transfer to warm plates and sprinkle with cinnamon sugar if desired, or transfer to an oven-proof platter if keeping warm, and don't add cinnamon sugar until serving. Leave the skillet off the heat for a minute. Put two to three more pieces of bread in the custard to soak.

Meanwhile, combine ¼ cup of the maple syrup and a third of the berries in a small skillet. Mash some of the berries with the back of a fork while

continued on p. 140 ›

› a good rain storm. Lucky for us, our chickens love droppers and splitters. Come August, frankly, we are all on a bit of a cherry-tomato high.

We put a lot of thought into producing a colorful mix of cherry tomatoes, so our pints are pretty sexy. Color is one thing, but flavor and convenience really seal the deal with farm stand customers. Pick up a pint and you can immediately start handing off cherry tomatoes to restless kids in the back seat. Libby will eat ripe Sun Golds like candy. Most kids will. Or you can take the little beauties straight home, slice them into your salad, and have instant summer on the plate. And you can even roast cherry tomatoes or tuck them into an easy gratin (p. 218) for powerhouse flavor—more quickly than a slow cooked tomato sauce.

The problem with the all-mini-veg farm stand, if you really wanted to go that way, is that you'd miss beefsteak tomatoes. That just doesn't compute, does it? So don't misunderstand me—we don't grow cherry ›

COOK'S TIP

We make French toast "to order," but if you want to serve it all at once, you can keep it in a warm (200°F) oven. Just don't mix and heat the syrup until serving.

the syrup is heating. When the syrup is bubbling and the fruit is warmed through and releasing its juices (2 to 3 minutes), pour it over the slices of cooked French toast and serve. (Don't let the syrup bubble for long or it will start reducing.) Reserve the syrup skillet.

Return the large skillet to medium heat, add another 1 tablespoon butter, and cook the second batch of soaked bread. Sprinkle with cinnamon sugar if desired. Make the second batch of berry syrup and pour over the toast. Repeat with the third and last batch of bread and syrup.

YOGURT, SUMMER BERRY & HOMEMADE MAPLE GRANOLA PARFAIT

SERVES 1

¼ cup Simple Homemade Maple Granola (p. 142)

1 tablespoon chopped well-toasted pecans

½ cup plain thick Greek yogurt (a little more if you like)

⅔ cup mixed berries (whole raspberries, black raspberries or blueberries, and/or sliced strawberries)

Honey or pure maple syrup, preferably local (optional)

I often make one of these parfaits for breakfast or a snack, but they're great for dessert, too. Assemble and eat right away for the best texture, or assemble ahead and refrigerate. While the granola will lose some of its crispness, the flavors have time to mingle—not a bad trade-off for a make-ahead. I like a lot of granola in my parfaits, but feel free to fiddle with the proportions here. This recipe makes one serving; multiply as you like.

Toss together the granola and pecans in a small bowl. Reserve about a teaspoon for the top garnish. Put one-third of the yogurt in the bottom of a 6- to 8-ounce glass (I like a sturdy water tumbler but a wine glass works for a fancier presentation, too). Sprinkle with one-third of the granola and top with one-third of the berries. Drizzle the berries with a little honey or maple syrup if you like, especially if they are not particularly sweet or are a bit under-ripe. Repeat the layers twice more with the remaining yogurt, granola, berries, and honey or maple syrup. Top with the reserved teaspoon of granola. Eat right away or cover loosely and refrigerate for up to 6 to 8 hours.

continued on p. 142 ›

› tomatoes to the exclusion of other tomatoes. Like most market gardeners who need to maximize sales in high summer, tomatoes of all types must be embraced (not such a bad thing, huh?). We grow beefsteaks and plums and sandwich tomatoes. Alas, we don't grow a lot of heirlooms, fascinating and quirky and emotionally appealing as they are. They yield less and suffer damage easily, so for our little farm, they don't make as much economic sense as hybrid tomatoes.

We could never go completely without heirlooms though, and I try new ones every year. Friends—and farm stand customers—sometimes pass their ›

› favorite seeds along to us. In fact, one lovely couple visiting from the Midwest last summer made a point of stopping by here to give us some seeds from a variety called Cherokee Chocolate. The couple had visited our farm stand the summer before and noticed we had Cherokee Purple tomatoes (my favorite heirloom for go-go tomato flavor). We are growing the Cherokee Chocolates this year, and I have ants in my pants waiting to taste one. (Me, patient? Not so much.)

I am always surprised at how popular the "sandwich" type tomatoes are. I guess it has something to do with their ubiquitous tomato-ness—round, perfectly red, medium-sized. Not the best flavor ever, but we're happy to grow them nonetheless since they ripen earliest. And if we can get "TOMATOES" written up on our chalkboard out on the road by July 4th, it's a good thing. Otherwise, we have to endure questions from visitors who've traveled from places like New Jersey and ›

SIMPLE HOMEMADE MAPLE GRANOLA

MAKES 2⅓ CUPS

2 cups regular oats (not quick-cooking)

½ teaspoon ground cinnamon

⅛ teaspoon table salt

2 tablespoons unsalted butter, melted

¼ cup pure maple syrup

I eat so much granola that I decided I'd better learn to make my own. I wanted something simple that wasn't doctored up with unnecessary additions. So I came up with this easy maple version, and I add nuts or dried fruits separately if I like, depending on the preparation (like the parfait on p. 141). I bake the granola to a toasty brown color for the best flavor. Color is the best way to tell doneness, too, since the granola won't crisp up completely until it cools out of the oven.

Heat the oven to 350°F. Cover two heavy-duty rimmed sheet pans with parchment paper. In a shallow mixing bowl, combine the oats, cinnamon, and salt. Toss well. Drizzle the melted butter over the oats and toss well until the oats are thoroughly coated. Divide the mixture between the two pans and spread in one layer. Bake until the oats are lightly browned, 13 to 15 minutes. Remove the sheet pans from the oven and drizzle the maple syrup equally over both. Use a silicone spatula to stir and scrape the syrup and oats together until the oats are well coated. (They will likely be piled up in the center of the pan at this point.) Use the spatula to spread the oats back out into one loose layer on each pan. (There will be some clumping.)

Return the pans to the oven and continue baking until the oats are a deep golden brown, another 12 to 15 minutes. Let the oats cool completely on the pans. Roll up the parchment paper with your hands to break up the crisp clumps, and scrape all the granola into an airtight container for storage. Keep at room temperature for up to 2 weeks.

CHOCOLATE CHOCOLATE-CHIP ZUCCHINI AND RASPBERRY MUFFINS

MAKES 12 MUFFINS

Unsalted butter, softened, for the pan (or baking spray or muffin cups)

1⅔ cups (7½ ounces) unbleached all-purpose flour, plus more for the pan

⅓ cup plus 1 tablespoon unsweetened cocoa powder (about 1 ounce total), sifted

1 teaspoon baking powder

½ teaspoon baking soda

½ teaspoon table salt

2 large eggs

⅔ cup granulated sugar

⅔ cup light brown sugar

1 tablespoon instant espresso granules, dissolved in 1 tablespoon hot water

1 teaspoon pure vanilla extract

½ cup vegetable oil

⅓ cup sour cream

1 cup finely grated zucchini (ends trimmed, unpeeled, about 1 medium 6- to 7-ounce zucchini)

¾ cup semisweet chocolate chips

4 ounces fresh raspberries

Confectioners' sugar, for dusting (optional)

At last—the perfect place for that one zucchini you can't get rid of. It's a bit sneaky, I know, hiding it in a chocolate muffin, but why not? Add fresh raspberries, too, and you have a seasonal snack that doubles as dessert or the perfect picnic take-along. The flavor of these moist muffins improves overnight, so make them ahead, wrap in plastic, and store at room temp or freeze.

Heat the oven to 350°F. Position a rack in the center of the oven. Butter and flour a 12-cup nonstick muffin tin. (Or use baking spray or muffin cup liners.)

In a medium mixing bowl, whisk together the flour, cocoa powder, baking powder, baking soda, and salt.

In the bowl of a stand mixer (or a large mixing bowl), beat the eggs and both sugars together on medium speed until smooth, lightened, and somewhat increased in volume, about 1 minute. Add the reconstituted espresso, the vanilla, oil, and sour cream and mix again for 1 minute. With the mixer running on very low speed, gradually add the dry ingredients into the wet, beating just until combined and stopping to scrape down the sides of the mixer when necessary. Add the zucchini and mix until just combined. Stir in the chocolate chips and raspberries. Pour or spoon the batter (a ⅓-cup measure works well) into the muffin cups. (They will be quite full.)

Bake until the muffins are fully risen in the middle and a wooden pick inserted in the center of a muffin comes out clean, 23 to 25 minutes. Let the muffins cool in the pan for 10 minutes and transfer to a cooling rack to cool completely. Dust lightly with confectioners' sugar if desired (and only if serving right away). Wrap any extras in plastic and store at room temperature or in the freezer.

› Virginia where tomatoes are already ripe. Most people don't realize that we have a very cool spring here and that field tomatoes before mid-July are rare. I understand their confusion about tomatoes. But I would be happy if people did not ask for eggplant and red bell peppers (or jeeze, butternut squash) in June, though.

THE FAIREST DAYS OF ALL
Two ladies pedal down the driveway on their old-fashioned Schwinn® bicycles. The driveway is now covered with crushed clam shells, so we hear the bikes coming. The ladies stop and smile at us from under their ›

› incongruous space-age bike helmets. Pulling something out of their wicker baskets, they say, "And how many people are living in your household this year?" We always want to answer "Sixteen!" but we know they won't fall for that. "Okay, here are your four free Fair tickets for this year. See you there!" And they pedal off.

With that, we know Fair week has begun. That—and the lumbering 18-wheelers heading up State Road with carnival rides stacked on their tractor beds. They start showing up on Monday and Tuesday, and I love to look across the street and watch them line up in the field. This is the reason we get free tickets to the Martha's Vineyard Agricultural Society's annual Fair—we are "abutting" neighbors. Which means we have to listen to bloodcurdling screams and smell cotton candy for four days straight.

Look, things could be worse. Basically, we just give in and give ourselves over to the Fair. And we have a total blast. I've turned into a real Fair geek, ›

VERY BERRY VANILLA CLAFOUTIS

SERVES 4

3 large eggs (at room temperature if possible)

½ cup unbleached all-purpose flour

⅓ cup heavy cream

⅓ cup whole milk

¼ cup pure maple syrup

2 tablespoons sugar

1½ teaspoons pure vanilla extract

¼ teaspoon freshly grated orange zest (optional)

½ teaspoon kosher salt

1½ tablespoons unsalted butter

8 ounces fresh blueberries, raspberries, and/or black raspberries

Confectioners' sugar

A clafoutis is just a big custardy, fruity, popover-y pancake. Technically it's a dessert, but it's perfect for brunch, too. When our blueberries and black raspberries are ripening and the hens are laying at warp speed, this is a no-brainer, because the batter is so darn quick and easy to make in the blender. Use any combination of fresh, not frozen, berries you like, but please include at least a big handful of blueberries.

Heat the oven to 375°F.

Combine the eggs, flour, cream, milk, maple syrup, sugar, vanilla, orange zest (if using), and salt in a blender. Blend on high to combine thoroughly.

Melt the butter in a medium (10-inch) heavy-duty, non-stick, ovenproof skillet over medium heat. Cook until the milk solids in the butter turn golden brown and the butter begins to smell nutty. Pour half of the batter into the pan and let it set for a few seconds. Arrange the berries on top and gently pour the remaining batter over all. Nudge some berries back to the middle if necessary. Let the skillet sit on the burner for a few seconds. Very carefully transfer the skillet to the oven.

Bake until the pancake is set in the middle (it will be puffed and browned around the edges but not in the middle), 22 to 24 minutes. Remove the skillet and let the pancake cool for a few minutes in the pan (it will deflate). Slide a flexible silicone spatula or two under and all around to loosen the pancake a bit and then transfer it to a cutting board. Sprinkle generously with confectioners' sugar, let cool for a few minutes more, cut into wedges, and serve straight off the board. (It's better warm than hot.)

Backyard Berry Ice Cream
Pie with Chocolate Sauce

BACKYARD BERRY ICE CREAM PIE WITH CHOCOLATE SAUCE

SERVES 8 TO 12

1¼ cups chocolate wafer crumbs (about 6 ounces, or about 25 to 27 Nabisco® FAMOUS™ Chocolate Wafers, pulsed in a food processor until fine)

¼ cup sugar

⅓ cup unsalted butter, melted

Kosher salt

½ recipe (about 1¼ pints) Backyard Berry Ice Cream (p. 148)

1 pint vanilla ice cream

1 recipe Chocolate Sauce (p. 150)

½ cup fresh raspberries or black raspberries, for garnish (optional)

When we were little, my best friend, Eliza, and I used to beg my mom to make her chocolate ice-box pie. Now I've updated Mom's pie to feature our Backyard Berry Ice Cream (p. 148), though you could certainly make it with store-bought black raspberry ice cream—or any other flavor you like. Make this ahead, as it needs time in the freezer. Once frozen, wrap it well if you plan to keep it for a few weeks. It's perfect for a July birthday party. (Libby and I ought to know!)

Heat the oven to 400°F. In a mixing bowl, combine the chocolate cookie crumbs, sugar, melted butter, and a pinch of salt. Stir with a silicone spatula or wooden spoon until well combined. Press into a 9-inch pie pan, creating as much edge up the sides of the pan as possible. Bake the crust for 7 to 8 minutes. Let cool and then chill in the fridge for at least an hour.

Remove the ice creams from the freezer and let them soften up just a bit. Heat the chocolate sauce briefly (do not overheat) to loosen it to drizzling consistency. Remove the chilled pie shell from the refrigerator.

Scoop or spoon alternating portions of both kinds of ice cream (about half of each) onto the bottom of the shell to cover it. Flatten this layer of ice cream slightly and drizzle with about 4 to 5 tablespoons of the chocolate sauce. Continue scooping alternating portions of ice cream onto the pie to create a second and final layer, flattening and smoothing slightly to make a uniform top. Drizzle with another 4 to 5 tablespoons of the chocolate sauce (rewarm if necessary). Freeze the pie until the top is firm, then cover it tightly with plastic wrap and foil. Freeze for at least several hours or overnight before serving. It will keep in the freezer (if very tightly wrapped) for several weeks.

continued on p. 148 ›

› which is surprising, since I don't really like scary rides or big crowds. But the Ag Fair is different. There are cute animals. Lots of them. Not just cute animals, but huge animals. Clydesdales and Percherons. Teams of oxen (my favorite—so stately). Sows and boars. And little animals— pygmy goats and baby calves and piglets. Every breed of chicken possible. Ducks and geese. All in the judging barn. And out in the ring, I can watch the ox pull or the dog show— or even the women's cast iron skillet-throwing competition (this is serious stuff) while Roy and Libby go spend an entire summer's coin jar over at the rides.

And you can actually eat good food here. Which we do. For four days straight, in between all our farm chores, we dash across the street to eat lunch and dinner. ›

› (I mean really, who lives across the street from a Fair—and has free tickets to it?! We have it good, I tell you.) Pulled pork from a local smoker who raises his own pigs on the Island, with a side of fresh corn salad and slaw, is my favorite. There's an entire booth just for grilled local corn on the cob, too. Fireman's burgers and the best ever french fries, the famous veggie tempura, barbecued ribs, fish tacos, design-your-own cup-cakes, fruit smoothies, root beer floats, frozen lemonade and ice cream for charity—in addition to all the usual fair fare. You plop down at a picnic table and you see at least a half dozen people you know.   ›

> COOK'S TIP
>
> For the best results, freeze the ice cream custard in two batches (unless you happen to have one of the large-capacity home ice cream makers). You'll have plenty to make the ice cream pie and still have some left over for midnight snacking.

Keep the extra chocolate sauce, covered, in the refrigerator to use for serving.

To serve, remove the pie from the freezer and soften slightly at room temperature for a few minutes. Cut into wedges. Warm the remaining chocolate sauce if using, and drizzle serving plates with it. Arrange wedges of pie over the sauce and garnish with a few berries next to it if you like.

BACKYARD BERRY ICE CREAM

MAKES ABOUT 4 CUPS ICE CREAM BASE OR 2½ PINTS ICE CREAM

....

12 ounces black raspberries or a mix of 6 ounces blackberries and 6 ounces raspberries

¾ cup plus 2 tablespoons sugar

2 tablespoons pure maple syrup

4 large egg yolks

2½ cups heavy cream

Table salt

1 teaspoon pure vanilla extract

Around the fourth of July, we start harvesting the black raspberries that grow wild all around the farm, and we make our first batch of homemade ice cream for the holi-day. All too quickly the black raspberry picking extrava-ganza is over, but the longing for the ice cream (and my favorite ice cream pie, p. 147) is still with us. So instead, I combine raspberries and blackberries for a delicious flavor base that comes pretty darn close to black rasp-berry. Despite the fruit base, this is a creamy, custardy ice cream—the kind I grew up making in Delaware.

In a blender, purée the berries until they are completely smooth. Strain the berry purée through a fine-mesh sieve into a 2-cup glass (liquid) measuring cup. Press on the solids to be sure to extract all of the juice. Stir in ¼ cup plus 2 tablespoons of the sugar and the maple syrup. (You should have about 1½ cups purée, or a little more.) Refrigerate the purée for at least 1 hour or up to 24 hours.

Fill a large, wide bowl halfway with ice and water. Put a smaller heat-proof bowl (a stainless-steel mixing bowl of at least 6-cup volume works well) in the ice bath. Have a strainer ready, too.

Whisk the egg yolks in a medium bowl and set aside. In a medium sauce-pan, combine the remaining ½ cup sugar with the cream and a pinch of salt. Heat the mixture over medium-high heat, stirring occasionally (but keeping an eye on it), until the sugar dissolves and the mixture is just starting to

continued on p. 150 ›

› But the best part? Thursday evening (drum roll please!): The doors to the Hall open. The crowds stream in. At last, the judging of pies, cakes, art, photographs, woodwork, pickles, flowers—and vegetables—is done. Ribbons are pinned everywhere, and we all race around to see who has won. We've all dropped our entries off on Wednesday evening or Thursday morning, and the anticipation is killing us.

I never understood this phenomenon until Roy and I entered our vegetables for the first time. Even that first year, we had to enter in the "professional" category, because we were selling vegetables. So from the get-go, we've been competing ›

bubble around the edges of the pan (3 or 4 minutes). Gently pour half of the cream into the egg yolks, whisking constantly to prevent the eggs from curdling. Pour the egg mixture back into the saucepan and cook over low heat (or medium low if your stove is electric!), stirring constantly and scraping the bottom of the pan with a heatproof cooking spoon until the custard thickens slightly to a more viscous consistency and coats the back of a wooden spoon (holding a horizontal line drawn through it with a finger), 3 to 5 minutes. Don't let the custard overheat or boil or it will curdle.

Immediately strain the custard into the bowl nestled in the ice bath. Stir the custard frequently over the ice bath until an instant-read thermometer registers 70°F. Add the vanilla extract and stir. Add all of the berry purée and mix well.

Chill the berry custard in the refrigerator for at least 4 hours or overnight. (I put mine in a 2-quart Pyrex glass measure and cover tightly with plastic. You can also divide the base in half at this point.)

Freeze half of the berry custard in your ice cream maker's canister according to the manufacturer's instructions. (If you have one of the newer super-large ice cream makers, you can freeze the whole batch at once. If making in two batches, keep the remaining custard in the refrigerator.) Transfer to an airtight container and lay a piece of plastic on the surface of the ice cream before freezing it, covered, for up to several days. Wash and rechill your ice cream canister, freeze the second half of the ice cream base, transfer it to an airtight container, and freeze.

CHOCOLATE SAUCE

MAKES 1 CUP

4 ounces semisweet or bittersweet chocolate, finely chopped

½ cup heavy cream

2 tablespoons sugar

1 tablespoon unsalted butter

Kosher salt

1 teaspoon pure vanilla extract

Put the chopped chocolate in a heatproof bowl. Combine the cream, sugar, butter, and a pinch of salt in a medium heavy saucepan over medium-high heat. Bring just to a boil, stirring constantly. Pour the hot cream mixture over the chopped chocolate and let stand for 1 minute. Stir until the chocolate is melted and smooth. Whisk in the vanilla.

LIBBY'S LEMON BLUEBERRY BUCKLE

SERVES 6 TO 8

Baking spray, for the pan

FOR THE CRUMB TOPPING

½ cup unbleached all-purpose flour

⅓ cup packed light brown sugar

3 tablespoons unsalted butter, cut into pieces

Table salt

FOR THE CAKE

1½ cups (6¾ ounces) unbleached all-purpose flour

2 teaspoons baking powder

½ teaspoon ground cardamom or ¾ teaspoon ground cinnamon

Table salt

½ cup unsalted butter, at room temperature

½ cup granulated sugar

¼ cup light brown sugar

2 teaspoons pure vanilla extract

1½ teaspoons freshly grated lemon zest

2 large eggs

½ cup sour cream

2½ cups fresh blueberries

Berries and cake and crumb topping—no wonder this is a favorite around the farm. Libby and I make it together after we snag our first blueberries of the season, and we all devour it straight from the pan. Theoretically, this is great with vanilla ice cream, but we rarely wait that long, and we eat it for breakfast, too. I use ground cardamom as the background spice here for an intriguing pairing with the lemon, but feel free to use cinnamon if you'd rather.

Heat the oven to 350°F. Spray a 9-inch square baking pan with baking spray, such as Baker's Joy®.

MAKE THE TOPPING

In a small bowl, combine the flour, brown sugar, butter, and ¼ teaspoon salt. Mix thoroughly with your fingers, mashing the butter into the flour and sugar, until the mixture is well combined and crumbly. Set aside.

MAKE THE CAKE

Stir together the flour, baking powder, cardamom, and ½ teaspoon salt. In the bowl of a mixer, combine the butter, both sugars, the vanilla, and lemon zest. Mix well on medium-high speed until light and fluffy, 2 to 3 minutes. Add the eggs one at a time and mix well on medium speed, stopping to scrape down the sides and bottom of the bowl after each addition. Add half of the flour mixture and mix on medium-low speed just until incorporated. Add half of the sour cream and mix on medium-low speed just until incorporated. Repeat with the remaining flour and sour cream. Fold in a little more than half of the blueberries.

continued on p. 152 ›

› against other farmers—and not in the home gardener category. To this day—we've now won a slew of blue, red, and white ribbons—I still think this is why we do well. The home gardener competition is fierce, with lots of entries. Farmers aren't as diligent about getting their entries in, so I don't think the competition is nearly as stiff. (Though I am told that the judges will not award ribbons at all if they don't think anything merits one!)

Regardless, every year when we walk in the Hall and see our cherry tomatoes and green beans—and potatoes and cosmos and squash and onions and even Roy's gladiolus—sporting a brightly colored ribbon, we are happy. What a kick. Actually, the whole vibe of that evening—the first night of the Fair—is uplifting. You can just feel the excitement, and it doesn't hurt that it's like a real date night for Roy and me, who've been working hard all summer. Now we get to relax and walk around on a warm summer night under the stars, holding hands, catching ›

› up with friends, eating an ice cream cone or sharing a fried dough with lots of confectioners' sugar. And all without having to drive anywhere or find a place to park!

On the Sunday side of Fair week, we are exhausted for sure. Traffic at the farm stand has been extra heavy, and we've been up every morning extra early. It's been a long week, this third week in August, but we wouldn't have it any other way. In fact, I think I know what I will be doing the third week in August for the rest of my life. So don't go planning a wedding or pull some other drastic stunt to try to get me off this Island. Because I'll be at the Fair.

Transfer the batter (it will be thick) to the prepared baking pan and spread it out as evenly as possible. Sprinkle with half of the crumb mixture. Sprinkle with the remaining blueberries and the remainder of the crumb mixture.

Bake until golden and set (a toothpick inserted will come out clean), about 50 minutes. Let cool in the pan for 20 minutes or so. Cut out squares and serve warm or at room temperature. Wrap leftovers tightly and keep at room temperature for 24 hours or in the freezer for several weeks.

PEPPERMINT LEMONADE SODA

SERVES 6

1 cup sugar

1 cup water

½ cup (loosely packed) peppermint leaves, plus 6 sprigs for garnish

Ice cubes

1¼ cups fresh lemon juice (from 6 to 7 lemons), plus 1 lemon, thinly sliced crosswise

4 cups plain seltzer water

Homemade lemonade—fresh lemon juice and simple syrup—gets even better with an infusion of peppermint and a sizzle from seltzer. A truly refreshing drink, it makes a lovely non-alcoholic cocktail, too. I love our red-stemmed peppermint for its candy-cane flavor, but if you use another mint, taste and smell it first, as some mints can be a bit funky. The simple syrup needs time to cool so plan ahead. (It keeps in the fridge.)

Make a mint-infused simple syrup: Put the sugar, water, and mint leaves in a small saucepan over medium-high heat. Bring just to a boil, stirring to dissolve the sugar, and remove from the heat. Let cool completely to room temperature. Strain the mint leaves and reserve the simple syrup. (If making ahead, refrigerate for up to 2 days.)

Arrange a few ice cubes, a lemon slice or two, and a mint sprig in each of six tall glasses. Combine the simple syrup, lemon juice, and seltzer in a pitcher, mix well, and pour over the ice in each glass. (Alternatively, if you are not serving six people at once, combine only the lemon juice and simple syrup and portion one-sixth of it, which is about a generous ⅓ cup, into each glass at a time. Add ¾ cup cold seltzer water to each glass.) Stir lightly and serve right away.

GREEN ISLAND
FARM
EGGS→

INDIAN SUMMER
AND
EARLY FALL
(AKA "THE BONUS SEASON")

SEPTEMBER IS THE SORCERER'S gift to farming. It tricks you into believing that every day on a farm is warm and sunny and magical, that fruits and vegetables will always tumble off plants in a profusion of flavor, that there's nothing better in the world than working outside.

And with this temporary suspension of reality, September offers another seductive gift—small snippets of time. For Roy and me, that means time when we can look at each other and acknowledge the questions that've swirled through our heads all summer: "Where are we going with this whole thing? Are we market gardeners or are we farmers? Can this lifestyle we're pursuing really be our business, too—a business with a decent income? Will we be able to stay here at the farmhouse for ›

The Beet Bar

THE BEET BAR

SERVES 4 TO 6

2 ounces fresh goat cheese

1 tablespoon milk

1 teaspoon roughly chopped fresh thyme leaves

1 cup roughly chopped toasted pecans, walnuts, or a mix

2 to 3 ounces aged goat cheese, such as Boucheron

2 to 3 ounces creamy blue cheese, such as Gorgonzola Dolce

1 to 2 cups baby leafy greens such as mizuna, tat soi, nasturtium leaves, or mâche, washed and dried

4 ounces very thinly sliced prosciutto, cut or torn into smaller pieces

1 recipe Balsamic Drizzle (p. 13)

1 recipe Quick-Roasted Beet Slices (below)

Don't laugh, but beets can be just the thing to get a party off on the right foot. I've noticed when I make my Quick-Roasted Beet Slices (which taste like candy) that people stand around the kitchen and snatch the beets straight off the sheet pan. With a little goat cheese, a few toasted walnuts or pecans, a slice or two of prosciutto, and some wispy greens nearby, they make their own roasted beet "sandwiches" (open-faced or closed). I call this The Beet Bar. Why not?

In a small bowl, mash together the fresh goat cheese, milk, and thyme leaves until smooth. (A small silicone spatula works well.) Transfer to a small decorative serving bowl if you like and cover loosely with plastic until serving.

Set out the toasted nuts, aged goat cheese, blue cheese, leafy greens, prosciutto, and Balsamic Drizzle on platters and in bowls, along with small serving utensils and spreading knives. Put trivets or wooden boards nearby for the sheet pans of roasted beets. Let the beets cool for a couple of minutes and then let everyone make their own appetizers. (Alternatively, transfer the beet slices to a nice platter and serve with everything else.)

QUICK-ROASTED BEET SLICES

SERVES 4 OR 5 AS AN APPETIZER OR 2 OR 3 AS A SIDE

1 to 1¼ pounds beet roots (6 to 8 small beets, stalks and leaves trimmed), washed and trimmed but unpeeled

1 teaspoon kosher salt

2 tablespoons extra-virgin olive oil

My world changed when I figured out how quickly and deliciously beets cook when sliced thinly and roasted. (And no peeling required!) This recipe can easily be cut in half or doubled. (Just don't crowd your oven; cook only two sheet pans at a time unless you have a convection oven.)

Heat the oven to 450°F. Line two large heavy-duty rimmed sheet pans with parchment paper.

› a while? (And does that mean we can plant asparagus?!)" Unwittingly, we actually think September is a good time to make decisions.

Stepping back from this stage, I look down at the characters and laugh. They are bewitched; their fate is a foregone conclusion. They never had a chance. The signs were all there.

First there was the free tractor. Then the offer of land.

In the fall of our second year at the homestead, a series of happy (let's return to the positive view of this story!) events conspired to move us across the line from market gardeners to farmers. Roy got a free tractor. And our landlord, Tom, offered us four acres to farm. ›

continued on p. 158 ›

Using a sharp, thin-bladed knife (such as a ceramic knife or a Santoku), slice each beet crosswise into rounds between ⅛ and ¼ inch. (There's no need for a mandoline—if your slices were paper thin, they'd burn!) If the beet root wobbles around, cut a thin piece off the bottom to stabilize it and continue slicing. Put the beet slices in a mixing bowl and toss thoroughly with the salt and olive oil.

Arrange the slices, evenly spaced, on the sheet pans (it's okay if they touch). Roast, rotating the sheet pans once halfway through cooking, until the beets are tender, shrunken, wrinkled, and glistening, 14 to 16 minutes. (Smaller beets will cook more quickly. The smallest slices will be black and crisp around the edges. Bigger pieces will be sweet and pliable. Both are fine.) Let cool for a few minutes and serve warm.

SPICY BOWL OF GREENS AND NOODLES

SERVES 4

Kosher salt

8 ounces dried udon noodles

1 teaspoon toasted sesame oil

2 tablespoons low-sodium soy sauce

1 tablespoon oyster sauce

1 tablespoon fresh lime juice

1 tablespoon rice wine or sherry

2 teaspoons light brown sugar

2 tablespoons chopped fresh ginger

3 tablespoons vegetable or peanut oil

1 cup thinly sliced shallots (about 4 ounces)

5 ounces cremini mushrooms, halved and sliced (about 2 cups)

1 tablespoon chopped fresh garlic

1½ teaspoons Asian chili-garlic paste

¼ teaspoon ground cinnamon

4 cups low-sodium chicken broth

5½ to 6 cups coarsely chopped Tuscan kale (aka Cavolo Nero, Lacinato) leaves (5 to 6 ounces after ribs removed, from one 9- to 10-ounce bunch)

¼ cup thinly sliced scallions (all parts), for garnish

East meets West here in a warming, good-for-you marriage of Italian greens and Asian flavors. You wouldn't think of kale in a traditional noodle-shop dish, but it's pretty darn friendly with the likes of ginger, garlic, soy, chili, lime, and, of course, pasta (aka udon noodles, in this case). I especially like using the silky-textured Tuscan kale in this. I like a generous amount of noodles, too, but you can use less if you like—just cook the noodles separately first. Substitute an equal amount of fresh udon if you can't find dried.

Bring a large pot of salted water to a boil. Add the udon noodles and cook until tender, about 6 minutes. (They will be tender in a little less time than most package directions indicate.) Drain in a colander, rinse briefly, and let dry a bit. Transfer to a bowl and toss with a big pinch of salt and the sesame oil.

In a small bowl, stir together the soy sauce, oyster sauce, lime juice, rice wine or sherry, brown sugar, and 1 tablespoon of the ginger. Set aside.

In a large (5- to 6-quart) Dutch oven or other soup pot, heat the vegetable or peanut oil over medium-low heat. Add the shallots, creminis, and ¼ teaspoon salt and cover; cook, stirring occasionally, until the shallots are well softened and just beginning to brown, about 5 minutes. Uncover and continue cooking, stirring frequently until the shallots and mushrooms are shrunken and lightly browned (the bottom of the pan will be brown, too), another 5 to 6 minutes. Add the garlic, chili-garlic paste, cinnamon, and the remaining 1 tablespoon ginger. Stir and cook until fragrant, about 30 seconds. Add the chicken broth, bring to a simmer, cover

continued on p. 160 ›

› Roy got the tractor because he gets up earlier than the paper boy. (I told you that. Actually maybe it's because he once was a paper boy.) He goes to get his job coffee at the general store one Friday, nabs the first copy of the weekly *Vineyard Gazette* fresh from the printer, turns to the classified, and sees an ad for a tractor. A tractor that needs to be removed from a property where it has been sitting unclaimed for three years. He calls the number, and the man says, "Wow, that was fast. You must get up early!" By the time he'd hung up the phone, Roy had agreed to take the tractor, sight unseen—and he immediately called a tow truck to meet him up there.

Roy arrived at the property and looked over the classic machine—a 1967 Ford. There wasn't a key in the ignition, but Roy thought, "Heck, while I'm waiting for the tow, I'll try my own Ford truck key on the tractor." The tractor started right up. The tow truck driver couldn't believe Roy's luck when he ›

partially, and cook gently for 5 minutes. Add the kale leaves, stir, cover partially, and cook until the kale is tender, 8 to 10 minutes more.

Remove the pot from the heat, add the soy mixture, and stir.

Arrange the noodles in four large wide or deep soup bowls. Use tongs to arrange a portion of kale in each bowl, then ladle the remaining broth and soup ingredients into each bowl, distributing evenly. Garnish with the sliced scallions and serve right away while very hot.

CURRY-COCONUT BUTTERNUT SQUASH SOUP

SERVES 6

2 tablespoons unsalted butter

1 tablespoon extra-virgin olive oil

2 cups medium-diced yellow onions (about 12 ounces)

Kosher salt

1 tablespoon chopped fresh garlic

1 tablespoon chopped fresh ginger

1½ teaspoons fresh Madras curry powder

1 tablespoon tomato paste

3 cups (packed; about 1 pound 8 ounces) Slow-Roasted Butternut Squash (p. 162)

3 cups low-sodium chicken broth

6 to 7 tablespoons coconut milk, well whisked until smooth

1 teaspoon fresh lime juice, plus more to taste

2 tablespoons chopped fresh cilantro

2 to 3 tablespoons toasted unsweetened coconut flakes, for garnish (optional)

Butternut squash is an embarrassingly friendly soup vegetable. It cozies up to any number of different flavors, leaving your creativity wide open. Plus when you purée it, you get a silky, elegant soup that still has enough body to feel filling, too. In this version, I go for a classic curry profile—subtly spicy and finished with a bit of coconut milk and lime, and I use roasted squash for even more flavor. Everyone loves this soup, which can be a starter or a main dish. Be sure to use regular coconut milk, not "lite."

In a medium (4- to 5-quart) Dutch oven or other wide soup pot, heat the butter and olive oil over medium heat. When the butter has melted, add the onions and ½ teaspoon kosher salt and stir. Cover and cook, stirring occasionally, until the onions are translucent and softened, 6 to 8 minutes. Uncover and cook, stirring frequently, until the onions are well browned, another 3 to 5 minutes. Add the garlic and ginger and stir until fragrant and well combined, about 1 minute. Add the curry powder and ¾ teaspoon kosher salt and stir well. Stir in the tomato paste and the squash, breaking it up a bit with a spoon. Add the chicken broth and 3 cups water. Whisk very well to break the squash apart. Bring to a boil, reduce to a gentle simmer, cover loosely (the lid should only be very slightly ajar), and cook for 15 minutes. Remove from the heat and let the soup cool for 15 to 25 minutes.

Purée the soup in three batches, adding 2 to 3 tablespoons of coconut milk to each batch as you blend. (Err on the side of less coconut milk at first until you taste. You can always blend in a little more on the third batch.) Be sure not to fill the blender jar more than two-thirds full—a little more than half is even better. Cover the blender lid partially with a folded dishtowel

continued on p. 162 ›

› arrived to haul the tractor back to our place.

Then one maple-cooled late afternoon, Tom came by to chat with Roy. At the kitchen window, I stood washing my hands, watching the two of them lean against the truck like men do. After a spell, they sauntered down to the fence line at the bottom of the property and stood talking for 15 or 20 minutes, gesturing at the field behind us. Back toward the house they walked, Roy stepping lively with a big smile on his face. I opened the screen door to say hello, and Roy said, "Honey, we're going to be chicken farmers."

Apparently Tom and Roy had shaken hands on a very friendly ›

› agreement for us to lease the four acres of fields behind us, with the option to use another four acres beyond that if we grew to need it. Part of the family property, this grassy land is supposed to be in agricultural production (for tax purposes), so when Roy suggested we put chickens (or I should say laying hens) on the land, Tom loved the idea. As a corollary, it was clear that Tom and his mother Drusilla were happy to have us continue to rent the homestead for the indefinite future. For Roy, who was coming off a long and painful work project as general contractor of a house renovation, the idea of doing a few less building projects and a little more farming was very appealing. ›

COOK'S TIP

You can store the cooked squash, tightly covered, in the fridge for up to 2 days. It may give off a little liquid, but that's no problem. Just drain it off or put the squash in a nonstick saucepan over low heat to cook off the excess moisture.

(leaving a vent opening uncovered to let steam out) to prevent hot soup from splashing on you. Combine the batches in a mixing bowl; rinse out the soup pot and return the soup to the pot.

Gently reheat the soup, stir in 1 teaspoon lime juice and the cilantro, and taste. Add more lime juice or salt as necessary. Serve the soup garnished with the toasted coconut, if desired.

SLOW-ROASTED BUTTERNUT SQUASH

MAKES ABOUT 3 CUPS SQUASH

Unsalted butter, slightly softened

Kosher salt

Pure maple syrup

3 to 3½ pounds butternut squash (about 2 small or 1 large)

Roasting is my favorite technique for extracting great flavor from fall squash. Because the squash halves roast cut side down, the skin acts as an insulator, and trapped moisture steams the squash through and makes it extra-tender. Plus, the cut sides get a bit caramelized. You can make dozens of things with the roasted squash, from soup (p. 161) and quick bread (p. 223) to stuffed pastas, side dishes, pizzas, and more. One pound of squash yields about 1 cup roasted flesh.

Heat the oven to 400°F. Line a heavy rimmed baking sheet with aluminum foil and then top with parchment paper. Rub the parchment all over with a little butter. Cut the squash in half lengthwise and scoop out the seeds (I use a big serving spoon). Arrange the squash halves (cut side up) on the sheet pan. (Alternate the neck ends with the round ends to fit the most on a pan.)

Sprinkle on a little salt and drizzle just a tiny bit of maple syrup over the squash. Then turn the halves over so that they lie cut side down on the baking sheets.

Roast the squash until the flesh is very tender (poke and prod the neck end with a finger to be sure), the skin is very browned and collapsed, and the edges of the undersides are caramelized, at least 1 hour and up to 1 hour 20 minutes, depending on the size of the squash. Let the squash cool on the sheet pans. Gently turn the squash over and scoop the flesh out with a serving spoon (or your fingers), leaving all the skin behind.

› Because of the 50 laying hens we'd purchased earlier that year, we'd become acutely aware of the demand for local eggs on the Island—and the opportunity in the market. While we knew we wanted to grow more vegetables (we already had the parts to build a hoop house), we also knew we needed a higher-volume, profitable business we could manage without hiring extra workers. With Roy's building skills and knack for salvaging materials (allowing us to build coops and pens more cheaply) and the land Tom was offering us, I could put together numbers that made the egg business work. ›

INDIAN SUMMER MINESTRONE WITH LATE TOMATOES AND BEANS

SERVES 6 TO 8

3 tablespoons extra-virgin olive oil

3 to 3½ ounces bacon (3 to 4 slices), diced

2 cups medium-diced onions (about 1 large or 2 medium onions, or 10 ounces)

2 cups medium-diced carrots (5 or 6 carrots, or 12 ounces)

1 cup diced, cored, fennel bulb (about ½ medium fennel bulb, tops removed)

Kosher salt

1 tablespoon chopped fresh garlic

½ teaspoon crushed red pepper flakes

¼ to ½ teaspoon freshly ground black pepper

4 cups coarsely chopped fresh plum tomatoes (include any juices or seeds that escape, about 8 plum tomatoes)

2 tablespoons chopped fresh oregano

2 cups small-diced butternut squash

3 cups sliced kale leaves (include tender stems if you like, but remove tougher, larger ribs)

One 2-inch piece Parmigiano-Reggiano rind, plus ⅓ cup grated, for garnish (optional)

6 cups low-sodium chicken broth

continued on p. 166

The night air gets chilly around here long before the last of the tomatoes and beans have come off the vine. This means I have an excellent excuse for making my favorite soup out of all the damaged veggies that aren't quite sellable on the farm stand—but aren't quite chicken food yet either (we rank somewhere in between!). Also, I get to use my favorite late-season beans (pole green beans and cranberry shell beans) in this delicious, full-flavored minestrone. If you use fresh cranberry beans, follow the basic cooking instructions in the Roman-Style Cranberry Beans recipe on p. 211.

In a large (5- to 6-quart) Dutch oven or other large soup pot, heat the olive oil over medium heat. Add the bacon, onions, carrots, fennel, and 1 teaspoon salt. Cover and cook, stirring occasionally, until the onions are translucent, 5 to 7 minutes. Uncover and continue cooking, stirring occasionally, until the veggies are a bit shrunken, the pan looks dry, and you are scraping browned bits off the bottom of the pan, 8 to 10 minutes.

Add the garlic, crushed red pepper, and black pepper and stir until fragrant, about 30 seconds. Add the tomatoes (and any accumulated juices) and oregano and cook, stirring occasionally, until the tomatoes are mostly broken down and have lost some volume (the mixture of veggies will look and feel thicker), 10 to 12 minutes. Add the butternut squash, kale, Parmigiano rind, chicken broth, 4 cups of water, and 1 teaspoon salt.

Bring to a boil, reduce to a simmer, and cook, stirring occasionally (and scraping the bottom of the pan with

continued on p. 166 ›

Indian Summer Minestrone
with Late Tomatoes and Beans

½ cup ditalini or other
tiny dried pasta

1½ cups diced green beans
(preferably pole green beans
or romano beans)

1¾ cups cooked fresh
cranberry beans or one
15½-ounce can pink beans,
pinto beans, or other beans of
your choice, rinsed and drained

1 teaspoon balsamic vinegar,
plus more if desired

¼ cup thinly sliced or chopped
fresh basil (optional)

a wooden spoon), for 5 to 7 minutes. Add the pasta and
cook for another 6 to 8 minutes, stirring and scraping
occasionally. Add the green beans and cranberry beans
(or canned beans) and cook for 4 to 5 minutes more.

Remove the pot from the heat, remove the Parmigiano
rind (if you can find it—otherwise just leave it in!), and
stir in the balsamic vinegar. Taste and season with salt or
more vinegar if desired. Serve the soup with the basil and
grated Parmigiano on the side for garnishing.

HERB AND LEMON–MARINATED FETA

MAKES ABOUT 1 CUP

4 ounces best-quality feta cheese, roughly crumbled or cut into ½-inch cubes

2 to 3 teaspoons (loosely packed) fresh thyme leaves

2 to 3 teaspoons (loosely packed) fresh oregano leaves

2 teaspoons freshly grated lemon zest

1 tablespoon chopped, pitted Kalamata olives

2 teaspoons chopped, drained oil-packed sun-dried tomatoes

Sea salt or kosher salt

½ cup extra-virgin olive oil, plus more if necessary

Whether you marinate it for a few hours or overnight, this tasty feta makes a great topping for crackers or crostini, vegetables (think grilled eggplant, roasted peppers, or sautéed greens), and burgers, or stuff it in a pita with salad greens. If you plan to put it out as an appetizer, marinate it in a shallow, straight-sided dish (such as a mini gratin pan or tapas dish) so you can serve it directly with a small spreading knife. Bring it to room temperature before serving.

Arrange the feta in one layer in a small shallow dish. Sprinkle the herb leaves, lemon zest, olives, and sun-dried tomatoes over and around the cheese. Taste the feta—if it is very creamy and clean-tasting, sprinkle it with a little salt. If it is salty, don't add salt. Pour the olive oil over top. (If you need a touch more to mostly cover the feta, add it.) Let the cheese marinate in the refrigerator for a few hours or overnight, and bring it to room temperature about 45 minutes before serving.

› The long warm Indian summer still lay unfurled ahead of us. I kept harvesting; the farm stand stayed open every day. The tidy rows of onions began to tip their green leaves over toward winter, the butternut squash vines stiffened and dried up, and the turnips got fat and happy. Even when the occasional frosty morning arrived to kiss the kale and make it sweet, we were far from done for the season. With 200 chickens on the way, a hoop house to build, and a business to plan, we were just getting started.

DON'T LAUGH (OR CRY)— ONIONS ARE THE "IT" VEG

"Drop the onion!" I came up behind the man and let him have it. No, not really, but I did tell this customer (the third one of the day who asked) that the onions simply weren't for sale. ›

ROASTED CARROT "FRIES" WITH ROADHOUSE DIPPING SAUCE

SERVES 3 TO 4

1 pound carrots, peeled, trimmed, and cut into pieces 2 to 3 inches long and ⅜ inch wide

2 tablespoons extra-virgin olive oil

Kosher salt

Roadhouse Dipping Sauce (below)

Like sweet potato oven-fries, carrot "fries" don't get crispy—but they do caramelize and taste super-delicious right out of the oven. In fact, like the roasted beets on p. 157, I serve them straight off the sheet pan—with or without a tasty little dipping sauce—for friends to munch on in the kitchen. You could certainly serve them as a side dish, too; just get them on to dinner plates quickly. Double the recipe for a crowd and be sure to use two sheet pans.

Heat the oven to 475°F. Line a large rimmed baking sheet with parchment paper. In a mixing bowl, toss the carrots with the olive oil and ½ teaspoon salt. Spread in one layer on the sheet pan. Roast until the carrot sticks are very well browned and tender, tossing once with a spatula if you like, 26 to 28 minutes. Let cool for a few minutes on the sheet pans, sprinkle with a little more salt, and serve warm with Roadhouse Dipping Sauce.

ROADHOUSE DIPPING SAUCE

⅓ cup mayonnaise

1 teaspoon freshly grated lemon zest

1 teaspoon fresh lemon juice

1 teaspoon Dijon mustard

1 teaspoon honey

½ teaspoon freshly grated ginger

In a small bowl, combine all the ingredients and stir well. Let sit for several minutes for the flavors to develop. Refrigerate if making ahead.

› (Like the sign on the table said. Jeeze.)

Who knew that people would want to buy onions at a farm stand? It doesn't seem like your sexiest veg, and you wouldn't think a farm stand onion would necessarily be that much tastier than a grocery store onion.

You, like me, would be wrong on both counts if you made these assumptions. (Didn't your mother ever tell you not to assume anything?!)

The confusion, for the poor customers, comes from the fact that we have to spread the onions out in the sun to "cure" them once we harvest them at the end of the summer. We pull them all up at once and ›

› lay them out on any available surface that has good air circulation (various tables in the yard) and turn them over frequently until the outer skin gets crackly and the neck is dry. Some of the varieties we grow produce onions the size of softballs, so it's a rather spectacular sight to see all of these big fat onions with long green withery tops lounging about. Mind you, people have to veer off course from the farm quite a bit to look at the onions. But veer they do. And fondle. And psychologically, I think they want them even more when they find out they're not for sale.

Lest you think I am very cruel, I didn't wind up hoarding all the onions. Eventually I sold some the first year, and more the next. But I had originally planted them to store and use for our ›

TUSCAN WHEAT BERRY SALAD WITH VEGGIES CRUDO

SERVES 6

¾ cup (winter or hard red) wheat berries

Kosher salt

¼ cup extra-virgin olive oil

2 tablespoons white balsamic vinegar

2 tablespoons fresh lemon juice

1 tablespoon fresh orange juice

1 tablespoon coarsely chopped fresh thyme

2 teaspoons chopped fresh garlic

2 teaspoons finely grated lemon zest

2 teaspoons black olive tapenade

2 teaspoons honey

Freshly ground black pepper

2 cups thinly sliced trimmed Brussels sprouts (5 to 6 ounces, cut in half first for easiest slicing)

1½ cups halved small cherry or grape tomatoes (6 to 7 ounces)

1 cup fresh raw corn kernels (from about 2 small ears)

1 cup small-diced cored fennel bulb (about ½ medium fennel bulb)

½ cup thinly sliced scallions (white and light green parts)

¼ cup chopped fresh flat-leaf parsley

¼ cup toasted pine nuts (optional)

There is a beautiful moment in the fall when we are pulling up fennel bulbs and harvesting little Brussels sprouts buds, but also still picking cherry tomatoes and enjoying the last of the sweet corn. That's when I make this season-shifting salad with lots of raw veggies, marinated in a bold Tuscan vinaigrette. Thanks to the nutty wheat berries and the raw veggies, this is a crunchy, healthy treat that's great for a party, too. It holds up well, so feel free to make it ahead.

In a Dutch oven or other large sauce pot, combine the wheat berries, ½ teaspoon salt, and 10 to 12 cups of water (enough to cover the berries by a few inches). Bring to a boil, reduce to a rapid simmer, and cook, partially covered, until the wheat berries are tender. Begin checking after 50 minutes, although this may take up to 90 minutes. (Most are usually done between 60 and 70 minutes. The berries should be pleasantly chewy. If you taste early and often, you'll get a sense of what "done" feels like—and what your "chewiness" preference is.) Drain and spread on a dishtowel to dry. Transfer to a small mixing bowl.

In a small bowl, combine the olive oil, vinegar, lemon juice, orange juice, thyme, garlic, lemon zest, tapenade, honey, ½ teaspoon salt, and several grinds of pepper. Whisk well. In a large, wide mixing bowl, combine the Brussels sprouts, tomatoes, corn, fennel, scallions, ½ teaspoon salt, and half of the parsley. Drizzle three-quarters of the vinaigrette over the veggies and toss well. To the bowl of wheat berries, add ½ teaspoon salt and the remaining vinaigrette; toss well. Let the veggies and the wheat berries sit for 20 minutes. Stir occasionally.

COOK'S TIP

Wheat berries take
60 to 70 minutes to
cook, but they can take
up to 80 or 90 minutes
if they are older or drier.
For convenience, you can
cook them a day ahead;
cool and refrigerate,
covered.

Add the wheat berries and most of the pine nuts (if using) to the bowl
of veggies, toss well, taste for salt, stir, and let sit again for 10 minutes.
Transfer to a serving bowl and garnish with the remaining parsley and pine
nuts. Serve at room temperature.

QUICK-ROASTED BUTTERNUT SQUASH AND PEAR SALAD WITH GINGER–LIME VINAIGRETTE

SERVES 6

2 tablespoons raisins or coarsely chopped dried cherries

2½ cups medium-diced (½-inch) butternut squash (11 to 12 ounces)

1 large firm-ripe pear (8 to 9 ounces), peeled, cored, and cut into ½-inch dice (about 1½ cups)

2 tablespoons canola or safflower oil

Kosher salt

6 to 7 cups (7 ounces) sturdy mixed baby winter salad greens, such as spinach, escarole, frisée, radicchio, endive, and/or baby kale, washed and dried

3 tablespoons extra-virgin olive oil

1 tablespoon white balsamic vinegar

2 tablespoons minced crystallized ginger

2 teaspoons fresh lime juice

½ teaspoon grated fresh ginger

¼ teaspoon freshly grated lime zest

Freshly ground black pepper

2 tablespoons finely chopped toasted skinned hazelnuts

6 small lime wedges, for serving

Veggies star front and center in this warm/cool, sweet/tangy winter salad. Diced butternut squash and pear roast together in no time thanks to a high-heat oven. Spooned over a bed of sturdy winter greens and garnished with a peppy ginger–lime vinaigrette, this is just the thing to serve friends before a bowl of chili or soup. I like to use crinkly spinach and fluffy frisée (or inner leaves of escarole) in my greens mix, but you can get creative as long as you choose hearty greens.

Put the raisins or cherries in a small bowl. Cover with 2 tablespoons hot water and let soften.

Heat the oven to 450°F. Line a heavy-duty rimmed sheet pan with parchment paper. In a mixing bowl, combine the squash, pears, canola or safflower oil, and ½ teaspoon salt. Spread the squash and pears in one layer on the sheet pan. Roast, flipping once or twice with a spatula, until the squash and pears are tender and nicely browned on at least one side, 30 to 35 minutes. Let cool on the baking sheet for a few minutes.

Put the salad greens in a large mixing bowl. Sprinkle with ¼ teaspoon salt. Have six salad plates ready. Whisk together the olive oil, vinegar, 1½ tablespoons of the crystallized ginger, the lime juice, fresh ginger, lime zest, several grinds of pepper, and a big pinch of salt. Drain the dried fruit and add it to the vinaigrette. Drizzle 3 to 4 tablespoons of the vinaigrette (with the dried fruit) over the greens, reserving 1 to 2 tablespoons. Toss well. Arrange a portion of the dressed greens on each of the

continued on p. 174 ›

› home cooking through the winter—one of my efforts to try and eat more local food year-round. I use a ton of onions in cooking, so I thought, well, this will be cool. We'll have our own onions, and hopefully carrots and turnips and kale, and we'll be golden. I also didn't originally think about selling the onions, because I can't see asking more than $2 a pound for onions, so they didn't seem like a big-bucks crop.

But my opinion on the profitability of onions changed. Perusing my stack of farm business books one night, I came across a chart on profitability of crops based on the amount of man hours put into them. Onions practically topped the chart, based on what you put into them and what you get out. But for a little bed prep work and mulching in springtime, you plant the baby onions—which cost mere pennies—and pull them out four months later, multiplied in size by a zillion.

In early summer, you can harvest some and sell them as spring onions if you like, or you ›

› can stand by and watch them all bulb up (fascinating!) and grow big tall green stalks. When the leaves begin to wither and lean over a bit, you help them along by bending the stalks at the neck.

Compared to say, green beans, the time you put into onions is piddling. If you were a really savvy number-crunching farmer, you'd take a hard look at this man-hours thing, which is serious stuff. However, we mostly use our intuition. If a crop is a lot of work, it has to either be sellable at a decent price or be a real draw to the farm stand.

And obviously, man-hours aren't the only thing you look at when choosing crops. ›

salad plates. Spoon a portion of the squash and pears on top of the greens. Drizzle with the remaining vinaigrette and garnish with the toasted hazelnuts and the remaining crystallized ginger. Serve right away, with the lime wedges on the side.

CHRISTMAS SLAW WITH SLIVERED PEARS, CRANBERRIES & PECANS

SERVES 8 TO 10

8 cups (about 1 pound 6 ounces) very finely sliced green cabbage

⅓ cup fresh lime juice

2 tablespoons sugar

1 tablespoon plus 1 teaspoon finely minced fresh ginger

1 teaspoon freshly grated lime zest

Kosher salt

2 large firm-ripe Bartlett pears (8 to 9 ounces each)

⅓ cup sour cream

⅓ cup thinly sliced scallions (light and dark green parts only)

⅓ cup very finely chopped dried cranberries

¼ cup roughly chopped fresh flat-leaf parsley

⅓ cup very finely chopped toasted pecans

Easy, pretty, delicious—how's that for great recipe PR? Tangy and light, this ultra-fresh slaw doesn't have a hint of the heaviness of sub-par slaws. I call it Christmasy because of little flecks of red (dried cranberries) and green (parsley and scallions), and because it would be great with ham and popovers for a Christmas brunch. But make it any time you find nice pears—or just feel like something light and bright.

In a large mixing bowl, combine the cabbage, lime juice, sugar, ginger, lime zest, and 1 teaspoon salt. Let sit, tossing occasionally, until softened but still somewhat crunchy, 30 to 40 minutes.

Peel the pears, cut them in half, and scoop out the cores and stems. Lay the halves cut side down on a cutting board and slice them very thinly lengthwise. Cut the slices lengthwise again into thin sticks.

Add the sour cream to the cabbage mixture and toss. Add the pears, scallions, cranberries, most of the chopped parsley, and most of the chopped pecans. Toss again.

Transfer to a serving bowl and garnish with the remaining parsley and chopped pecans. Serve right away.

BABY KALE AND BLOOD ORANGE SALAD WITH FETA AND TOASTED ALMONDS

SERVES 6 TO 8

3 blood oranges

2 tablespoons extra-virgin olive oil

2 tablespoons red-wine vinegar

1 tablespoon honey

Kosher salt

8 cups baby kale leaves or thinly sliced Tuscan kale leaves (ribs removed first), 7 to 8 ounces

½ cup crumbled best-quality feta cheese

¼ cup toasted sliced almonds

I was skeptical about kale salads at first, as I'm not fond of the chewy texture of raw kale. But once I realized how a bracing vinaigrette can soften the leaves (acting more like a marinade), I was hooked. I still prefer the softer texture of baby kale leaves (look for them packaged in grocery stores and at farm stands), but if you can't find them—and you don't mind a slightly toothy texture—thinly sliced Tuscan kale is a good substitute. All that said, this is a stunning and delicious salad, and, of course, quite good for you! The salad is tastiest with blood oranges, so make it when they're in season.

Using a rasp-style grater, remove ½ teaspoon of zest from one of the blood oranges. Cut the zested blood orange in half and juice it. Set aside 2 tablespoons of juice (and drink any remainder!). Peel and thinly slice the remaining two blood oranges crosswise (you should have about 16 slices). Set aside.

In a small bowl, combine the 2 tablespoons blood orange juice, the blood orange zest, olive oil, red-wine vinegar, honey, and ¼ teaspoon salt. Whisk well. Put the kale leaves in a large mixing bowl and sprinkle with ½ teaspoon salt. Pour the dressing over the kale and toss well with your hands, rubbing the dressing into the leaves as you toss. Let sit at room temperature, tossing occasionally, for 30 minutes.

Arrange the kale in a large shallow serving bowl or portion the kale onto six or eight salad plates. Arrange the blood oranges over or next to the greens and garnish with the crumbled feta and the toasted almonds. Serve right away.

› A disadvantage to onions is that they take up a lot of space for a long time. That same bed could be used for a crop of carrots, a round of arugula, and a planting of cranberry beans. But frankly, it's kind of a relief to me to have some beds that I actually can't fuss with. It feels swell to simply walk past the neat rows of green stalks all summer, admire their beauty, and then collect all the goodies in the fall.

We've also come up with a partial solution to the space issue. We now grow the onions (in addition to the potatoes) outside of the deer-fenced market garden area. Nothing really likes to munch on onions, so we plant them in rows on the outside of the fence. ›

› I am happy now that we have enough onions to "share" with our farm stand customers. (My sister tells me I wasn't a really good sharer as a child. I think this is not true. I think I was only trying to protect my stuff from my marauding big sister, who even broke into my piggy bank. I love my sister, though. I would share my onions with her.)

Everyone should get to eat a fresh onion some time—they're exquisitely crisp and juicy and not at all wonky. Really, try one.

AN EMBARRASSMENT OF SQUASHES

Carnival Squash. Acorn Squash. Butternut Squash. Delicata Squash. Mini pumpkins. In our first market garden, we got a little carried away with the whole winter squash thing. We ›

MARINATED ROAST CHICKEN AND HARVEST VEGGIES WITH HERBED PAN SAUCE

SERVES 4

5 tablespoons extra-virgin olive oil

3 tablespoons balsamic vinegar

3 tablespoons dry white wine

3 tablespoons honey

2 tablespoons Dijon mustard

2 tablespoons fresh lemon juice

2 tablespoons fresh orange juice

2 tablespoons tomato paste

1 tablespoon plus 1 teaspoon minced fresh garlic

2 teaspoons freshly grated lemon zest

1 tablespoon chopped fresh thyme, plus a few sprigs for garnish

1 tablespoon chopped fresh rosemary, plus a few sprigs for garnish

1 tablespoon chopped fresh sage, plus a few sprigs for garnish

Kosher salt

2 bone-in, skin-on medium-sized chicken breast halves (about 1½ pounds total; I like Bell & Evans®)

4 bone-in, skin-on chicken thighs (about 1¼ pounds total; I like Bell & Evans)

continued on p. 178

In a world of boneless chicken breasts, sometimes folks forget how tasty chicken on the bone (and with the skin!) is. We have a great technique for marinating and roasting chicken pieces (no whole chicken to carve afterwards) that incorporates lots of fall veggies and herbs from the garden and makes its own delicious pan sauce while it cooks. It's a great destination for carrots, which soak up all the lovely flavors in the pan, but I also add potatoes and onions to make this truly a one-pan meal.

Four hours or up to 24 hours ahead, marinate the chicken: In a small bowl, combine 3 tablespoons of the olive oil, the balsamic vinegar, wine, honey, Dijon, lemon juice, orange juice, tomato paste, garlic, lemon zest, 2 teaspoons each of the herbs, and ¼ teaspoon salt. Whisk until thoroughly combined.

Put all the chicken pieces in a mixing bowl. Use a paring knife to poke a few holes in each chicken piece. Add the orange slices to the bowl with the chicken. Pour the marinade over the chicken and toss well. Cover very tightly and refrigerate for at least 4 hours or up to 24 hours. (Remove 30 minutes before cooking.)

Heat the oven to 400°F. Toss the veggies in a bowl with 1 teaspoon salt, the remaining 2 tablespoons olive oil, and the remaining 1 teaspoon each of thyme, rosemary, and sage.

Uncover the chicken and transfer just the chicken pieces and orange slices (reserving the marinade) to a 10- x 15-inch shallow roasting or baking dish (such as

continued on p. 178 ›

Marinated Roast Chicken and Harvest
Veggies with Herbed Pan Sauce

½ small orange, cut stem to base, ends trimmed and thinly sliced into half-moons

10 to 12 ounces carrots (5 to 6), trimmed, peeled, and cut into pieces about 3 inches long and ¾ inch wide

½ pound baby potatoes (1 ounce each or no wider than 1½ inches, about 8), halved

½ pound small yellow onions, quartered, or medium onions cut into 1-inch wedges (3 to 4 small or 2 medium)

Pyrex). Season the chicken on both sides with a little salt and turn it skin side up. Transfer the veggies to the pan and arrange around the chicken pieces. (It will be very snug—don't worry, things will shrink.) Scrape the reserved marinade over the chicken and the veggies, distributing it as evenly as possible.

Roast the chicken and veggies for 30 minutes. Baste the chicken with the pan juices and continue roasting, basting every 10 minutes to darken up the skin and veggies, until the veggies are tender and the chicken pieces are deeply browned, about another 35 minutes.

Remove the pan from the oven and transfer the chicken breasts to a cutting board. Cut each breast in half with a sharp chef's knife. Transfer the breast pieces, along with the chicken thighs, all the veggies, and the orange slices to a warm serving platter and arrange nicely. Tent loosely with foil if you like.

Holding the roasting pan with a potholder (better yet, enlist a helper for this), tip the pan and pour all the juices into a gravy separator. Let sit for a few minutes so that the fat rises to the top; then transfer the juices (now a pan sauce!) to a serving vessel.

Garnish the chicken and veggies with the herb sprigs and serve family-style, passing the pan sauce at the table. Or plate the chicken and veggies (serve everyone one-half breast and one thigh) and spoon over a bit of sauce.

ROASTED BUTTERNUT SQUASH RISOTTO WITH THYME, PARMIGIANO & TOASTED PINE NUTS

SERVES 4

3 cups small-diced peeled butternut squash (about 14 ounces)

3 tablespoons extra-virgin olive oil

Kosher salt

4 cups (1 quart) low-sodium chicken broth

2 tablespoons unsalted butter

1 large shallot, finely diced (about ½ cup)

1½ cups arborio or carnaroli rice

¼ cup apple cider

¼ cup dry white wine

1½ teaspoons chopped fresh thyme

½ cup plus 2 tablespoons grated Parmigiano-Reggiano or aged Gouda

Freshly ground black pepper

2 tablespoons chopped toasted pine nuts (optional)

Comforting risotto is a perfect vehicle for showcasing fall veggies. In this recipe, taking the little extra step of roasting the butternut squash first ensures a deeply flavored rice dish. (Quick-roasting diced squash actually doesn't take long, but be sure you get the squash nicely browned.) Fresh thyme and Parmigiano give even more flavor here, and an optional dusting of toasted pine nuts is a nice finish. This is great on its own or delicious with grilled or roasted sausages.

Heat the oven to 450°F. Line a heavy-duty rimmed sheet pan with parchment paper. Toss the squash with 2 tablespoons of the olive oil and ½ teaspoon salt. Spread the squash in one layer on the sheet pan. Roast, flipping once with a spatula if you like, until the squash is tender and very nicely browned, 25 to 30 minutes.

In a medium saucepan, heat the chicken broth over medium heat. If the broth simmers, reduce the heat to low, or just below a gentle simmer.

continued on p. 180 ›

› tried too many varieties and of course planted them a little too close together, so we wound up with a nearly impenetrable canopy of giant squash leaves in one corner of the garden that was nevertheless as beguiling and seductive as the poppy field in the "Wizard of Oz." We never sent Libby in alone, for fear she wouldn't come back out.

So it was kind of ironic when we wound up moving over to the farmhouse right in the middle of squash harvest time—and found acres of squash growing not far from our new backdoor. That year, our friends at Morning Glory Farm were also growing squash (in addition to corn) on the land they leased from the Hickies. We ran into Jim Athearn on a walk one day and he said we were welcome to "glean" the squash field after they harvested. So glean we did. ›

› (This was before a fabulous group called the Island Grown Gleaners was formed to glean farmers' fields and bring vegetables to the elderly and needy. It's a great service and also rescues veggies that might otherwise be wasted.)

We went around the edges of the field and up and down the rows, looking for odd squash that had been left behind. Now here was some serious squash variety! Hubbards. Sweet Dumplings. Buttercups. Red Kuri. We loaded up a couple of canvas shopping bags and lugged our treasure back to our front porch, where we arranged all the squash (including our own) on the steps around the geraniums. The idea was to keep everything outside in the cool air. ›

In a small (4- to 5-quart) Dutch oven or other wide, shallow pot, heat the remaining 1 tablespoon olive oil with 1 tablespoon of the butter over medium-low heat. (Cut the other tablespoon of butter into pieces and set aside.) Add the shallots and a pinch of salt, cover, and cook, stirring occasionally, until softened and somewhat shrunken, 4 to 5 minutes. Uncover and continue cooking, stirring frequently, until lightly browned, 3 to 5 minutes.

Add the rice and cook, stirring, until the edges of the grains are beginning to look a bit translucent, about 2 minutes. Add the apple cider and the wine and cook, stirring, until the liquid is absorbed, about 30 seconds.

Ladle ⅔ to ¾ cup broth over the rice (enough to cover it), stir, and cook until the liquid is mostly absorbed (and a spatula leaves a wide path when stirring), 3 to 4 minutes. (Bigger bubbles will form in the rice as the liquid reduces. If the liquid is reducing too quickly, turn the heat down a bit.) Continue adding the broth, ⅔ to ¾ cup at a time, and stirring almost constantly, until the rice is firm-tender (still firm to the bite but not crunchy in the middle—start tasting after 15 minutes), about 20 minutes total. You will most likely use all of the broth; if you need a bit more liquid or want to loosen the risotto up a bit at the end, add a little hot water.

Gently stir in the butternut squash, the remaining butter, the thyme, cheese, ¼ teaspoon salt, and several grinds of pepper. Remove from the heat and stir again. (You want to break up the squash a little bit so that the flavor gets around the rice, but don't break it up completely.) Serve right away, garnished with the toasted pine nuts (if using).

AUTUMN POT ROAST WITH ROASTED ROOT VEGGIE GARNISH

SERVE 6

3 tablespoons olive oil

One 4- to 4½-pound boneless beef chuck roast, tied

Kosher salt

Freshly ground black pepper

1 tablespoon unsalted butter

⅔ cup finely diced leeks, (white and pale green parts) well washed but not dried

⅔ cup finely diced carrots

⅔ cup finely diced celery

1 tablespoon chopped fresh garlic

½ cup sherry or brandy

2 tablespoons tomato paste

1 tablespoon chopped fresh thyme

1½ teaspoons black olive tapenade

2 whole dried bay leaves

1½ cups red wine (such as Merlot) or dry white wine

1½ cups low-sodium chicken broth

1 recipe Roasted Root Medley (p. 184)

1 to 2 tablespoons chopped fresh flat-leaf parsley (optional)

My favorite cut for pot roast is chuck, and I snap it up when I see it. I know a nice gentle braise of this tasty cut will be a great excuse to pile on a medley of roasted root vegetables as a garnish. That's right—roasted vegetables. While naturally I include some chopped veggies in the braising liquid, I also like to cook some root veggies separately so that they maintain their flavor and shape. They make a nice finish to this brothy, meaty dish, which you can also serve over mashed potatoes. I like to serve this in shallow, wide bowls.

Position a rack in the center of the oven and heat the oven to 325°F. In a large (5- to 6-quart) Dutch oven, heat 2 tablespoons of the oil over medium heat. Season the roast all over with about 1 teaspoon salt and freshly ground pepper. Add the roast to the pot and cook, turning with tongs, until nicely browned on the bottom, about 5 minutes. Turn the roast over and cook until brown on the other side, about 4 minutes. (If you like, you can also turn the roast on its sides and cook each for 1 to 2 minutes, but watch the pan and turn down the heat if the pan is getting a very dark brown.) Transfer the roast to a plate. Pour off all but a thin layer of fat from the pan.

Reduce the heat to medium low. Add the remaining 1 tablespoon oil and the butter. Add the leeks (with any water clinging to them), carrots, and celery, and season with a pinch of salt. Stir and cover. Cook, stirring, until the veggies are softened and lightly browned, 7 to 9 minutes. Uncover, add the garlic, and stir until fragrant, about 30 seconds.

› Looking out the screen door from the kitchen every morning, I could see those squash, and it didn't take me long to make up my mind: I wanted to know what they all tasted like, side by side. Maybe a winter squash taste test is a little nerdy, but I figured it would make good blog fodder, and honestly, I really wanted to see the color, feel the texture, and understand the nuances. Naturally, I subjected Roy to the taste test, too. I cut one of each squash variety in half, roasted it cut side down, and scooped out a spoonful of the soft flesh—each one a remarkably different color, ranging from pale gold to deep reddish brown—for us to nibble. The darker the flesh, the more I liked it (Red Kuri rocked), though Roy appreciated the light "squashy" sweetness of the Acorn. We also discovered that we had picked our own squash too early—now I've learned to wait until the stems are dry and brittle before picking. ›

continued on p. 184 ›

› In the taste test, butternut was an all-around winner for color, flavor, and texture—and to me, it is still the most versatile cooking squash, too, especially because it can be peeled without dealing with ridges and bumps. I never tire of making a new version of velvety butternut squash soup—the one on p. 161 with a little bit of curry and coconut milk, is the best yet, according to my dear friend and recipe tester Eliza Peter. (You should trust her. She's a great cook.)

I use slow-roasted squash in quickbread (p. 223) and quick-roasted butternut in warm salads, risotto (p. 179), burritos (p. 189) and simple sides. It simply isn't fall without butternut squash, and because space is still a bit of an issue for us, we concentrate now on only growing this one versatile squash variety for the farm stand. But that doesn't mean I don't have visions of fields of Cinderella pumpkins, and...well, that's probably enough about my visions.

Pour the sherry or brandy into the pot and cook, stirring to scrape up any browned bits on the bottom of the pot, until the liquid is reduced to about 2 tablespoons, 1 to 2 minutes. Add the tomato paste, thyme, tapenade, and bay leaves, and cook, stirring, until well distributed and fragrant, 30 seconds to 1 minute.

Put the roast back into the pot. Pour the wine, chicken broth, and 1½ cups water over and around the roast. (The liquid will come about two-thirds of the way up the roast.)

Bring the liquid to a simmer, cover, and put the pot in the oven. Cook, turning the roast with tongs about every 45 minutes, until it is fork-tender, about 3 hours. Remove the pot from the oven, but if you're not ready to serve, keep it covered. It will stay hot for 45 minutes. Transfer the roast to a cutting board.

Remove the bay leaves from the broth and skim the fat from the surface with a spoon. Alternatively, transfer the broth to a bowl and refrigerate briefly to make removing the fat easier.

Cut the strings from the roast and cut the roast into slices (or if it is falling apart, just pull it off in chunks) and arrange in six shallow serving bowls. Spoon some broth over the meat and top each serving with a portion of the Roasted Root Medley. Spoon over a little more broth if you like. Garnish with chopped parsley (if using).

ROASTED ROOT MEDLEY

1 medium turnip (7 ounces), trimmed but not peeled, cut into ½-inch dice (about 1½ cups)

3 medium carrots, cut into ½-inch dice (about 1 cup)

2 yellow potatoes (about 12 ounces), unpeeled, cut into ½-inch dice (about 2½ cups)

½ pound peeled butternut squash, cut into ½-inch dice (about 2 cups)

These veggies make a great garnish for thick slices of pot roast, but they are delicious on their own as a side dish, too, or as part of a warm salad.

Heat the oven to 450°F. Line a large heavy-duty rimmed sheet pan with parchment paper. In a large mixing bowl, toss the diced vegetables with the olive oil, thyme, and 1 teaspoon salt to thoroughly coat. Spread the vegetables in one layer on the sheet pan. Roast for 15 minutes; use a

CARROTS AND KALE AND MINESTRONE AND MEATLOAF, OH MY!

All this talk about squash and onions and soup and I can't help but think about minestrone—alchemy in a pot. It really is pure magic when practically everything from the fall garden winds up simmering together on the stovetop and turns into something so soul-satisfying that you will never regret a minute of the hard work you've put into growing those vegetables or the time it's taken you to chop them up. You will be nurtured in the very best way.

Into our minestrone (p. 164) goes a sweet, tasty carrot or two or three—ones we've harvested from our third or fourth planting of the year. We love a variety called Nelson, and we cannot even put "carrots" on the farm stand sign or we will cause traffic accidents. The longer we wait, the sweeter they are. But of course, we know how patience goes around here....

Little crunchy kale leaves—any of several varieties we grow that have survived a plague ›

4 tablespoons extra-virgin olive oil

2 teaspoons chopped fresh thyme

Kosher salt

flat spatula to flip some of the veggies over for more even browning. Roast for 15 to 20 minutes more, or until all the veggies are tender and nicely browned in places, a total of 30 to 35 minutes.

SPICY SHRIMP, KALE, CHORIZO & WHITE BEAN RAGOÛT

SERVES 4

2 tablespoons olive oil

4 ounces chorizo, preferably
Portuguese cured, cut into
thin half-moon slices

1 tablespoon unsalted butter

½ cup medium-diced onions
(about ½ medium onion)

½ cup medium-diced
cored fennel bulb (about
⅓ medium fennel bulb)

When I smell this dish simmering on the stove, I get a
smile on my face. Part Spanish, part Portuguese, part
Creole, it's wholly satisfying. It doesn't take as long to
make as a stew, but a few tricks, starting with a sauté of
late-season garden veggies, give it an intensely flavored
broth. A pinch of saffron, a generous addition of crushed
red pepper, lots of garlic, and sautéed chorizo flavor the
broth, too. This healthy ragoût is great over rice or with
crusty bread.

½ cup medium-diced red bell pepper (about ½ medium pepper)

Kosher salt

1 tablespoon minced fresh garlic

¼ teaspoon (generous) crushed red pepper flakes

Small pinch of saffron threads (14 to 16 threads), crushed with a pestle or a wooden spoon handle

1½ cups coarsely chopped seeded plum tomatoes (5 to 6 small)

2 cups chicken broth (see Cook's Tip)

4 cups (loosely packed, about 3½ ounces) very thinly sliced kale (ribs removed before slicing)

1 pound jumbo (21 to 25 count) frozen uncooked shrimp, thawed, peeled, deveined, and each cut into 2 or 3 bite-size pieces

One 15-ounce can small white beans (I like Goya), drained and lightly rinsed

Cooked rice, for serving

2 tablespoons chopped fresh flat-leaf parsley (optional)

4 lemon wedges, for serving

Crusty bread, for serving (optional)

In a large (5- to 6-quart) Dutch oven, heat the olive oil over medium heat. When the oil is hot, add the chorizo and cook, stirring, until shrunken and browned, about 3 minutes. Transfer the chorizo to a plate with a slotted spoon.

Turn the heat to medium low and add the butter, onions, fennel, bell peppers, and ½ teaspoon salt. Cook, stirring frequently, until most of the onions and fennel have lost their opacity, 7 to 8 minutes. Add the garlic, red pepper flakes, and saffron. Cook, stirring, until fragrant, about 30 seconds. Add the plum tomatoes and cook, stirring and scraping constantly, until the tomatoes are collapsed and soft and the mixture is thickened to a loose paste, about 5 minutes.

Add the chicken broth and the kale, stir well, and bring to a simmer. Cover loosely and cook, stirring once or twice, for 5 minutes. Uncover, add the shrimp, the cooked chorizo (and any accumulated juices), and the beans. Bring back to a low simmer, cover loosely, and cook, stirring once or twice, for 2 to 3 minutes, or until the shrimp are cooked through. Remove the pot from the heat.

Spoon cooked rice into four shallow bowls. Spoon the ragoût over the rice and garnish with some of the parsley (if using). Put a small plate of lemon wedges on the table for squeezing over the ragoût. Serve right away, with crusty bread on the side, if you like.

› of cabbage worms—wind up in the pot, too. (My favorite is a brilliant purple version of Tuscan kale.) And something so pretty you will gasp in delight—and cry when you see the color fade with cooking. It's a cranberry bean. I pretty much grow them for two reasons—to gaze at the gorgeous pink and white mottled pods, and to make minestrone. Oh, and also to cook Roman Beans (p. 211) with lots of garlic and pancetta. The beans have a smooth, buttery texture when cooked.

Let's see. We pull a nice crisp fennel bulb and dice that up for the pot. Oh, and we still have tomatoes ripening so we get to use those instead of canned ›

Butternut Squash and Smoky Black Bean Burritos with Queso Fresco and Pepitas

BUTTERNUT SQUASH AND SMOKY BLACK BEAN BURRITOS WITH QUESO FRESCO AND PEPITAS

MAKES 5 BURRITOS

1¼ pounds ½-inch diced butternut squash (about 4¼ cups)

Extra-virgin olive oil

Kosher salt

1 tablespoon unsalted butter

1 tablespoon fresh orange juice

1 tablespoon plus ½ teaspoon pure maple syrup

1 teaspoon fresh lime juice, plus one or two lime wedges for assembling

⅛ teaspoon ground cinnamon

2 teaspoons minced fresh garlic

Two 15½-ounce cans black beans, drained and rinsed

2 teaspoons adobo sauce from a can of chipotles in adobo

½ cup low-sodium chicken broth (or water seasoned with a pinch of salt)

5 burrito-size (10-inch) flour tortillas

¾ cup (4 ounces) crumbled queso fresco (or a combination of feta and fresh goat cheese)

¼ cup toasted pepitas

½ cup loosely packed cilantro leaves and/or tender sprigs

1 avocado, peeled, pitted, and sliced (optional)

Years ago, I often escaped from work at lunchtime to eat a favorite black bean burrito from a tiny Mexican restaurant down the street. I used that memory to inspire this burrito and added roasted butternut squash and a bit of spice. The combo is really satisfying, especially with the crunch of pepitas and the freshness of cilantro and queso fresco. Serve these cut in half on the diagonal—on their own for lunch, or with a side of rice and a green salad for dinner. And a cold beer or Mexican soda, of course.

Heat the oven to 450°F. Line a large heavy-duty rimmed sheet pan with a piece of parchment paper. In a mixing bowl, toss the squash with 2 tablespoons olive oil and 1 teaspoon salt. Spread the squash in one layer on the sheet pan. Roast, flipping once or twice with a large spatula, until the squash is tender and nicely browned around the edges, 25 to 30 minutes. Transfer to a mixing bowl. Turn the oven down to 250°F.

Melt the butter over medium-low heat in a small saucepan. Add the orange juice, 1½ teaspoons of the maple syrup, the lime juice, and cinnamon; whisk well until combined and remove from the heat. Drizzle the butter mixture over the roasted squash and toss gently.

In a medium saucepan, heat 1 tablespoon olive oil over medium-low heat. Add the minced garlic and cook until softened and fragrant. Add the black beans, adobo sauce, the remaining 2 teaspoons maple syrup, and the chicken broth or water and stir well. Bring to a simmer, cover, and

continued on p. 190 ›

› ones in the soup. Our Juliet plum tomatoes work great. There are plenty of green beans still coming on, and slicing the kernels off an ear of corn is a nice addition, too. Our warm fall maritime climate means herbs, both tender and woody, are ridiculously happy, so we toss in some fresh oregano and fresh basil, too. Surprisingly, though my favorite minestrone (p. 164) starts with bacon, I don't always use it. I've found that simmering a Parmigiano rind—as well as adding deeply flavored vegetables like cabbage and mushrooms to a minestrone—turns out a delicious vegetarian rendition, too. ›

cook, stirring, for 5 minutes. Uncover and continue cooking, stirring frequently until the liquid has been mostly absorbed, another 4 to 6 minutes. (The beans will look a bit creamy.) Remove from the heat and keep partially covered until ready to use.

Wrap the tortillas in foil and put in the oven to heat until just warm and pliable, 5 to 10 minutes. (Alternatively, warm the tortillas between two damp paper towels in the microwave for a few seconds. Do not over-warm or they will get stiff or rubbery.) Lay all 5 tortillas flat on a counter or other surface.

Using a large serving spoon or slotted spoon, spoon a portion (about ½ cup) of the warm black beans onto the lower center of each tortilla (the side closest to you), forming a rough shape a little bigger than a deck of cards. Top the beans on each tortilla with a portion of butternut squash,

distributing it as evenly as possible. Top the squash on each tortilla with a portion of queso fresco, some of the pepitas, the cilantro, and avocado slices (if using). Squeeze a little lime juice over the filling in each burrito.

Wrap each burrito: Start by folding up the bottom (the side closest to you); then fold the two sides in, keeping the filling layered and compact. Then roll the whole burrito tightly over on itself to close it. Cut each burrito in half on a sharp diagonal and arrange the two halves on a plate.

BRAISED CHICKEN THIGHS WITH CHIPOTLE-PLUM TOMATO SAUCE

SERVES 4

1 teaspoon chili powder

½ teaspoon unsweetened cocoa powder

½ teaspoon ground cumin

½ teaspoon ground coriander

¼ teaspoon sugar

⅛ teaspoon ground cinnamon

Kosher salt

1 tablespoon minced fresh garlic

1 serrano pepper, thinly sliced crosswise

8 small bone-in, skin-on chicken thighs (about 2½ pounds total; I like Bell & Evans)

Freshly ground black pepper

2 tablespoons extra-virgin olive oil

1 medium onion (5 to 6 ounces), diced (about 1 generous cup)

continued on p. 192

One cool summer night, I made up this braised chicken dish using our extra plum tomatoes and my favorite chili spices. The bold flavors were so terrific—warm and spicy and fragrant—that I wound up making this dish again and again in the early days of fall while we still had some plum tomatoes. We usually eat the chicken and its spicy sauce over a fluffy white rice pilaf, but it would be good with any grain or polenta, too. The braise takes a little time to come together, but the flavor is worth it.

In a small bowl, stir together the chili powder, cocoa powder, cumin, coriander, sugar, cinnamon, and ½ teaspoon salt. In another small bowl, combine the garlic and serranos. Season the chicken pieces with 1 teaspoon salt and freshly ground pepper.

In a large (5- to 6-quart) Dutch oven, heat the olive oil over medium heat. Add 4 chicken thighs, skin side down. Cook without moving until the bottom is golden brown, about 4 minutes. Using tongs, carefully turn the thighs over and cook until the other side is golden, 3 to 4 minutes.

continued on p. 192 ›

› It's that alchemy thing, I guess. I just think the flavors of the fall garden—the roots, the herbs, the beans, the greens, the squash—all play so well together that you can combine them artfully in any number of ways. Why, I even use the kale-carrot-onion-herb combo in a terrific Winter Green Market Meatloaf (p. 194). I guess what I'm saying is that fall vegetables are humble and forgiving and perfect for the cook or gardener who may be short on experience but long on enthusiasm.

STINKY VEGETABLES 'R US

And then there are those late-fall vegetables that everyone loves to turn up their nose at—turnips and rutabagas and Brussels sprouts. Stinky veg. Well, lately Brussels sprouts have become something of a media darling, but I don't think turnips will be starring in their own reality TV show anytime soon. But we like them. More to the point, Roy, Mr. Meat and Potatoes, likes them. I can't for the life of me figure this out, ›

› but I suspect it might be a sentimental thing. As a teenager, Roy spent a summer working on his uncle's farm in Scotland (where supposedly his summer sweetheart was the Junior Miss of Scotland...), and they grew a lot of turnips. Mostly for the sheep, but the family ate them too. "Time to hoe the 'neeps, lad," Roy's uncle would say to him, probably when he'd been spending too much time with Miss What's-her-name.

I've cozied up to turnips by roasting or sautéing them and pairing them with something a little bit sweet, like the Turnip, Sweet Potato & Apple Sauté (p. 201) and the Honey-Roasted Baby Turnips and Cremini Mushrooms (p. 208). And farm ›

¼ cup dry red wine

1 pound ripe plum tomatoes, cored, seeded, and diced (2⅓ to 2½ cups)

½ cup low-sodium chicken broth, plus more if needed

1 teaspoon adobo sauce from a can of chipotles in adobo

Cooked white rice, for serving

2 tablespoons chopped fresh cilantro

Transfer the thighs to a plate or platter. Add the remaining 4 thighs to the pot and cook on both sides until golden. Transfer to the plate with the other thighs.

Spoon some of the fat out of the pot (about half, leaving enough to generously cover the bottom). Turn the heat to medium low, add the onions and a pinch of salt, stir, cover, and cook, stirring and scraping frequently, until the onions are softened and browning around the edges, 5 to 6 minutes. Uncover, add the garlic and serranos, and cook, stirring, until fragrant, about 30 seconds. Add the spice mixture and cook, stirring, until fragrant and darkened, about 1 minute. Add the red wine and cook, stirring and scraping, until the wine is reduced and a bit thickened, about 1 minute.

Add the tomatoes, chicken broth, and adobo sauce. Stir well, cover, and bring to a gentle simmer. Cook until the tomatoes are well softened, about 5 minutes.

Return the chicken thighs (and any juices they've released) to the pot, snuggling them into the sauce in one layer. Partially cover the pot and lower the heat as much as necessary to maintain a gentle simmer. Cook until the chicken thighs are tender and cooked through (check by removing one and slicing into it) and the sauce has reduced a bit, about 40 minutes.

Remove the pot from the heat. Arrange 2 thighs over a portion of rice on each plate. Stir half of the cilantro into the sauce and spoon over the thighs and rice. Garnish with the remaining cilantro.

› stand customers like them with their burly greens attached. (We grow the purple-topped variety, which are quite pretty.) It's a good thing we've embraced turnips and rutaba-gas, because we do a much bet-ter job of growing them than growing Brussels sprouts.

Actually, growing Brussels sprouts isn't hard, and their massive stalks are so totally brag-worthy that you've got to go for it. But keeping the cab-bage worms (produced by an innocuous-looking little white butterfly) from destroying them requires near mummification in white fabric row cover. Lift that cover off, one butterfly gets in, and the game is up. That—and the 100 days you wait for the sprouts—can be frustrating.

Usually you can salvage the ravaged sprouts, though I cer-tainly don't sell them at the farm stand. I take them into the kitchen and peel the leaves away from the core, looking for any bugs that might still be hanging around (soaking in water helps, too). But then I am left with the gift of a beautiful ›

WINTER GREEN MARKET MEATLOAF

SERVES 4 TO 6

¾ cup fresh breadcrumbs (about 1 English muffin)

3 tablespoons milk

½ cup ketchup

2 tablespoons Worcestershire sauce

2 tablespoons brown sugar

1 tablespoon low-sodium soy sauce

1 tablespoon Dijon mustard

1 large carrot (about 3 ounces), coarsely chopped

1 small onion (about 4 ounces), coarsely chopped

4 large cloves garlic, peeled

1 small serrano pepper, seeds and ribs removed, cut into 3 or 4 pieces

2 cups (packed) coarsely chopped kale (about 2 ounces)

2 tablespoons unsalted butter

Kosher salt

1 pound 80-85% lean ground beef

½ pound ground pork

3 ounces crumbled good-quality feta

1 large egg

Freshly ground black pepper

2 tablespoons (lightly packed) chopped fresh oregano

Yes, there's actually kale in this incredibly moist and flavorful meatloaf. (It works, really!) I made this one day after a visit to our Winter Farmers' Market, where I got all the veggies, the ground meat, and even local feta. Most of these veggies are still kicking around our garden in early winter, too, but you can collect them at the grocery of course, as well. Tossing the veggies and plenty of gar-lic into the food processor makes a finely minced mixture perfect for lightening up meatloaf. This is delicious left-over—reheated or even cold, pâté style.

Heat the oven to 350°F. Line a large rimmed heavy-duty baking sheet with parchment paper.

Put the breadcrumbs and milk in a small bowl and mix. Let sit. In a small bowl, whisk together the ketchup, Worcestershire, brown sugar, soy sauce, and Dijon.

In the bowl of a food processor, combine the carrots, onions, garlic, serranos, and kale. Pulse until very finely chopped, scraping down the sides as necessary to incorpo-rate the kale.

In a medium (10-inch) nonstick skillet, melt the butter over medium-low heat. Add the chopped veggies and ½ teaspoon salt. (The pan will be crowded.) Cook, stirring, until gently softened and very fragrant, about 5 minutes. Transfer to a plate and let cool (about 10 minutes).

In a large mixing bowl, combine the beef, pork, feta, egg, several grinds of pepper, the oregano, ½ teaspoon salt, the breadcrumb mixture, and 3 tablespoons of the ketchup mixture (reserve the rest for brushing on the loaf). Using your hands, mix all of the ingredients together thoroughly without mashing too much. Transfer the mixture to the baking sheet and shape into a long, narrow loaf (about 9 inches long

and 4 inches wide). Spoon the rest of the ketchup mixture down the length
of the top of the loaf and gently spread or brush it over the sides.

Bake the meatloaf until an instant-read thermometer registers 160° to
165°F, 55 to 60 minutes. Let rest for 5 minutes before slicing and serving.

CARAMELIZED CARROTS AND SHALLOTS WITH SPINACH AND CITRUS BROWN BUTTER

SERVES 3 OR 4

1 tablespoon fresh orange juice

1 tablespoon fresh lemon juice

½ teaspoon freshly grated lemon zest

1 pound carrots

4 shallots (6 to 7 ounces total)

3 tablespoons extra-virgin olive oil

4 to 5 fresh thyme sprigs

Kosher salt

2 cups (loosely packed) fresh baby spinach leaves (about 1½ ounces)

2 tablespoons unsalted butter

"Slow" sautéing is one of my favorite techniques for root veggies; they gently cook through in the skillet while they're browning, too. The carrots in this deeply delicious side dish pick up a lot of flavor from the shallots, and a citrus brown-butter drizzle, along with a few baby spinach leaves, brings it all together in a big way at the end. (Make the brown butter while the carrots are finishing cooking.) Serve this dish with roast pork—or eat the whole thing yourself for a fabulous vegetarian supper.

In a small bowl, combine the orange juice, lemon juice, and lemon zest.

Peel and trim the carrots and cut them into pieces that are 2 to 3 inches long and ⅜ to ½ inch wide. Peel the shallots, cut them in half, and trim just the hairy part off of the root end (keeping the root end mostly intact will help hold wedges together). Put the shallot halves cut side down on a cutting board and slice them into wedges about ¾ inch wide.

In a large (12-inch) nonstick skillet, heat the olive oil over medium heat. When the oil is hot, add the carrots, shallots, thyme sprigs, and ¾ teaspoon salt. Toss well. Cover the pan and cook, stirring occasionally, until the shallots are limp and have lost their opacity, and a few of the carrots are just starting to brown, 8 to 9 minutes. Uncover and continue cooking, stirring more frequently, until all the carrots are shrunken and tender and most are browned (the shallots will be very brown), 10 to 12 minutes. Add the spinach leaves and toss with tongs just until wilted. Remove the pan from the heat and remove the thyme sprigs.

In a small skillet or saucepan, melt the butter over medium-low heat. Cook, swirling occasionally, until the milk solids in the butter turn a nutty

continued on p. 198 ›

› pile of Brussels sprout leaves in varying shades of green. I use them to make a holiday-worthy side dish with buttery, silky leeks, and it pretty much erases any bad memory.

But I'm probably not helping the cause of cruciferous vegetables with this talk, so please don't despair. Not only are these veggies totally transformed with the kiss of high heat—go ahead and try Roasted Brussels Sprouts with Pomegranate Dressing (p. 216) if you're not converted yet—but you will get the sweetest, tastiest varieties at a farm stand or farmers' market, especially after a frost. (Plenty of farmers either don't have cabbage worms or do a much better job of scaring them off.) Since winter farmers' markets are gaining in popularity (we have one here on the Island at the Ag Hall across the street from us), these veggies are a great way to eat local in the shoulder seasons. ›

FARMER COMES HOME: A DOG TALE

October on the farm is simply stunning. Forget that I told you that, or I might have to kill you. It's a Vineyard secret—fall is much nicer than summer for visiting. This time of year, I start writing blogs about nature walks and golden light and Monet-esque haystacks. Between that and waxing on rhapsodically about root vegetables, I'm sure there are legions of blog readers out there covering their eyes and ears saying, "Stop! Stop! We get it! You love fall." (That is, if they keep reading at all. And, okay, maybe I don't have legions of blog readers.)

I am unapologetic. And if October weren't already my favorite month, now I will forever think of it as the month we brought the Farm Dog home to live with us.

We needed a real pet. We had Ellie the Lovebird, who moved with us from the apartment to the farmhouse. But she was never a very satisfactory companion, as far as I was ›

brown color, 6 to 8 minutes. Remove the pan from the heat and let cool for a few minutes. Add the citrus juice mixture to it.

Scrape and pour the citrus brown butter over the carrot mixture. Toss well and taste for salt, adding more if necessary. Transfer to a serving platter or plates and serve right away.

"MAC 'N CHEESE" WITH KALE, GOAT CHEESE & SUN-DRIED TOMATOES

SERVES 4 TO 6

2 teaspoons extra-virgin olive oil, plus more for the pan

½ cup fresh breadcrumbs (I like English muffin crumbs)

⅓ cup plus 2 tablespoons freshly grated Parmigiano-Reggiano

Kosher salt

¼ cup thinly sliced drained oil-packed sun-dried tomatoes

1 teaspoon balsamic vinegar

4 ounces fresh goat cheese, crumbled while still cold

8 ounces elbow-shaped pasta

8 ounces stemmed fresh kale (¾ to 1 pound before stemming), sliced, chopped, or torn into bite-size pieces

2 large cloves garlic, smashed and peeled

One 1-inch piece fresh ginger, sliced into thin coins and smashed

¾ cup milk

¾ cup heavy cream

I'm all about finding tasty ways to get folks to eat more kale, and this baked pasta does the trick. Creamy goat cheese blends with a light sauce that's infused with garlic and ginger to make a sophisticated "mac 'n cheese." The ingredients list and directions are long, but once you get started, you'll find this dish comes together in no time and is satisfying to make and eat. A great vegetarian supper, this also could share the plate with sausages or pork chops. Use any kind of kale you like here.

Heat the oven to 375°F. Rub a 2-quart shallow gratin or other similar-size baking dish with olive oil. Combine the breadcrumbs, 2 tablespoons of the Parmigiano, the 2 teaspoons olive oil, and a pinch of salt in a small bowl. Put the sun-dried tomatoes, balsamic vinegar, and crumbled goat cheese in a large mixing bowl.

Bring a large pot of salted water to a boil. Cook the pasta until al dente, according to the package instructions. Reserving the pasta water in the pot (to use again for the greens), transfer the pasta with a large slotted spoon to a colander and drain well. Transfer the pasta to the mixing bowl with the goat cheese and sun-dried tomatoes.

Freshly ground black pepper

Pinch of cayenne

2 tablespoons unsalted butter

2 tablespoons unbleached all-purpose flour

Sprinkle the pasta with ¼ teaspoon salt and gently toss with the other ingredients.

Return the pot of water to a boil, add the kale, and cook until the greens just lose their toothiness, 3 to 5 minutes. Drain the greens in the colander, rinse with cool water, and press out as much water as possible. Add the greens to the bowl with the pasta, gently breaking them up a bit (they will be clumping). Mix gently with the other ingredients.

In a small heavy saucepan, combine the garlic, ginger, milk, and heavy cream. Watching carefully, bring to a boil over medium-high heat. Remove the pan from the heat and let sit for 5 to 10 minutes to let the flavors infuse the cream. With a fork, remove as much of the smashed ginger and garlic pieces that you can. Season with ½ teaspoon salt, a pinch of cayenne, and a few grinds of fresh pepper.

In another small saucepan (nonstick works well), melt the butter over medium-low heat. Add the flour and whisk it with the butter until well combined. Cook for 1 minute, stirring constantly. Add the milk/cream mixture to it in a steady stream, whisking constantly. Turn the heat to medium and bring the sauce to a simmer, whisking constantly. (Adjust the heat to medium high if necessary.) The sauce should be velvety, smooth, and creamy, and will coat the back of a spoon. Immediately remove the sauce from the heat and gently stir in the remaining ⅓ cup Parmigiano. Pour over the bowl of pasta and greens. Mix thoroughly and transfer the pasta-greens mixture to the prepared baking dish, scraping the bowl as necessary. Arrange the pasta mixture evenly in the pan (which will be quite full) and top with the breadcrumb mixture.

Bake until the top is golden brown and the sauce is bubbling below the surface, about 30 minutes. (The sauce will be mostly absorbed as the pasta cools.) Let cool for a few minutes and serve warm.

› concerned. In fact, she fell in love with Roy and subsequently attacked me whenever I went anywhere near her. Charming. Ellie went away a while back.

Then we got Cocoa Bunny, mostly for Libby, from Little Leona's Pet Shop. Soft and cute and furry, Cocoa Bunny is nevertheless not very cuddly. A bit skittish, I'd say. Cocoa Bunny's cocoa-puffs (droppings) do make an excellent addition to the compost pile, though, and she reigns over the backyard— and the chickens—like the Queen she is.

Along with Cocoa Bunny, that initial batch of baby chicks pretty much filled our animal quota for the first summer at ›

TURNIP, SWEET POTATO & APPLE SAUTÉ

SERVES 5

2 teaspoons honey

1 teaspoon apple cider vinegar

2 tablespoons extra-virgin olive oil, plus more as needed

2 tablespoons unsalted butter

12 ounces purple-topped turnips (about 4 small), ends trimmed but unpeeled, cut into medium (½-inch) dice (about 2⅓ cups)

12 ounces sweet potatoes (about 2 small), ends trimmed but unpeeled, cut into medium (½-inch) dice (about 2¾ cups)

Kosher salt

1 Honey Crisp (or other crisp-firm) apple, peeled, cored, and cut into medium dice (about 1½ cups)

1 large or 2 small onions, cut into medium dice (about 1½ cups)

2 teaspoons minced fresh garlic

Freshly ground black pepper

1 tablespoon minced fresh flat-leaf parsley

2 tablespoons finely chopped toasted pecans (optional)

Turnips and sweet potatoes take a slow turn in the skillet in this silky sauté. Apples and onions join the sweet potatoes in countering the sharp notes of the turnips, and a drizzle of honey and cider vinegar play up all the flavors. (Choose small or baby turnips for the mildest flavor.) Serve this hearty side dish with grilled sausages and a light arugula salad on a crisp fall night, or serve it like hash with a fried egg for breakfast.

Combine the honey and vinegar in a small bowl. Whisk well and set aside.

In a large (12-inch) nonstick skillet, heat the olive oil and 1 tablespoon butter over medium-high heat. When the butter has melted and is bubbling, add the turnips, sweet potatoes, and 1 teaspoon salt. (The pan will look crowded.) Stir and toss well. Reduce the heat to medium, cover partially, and cook, stirring occasionally, for 12 minutes. (You should see browning after 8 to 10 minutes. Listen to the pan; you should hear a gentle sizzle, not a loud one. If the vegetables are browning too quickly or sizzling too loudly, reduce the heat a bit.) Uncover, add the remaining 1 tablespoon butter, the apples, onions, and ¼ teaspoon salt, and continue to cook, stirring occasionally. Turn the heat down slightly if necessary, and cook until the turnips and sweet potatoes are nicely browned and tender and the onions are translucent, another 12 to 14 minutes.

Fold in the garlic and cook until fragrant, about 1 minute. Remove the pan from the heat, taste, and season with more salt and freshly ground pepper if desired. Sprinkle the honey/vinegar mixture over the top, add the parsley, and stir. Transfer to a serving platter or individual plates and garnish with the toasted pecans, if desired.

› the farmhouse. We'd get a dog someday, we told ourselves.

Someday always comes when you least expect it. Like, say, during a toilet-paper-and-dental-appointment run. (This is an Islander's idea of a good day off—take the ferry to the mainland to stock up on necessities and get your teeth cleaned. How much fun is that? At least there's usually a latte from Starbucks® in the deal.) This particular warm October day, we were driving back from Hyannis to Falmouth, a little ahead of our ferry schedule. Windows rolled down, I drifted in and out of a catnap, slouching on the slippery front seat of Roy's truck.

"We just passed the MSPCA," Roy announced.

"Turn around," I said abruptly, opening my eyes. "I was just dreaming of a dog." (Really, I was.)

"Okay," Roy said, "We'll just look." Ha. Two dog lovers do not visit an animal shelter without coming home with a dog, don't ya know?

We walked in and were led back to the kennel area. Oh. Yikes. It had been a long ›

› time since I'd been to a shelter, and I didn't realize how many animals would be there. We sort of skittered up and down the rows, went to the outdoor kennels, and circled back. I had stopped to chat with a big yellow dog who was making eloquent barking speeches to the kennel at large, when I heard Roy say from around the corner, "Come here, Susie. There's a black Lab over here."

I came around the corner and a skinny little black dog—definitely part Labrador and surely part something else—looked at me with a crooked smile, put his paw through an opening in the cage to touch me, and then rolled over on his back. I petted him as much as I could before walking away. Roy and I walked around silently for maybe 2 more minutes, looked at each other, and went back to pet "Andy" again. (They name the unnamed dogs alphabetically as they come in. This dog, maybe 6 or 8 months old, had been found wandering in Mashpee three weeks earlier, and no one ›

SLOW-SAUTÉED GREEN BEANS WITH SHIITAKES AND PROSCIUTTO

SERVES 4

2 teaspoons pure maple syrup

2 teaspoons sherry vinegar

3 tablespoons extra-virgin olive oil

1 pound green beans, trimmed

7 to 8 ounces fresh shiitake mushrooms, stemmed and halved (or quartered if large)

8 cloves garlic, peeled and halved

2 ounces thinly sliced prosciutto, torn into small (1- to 2-inch) pieces

4 medium sprigs fresh rosemary

Kosher salt

You won't believe how crowded the pan is when you first load it up with all these veggies; but with this terrific (and straightforward) technique, the veggies will slowly soften, brown, and shrink into a delicious and tender tangle of deep flavor. For the most even cooking, pick beans that are all about the same thickness (or close anyway!); steer away from really thick beans or teeny tiny ones.

In a small bowl, combine the maple syrup and sherry vinegar.

In a large (12-inch) nonstick skillet, heat the olive oil over medium heat. Add the beans, mushrooms, garlic, prosciutto, rosemary, and 1 teaspoon salt. Toss well with tongs to coat. Cover the pan and cook, stirring occasionally, until all the green beans have turned bright green, are beginning to turn brown, and have begun to lose their stiffness, 10 to 12 minutes. Uncover and cook, stirring more frequently, until all the beans are very deeply browned (the mushrooms and garlic will be browned and tender, too), 15 to 18 more minutes. Remove the pan from the heat and taste a bean and a mushroom for salt. Season lightly if necessary (the mushrooms may have absorbed more of the salt). Stir in the maple-vinegar mixture. Remove the rosemary sprigs and transfer to a serving platter or plates. Eat right away.

Roasted Beet "Jewels" with Cranberries,
Toasted Pecans & Balsamic Butter

ROASTED BEET "JEWELS" WITH CRANBERRIES, TOASTED PECANS & BALSAMIC BUTTER

SERVES 4

1½ pounds beets (preferably half red and half golden), topped and tailed but not peeled

1 tablespoon plus 1 teaspoon extra-virgin olive oil

Kosher salt

1 tablespoon fresh orange juice

1 tablespoon seedless red raspberry jam

1 teaspoon balsamic vinegar

1½ tablespoons unsalted butter, cut into 6 pieces and chilled

¼ cup very finely chopped dried cranberries

1 teaspoon chopped fresh thyme

½ cup chopped toasted pecans

Small fresh parsley or mint leaves, for garnish (optional)

This easy and delicious side dish is a great way to introduce people to roasted beets—or beets in general. You'll love it too, because the small-diced beets cook in only 25 minutes—no boiling or long slow roasting here! This is just as great to make with summer beets as fall beets, and would be a welcome addition to the Thanksgiving table. You can also make this dish by substituting carrots for half of the beets.

Heat the oven to 450°F. Cover two heavy-duty sheet pans with parchment paper. Keeping the red and golden beets separate (if using both colors), cut them into medium-small dice (no more than about ½ inch). Put each color in a bowl and toss with 2 teaspoons olive oil and ½ teaspoon kosher salt. Transfer each bowl of beets to separate sheet pans and spread in one layer. Roast until the beets are tender and shrunken, about 25 minutes. (Rotate the baking sheets to opposite racks halfway through cooking for more even cooking.) Transfer to a mixing bowl.

Put the orange juice, raspberry jam, and balsamic vinegar in a small saucepan over medium-low heat. Stir or whisk continuously (don't walk away!) until the jam is completely melted and the sauce is slightly more viscous (it may be steaming but it should not boil), 2 to 3 minutes. Remove the pan from the heat and immediately add the cold butter. Swirl the pan until the butter is melted and the sauce is slightly creamy. Add the cranberries and thyme and stir. Pour and scrape the balsamic butter with the cranberries over the roasted beets and mix and toss gently. Add most of the pecans and stir gently again. Transfer to a serving bowl and garnish with the remaining nuts and herb leaves (if using).

› had come looking for him at the pound, so he'd been moved to the MSPCA.)

It wasn't long before we were talking with the managers. They said we should take "Andy" out for a walk to see what we thought. If we were interested, we'd need to get our landlord on the phone for permission to have a pet at our rental. The dog pulled and skipped down the sidewalk, while Roy said, "He's a nice dog, but I think we should wait. It's not time yet."

"Okay," I agreed, not wanting to be the one to push it. We walked a little more and came back up to the front door.

"Well, maybe you should call Tom," Roy said.

"Okay," I said, happy Roy had changed his mind. Tom, a dog lover, thought it was a great idea. ›

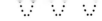

› As we left the MSPCA, Roy said to the women working there, "This is one lucky dog. He doesn't know it, but he's going to live on a farm on Martha's Vineyard! When he gets there, he'll be writing back to his old pals in the husgau, saying, 'Guys, guys, you won't believe this. I scored! This is one sweet deal!'"

On the front seat of the big truck, the dog sat between us, staring out the window. "What shall we name him?" I said to Roy. We had maybe thrown around three or four lame names when Roy suddenly said, "How about Farmer?"

"Farmer, you're going on your first ferry ride," we told him as we pulled up to the kiosk in Woods Hole to get our tickets. That may have been one of the best days of Farmer's life— except for the day a week later when we went for his second ferry ride to go pick up Libby for the weekend.

"A little girl! Well, this is all just too great," Farmer said, jumping all over her, his helicopter ears sticking straight out and his tongue hanging out ›

A BED OF BUTTERY BRUSSELS SPROUT LEAVES AND SILKY LEEKS

SERVES 3 TO 4

12 ounces Brussels sprouts

2½ tablespoons unsalted butter

Kosher salt

1 tablespoon extra-virgin olive oil

1½ cups thinly sliced leeks (white and pale green parts; about 3 medium), rinsed well but not dried

1 tablespoon dry white wine

2 teaspoons coarsely chopped fresh thyme

1 tablespoon heavy cream

Freshly ground black pepper

2 tablespoons coarsely grated Parmigiano-Reggiano

2 tablespoons finely chopped toasted hazelnuts or walnuts (optional)

Sometimes dense Brussels sprouts can cook unevenly, but one fun solution to this problem is to pare away the leaves from the core and cook only the leaves. It might seem fussy, but disrobing a sprout is easier than you'd think. You can then cook the leaves quickly in a hot pan for an almost instant side dish—and great nutty flavor. Or go one step further and toss the sprouts with silky leeks for an elegant "bed" for sear-roasted fish or beef.

To peel the Brussels sprout leaves off their core, begin by trimming a small piece off the stem end. Peel away the leaves that naturally fall off after trimming. (Discard any bruised leaves and begin a pile with the rest.) Continue trimming a bit off the stem end and peeling away leaves as they loosen. After just a few slivers, it's helpful to go ahead and cut the sprout in half and notch the core out with a generous V-shaped cut. The more tightly packed leaves will then come apart more easily. Continue trimming the base and peeling leaves away until you wind up with a big pile of leaves.

Heat 1 tablespoon of the butter in a large (12-inch) nonstick skillet over medium-high heat. When the pan is hot and the butter is foaming, add all of the leaves and ¼ teaspoon salt. Toss briefly, then let sit for 1 minute to let the bottom leaves begin to wilt and brown. Toss again and let sit for several seconds. Continue cooking and tossing, about another 2 minutes total, until all the leaves are lightly browned and mostly wilted. You will smell a nice nutty aroma. (Do not overcook.) Transfer all the leaves to a plate.

Let the skillet cool for a couple minutes, then return it to medium-low heat. Add the remaining 1½ tablespoons butter and the olive oil. When the butter is melted, add the leeks (with any water clinging to them) and ¼ teaspoon salt. Cover and cook, stirring occasionally, until the leeks are

well softened, 5 to 7 minutes. Uncover and continue cooking, stirring more frequently, until the leeks are very shrunken and browned in places, 6 to 8 more minutes. Add the white wine and cook, stirring, until it is absorbed. Return the Brussels sprout leaves to the pan and stir. Add the thyme, cream, and a few grinds of black pepper. Cook briefly, stirring, until the cream is mostly absorbed. Remove the pan from the heat and stir in the Parmigiano. Taste for salt, sprinkle with the toasted nuts, if using, and serve right away.

› between his broken teeth. "I am one lucky dog."

› between his broken teeth. "I

HOOP HOUSE DREAMS

With a farm dog, a tractor, and four new acres, we pretty much got everything two farmers could ask for in one fall season. I still longed for fruit trees, and would occasionally (and pretty obviously) flip through the fruit-tree catalogues, circling varieties that supposedly would produce fruit nearly instantaneously (or at least in two years) and would never get any diseases (right). I'd leave the catalogues open and lying on the coffee table so Roy could see them. He'd pick them up, give me that look, and ›

HONEY-ROASTED BABY TURNIPS WITH CREMINI MUSHROOMS

SERVES 4

1 pound unpeeled baby turnips or small to medium purple-topped turnips

8 ounces cremini mushrooms

Six 3-inch fresh rosemary sprigs, plus 3 more for garnish (optional)

Kosher salt

2 tablespoons extra-virgin olive oil, plus more for the pan

2 tablespoons honey, plus more for drizzling

1 tablespoon white balsamic vinegar

1 tablespoon finely minced crystallized ginger

Since I'm a color freak, I get pretty excited when this dish comes out of the oven; not only are the veggies shiny, but they're the most wonderful golden brown. I'd call it the color of deliciousness. Honey does the trick here, of course. During the first half of cooking, the turnips and mushrooms will give off some moisture, helping to cook the dense turnips through. After that, the glazing begins, so stir frequently and scrape the corners of the pan when you do. Serve this with roasted pork loin or turkey.

Heat the oven to 450°F. Rub a 9- x 13-inch baking dish all over with a bit of oil. (A glass ovenproof baking dish such as Pyrex works best for this recipe.)

If using baby turnips, trim and cut them into quarters or sixths. If using small to medium purple-topped turnips, trim them and cut them in half horizontally. Then cut each half into wedges or pieces about ¾ inch thick. Cut the mushrooms into quarters if they are large or in half if they are small. Combine the turnips, mushrooms, rosemary sprigs, and ½ teaspoon salt in a large mixing bowl.

In a small mixing bowl, combine the olive oil, honey, balsamic vinegar, crystallized ginger, and a pinch of salt. Whisk well. Drizzle and scrape the mixture over the turnips and mushrooms. Toss thoroughly. Transfer the veggie mixture to the baking pan, scraping out all dressing from the pan.

Cook, stirring occasionally at first, but every 5 to 10 minutes when browning begins, until the turnips are tender when pierced with a knife and the veggies are golden and glazed, about 40 minutes. (If the bottom of the pan gets too brown during cooking, stir in 1 or 2 tablespoons water.)

Remove the rosemary sprigs and transfer the veggies to a serving platter. Drizzle just a tiny bit of honey over all, sprinkle with salt, and garnish with fresh rosemary sprigs (if using).

SIMPLE GRILLED PINWHEEL ONIONS

**SERVES 2 OR 3
AS A CONDIMENT**

1 large yellow onion
(10 to 12 ounces)

Olive oil or vegetable oil

Kosher salt

This is more like a tip or a technique than a recipe, but it's a good one, I promise! You'll have to buy a silly thing at the grocery store, though—a package of turkey lacers. These tiny skewers are perfect for keeping the rings in a slice of onion together on the grill. After grilling, wrap your onion slices in a foil package to finish cooking all the way through. Then serve them with steak, top a burger (p. 103), or use them in a salsa (p. 73).

Heat a gas grill to medium.

Trim the ends of the onion and cut it crosswise into thick (½-inch) slices. Lay the slices on a baking sheet or other flat plate or tray. Thread a turkey lacer sideways through each ring, starting on the outside and poking straight through the center ring and out the other side so that all the rings in a slice are skewered together. Brush the slices generously with oil on both sides and sprinkle with salt.

Put the slices on the grill and cook without moving for 3 or 4 minutes. Turn the slices to a different angle and continue grilling for 2 to 4 more minutes, or until they are well marked on the bottom. Flip the slices over and cook until the new bottom side is well marked (turning to a different angle once again), another 5 to 7 minutes.

Transfer the skewered slices from the grill to a plate (or a big piece of foil), arranging them in stacks. Cover the plate tightly with foil (or seal the foil up). Let sit for 10 to 15 minutes. Unwrap, unskewer, and serve, or chop to use in other dishes.

› mouth, "No." Too much trouble for too little return. (That story is not over.)

Fortunately, our next-door neighbors pleaded with us to gather the pears from their two trees—and to sell them at the farm stand. Um, okay. We can take those off your hands. (I had a blast making up new desserts with pears, too, and Honey-Vanilla Roasted Pears, p. 236, are now a house fall favorite.) And another Up-Island friend invited us to pick apples (to eat, not sell) from a beautiful towering old tree behind their pre-Revolutionary home. This involved ladders and that fruit-picking tool that looks like a lacrosse stick. Libby loved it. We even went to pick wild cranberries and wild grapes over ›

> **COOK'S TIP**
>
> Wrapping grilled onions in foil to "finish" cooking ensures a pleasing, silky texture. You can use this same trick to finish cooking thick portabella mushrooms or eggplant slices.

ROMAN-STYLE CRANBERRY BEANS WITH GARLIC, PANCETTA & ARUGULA

SERVES 4

2 cups (10 ounces) shelled fresh cranberry beans (from 1¼ to 1½ pounds of pods)

Kosher salt

2 small sprigs fresh rosemary, plus 1½ teaspoons chopped fresh rosemary

1 large clove garlic, smashed, plus 2 teaspoons minced fresh garlic

4 very thin slices of pancetta (about 1 ounce total)

1 tablespoon extra-virgin olive oil, plus more for drizzling

½ teaspoon white balsamic vinegar

2 cups (loosely packed) baby arugula (about 1 ounce)

If you stumble on the stunning pink-podded cranberry beans at a farm stand or farmers' market, take them home and cook them simply to experience their creamy and supple texture. (Then try some in a soup, like the minestrone on p. 164.) Italians grow a virtually identical bean they call Borlotti, and you might see them in an Italian restaurant prepared like this, with lots of garlic and pancetta, and maybe a few greens. Sadly, the pink and white stripey color of the beans fades when cooked.

In a medium saucepan, combine the cranberry beans, ½ teaspoon salt, the rosemary sprigs, smashed garlic clove, and 4 cups water. Bring to a boil, reduce to a simmer, and cook gently until the beans are tender, 20 to 25 minutes. (You should be able to mash them lightly with the back of a spoon.)

Transfer the beans with a slotted spoon to a bowl; reserve the saucepan of cooking liquid. Remove the garlic and rosemary leaves from the beans.

In a medium (10-inch) heavy nonstick skillet, cook the pancetta over medium-low heat until it is golden brown and crisp, 10 to 12 minutes. Transfer the pancetta to paper towels to drain. Let the pan rest off the heat for a minute. Add the olive oil to the skillet and return it to the heat.

When the oil is hot, add the minced garlic, and cook, stirring, until it is fragrant and softened, 30 seconds to 1 minute. Add the beans, ½ teaspoon kosher salt, ½ teaspoon chopped rosemary, and about ¼ cup of the cooking liquid. Turn the heat to medium high and cook, stirring frequently, until most of the cooking liquid has been absorbed, about 2 minutes. Add the vinegar and another ½ teaspoon chopped rosemary to the beans.

Arrange most of the arugula in four shallow dishes and top with some beans. Drizzle a small amount of olive oil over each. Crumble the pancetta over the beans, sprinkle on the remaining rosemary and arugula, and serve.

› on Chappaquiddick Island. (I know, those don't grow on trees, but any local fruit is good in my book, especially with winter on the way.)

But there was one thing we both seriously wanted, and we'd been planning and putting it off since spring. That thing was a hoop house. You've probably seen one at a garden nursery or maybe on a farm you've passed while driving down the highway. But if not, you can basically think of it as a plastic greenhouse. Usually the plastic (clear polyethylene film) is stretched over half-round hoops (made of piping); the whole thing is anchored to the ground with lumber and ties. Doors and/or fans or screens are installed at either end to control temperature and airflow. Hoop houses can be short or long, small or gargantuan, depending on the ›

COOK'S TIP

If you don't plan to eat all the beans right away, save a little extra cooking liquid for reheating.

Slow-Roasted Beefsteak Tomatoes

SLOW-ROASTED
BEEFSTEAK TOMATOES

MAKES 16 TO 20 ROASTED
TOMATO HALVES

1 cup extra-virgin olive oil,
plus more as needed

4 to 5 pounds large ripe
beefsteak tomatoes

Kosher salt

Sugar

I'm an unapologetic roasted tomato fanatic. It's pretty much all about the intense smoky-sweet flavor, yet it's about versatility, too. In fact, roasted tomatoes are so useful that I've included two methods in this book. The first (p. 84) is a genius quick-roasting method for small, meaty tomatoes. It yields big flavor in less time. The method here is for juicy beefsteaks (heirlooms welcome!), which need slower roasting to release all that excess moisture and concentrate sugars. These are a gorgeous, rustic, delicious treat. Any leftovers find a great destination as a sauce, puréed with roasted red peppers (p. 215).

Heat the oven to 325°F. Line a heavy-duty rimmed baking sheet first with aluminum foil and then with parchment. (The foil makes cleanup much easier, while the parchment prevents sticking.) Drizzle and rub a little olive oil over the parchment.

Cut each tomato in half through the equator (crosswise—not from stem to blossom end) and gently poke the seeds (but not the ribs) out of each cavity. Put the tomato halves, cut side up, on the baking sheet and season each with a small pinch of salt and a big pinch of sugar. Drizzle the 1 cup of olive oil in and around the edges of each tomato half.

Roast the tomatoes for about 2½ hours, or until the color is a dark brick red and the tomatoes have flattened and collapsed somewhat (they will collapse more out of the oven). Let them cool for at least a few minutes on the sheet pan. Serve warm or at room temperature. Store in a covered container in the refrigerator for a week or in the freezer for 2 to 3 months.

› farm and the use. The main advantage of a hoop house to a small farmer or market grower is season extension—because the structure retains heat, it creates an environment where crops can be started earlier and grown later. But it can also be useful in the regular season (for heat-loving crops) because it offers so much protection from wind and other environmental damage. The second major advantage is a place to grow and harden off seedlings to use as starts on the farm and/or to sell.

And, um, it's a pretty swell place to hang out on a rainy day. I know that now. ›

COOK'S TIP

Roasting is also a great way to preserve the last of the season's tomatoes. Layer roasted tomatoes in plastic food storage containers (cover each layer with plastic wrap) and store tightly sealed in the freezer for up to 3 months. Texture suffers but flavor sure doesn't. Just one or two can add a real boost to a weeknight sauté, a pan sauce, or a soup.

› Yet while we both knew instinctively that this hoop house was sure to give us a leg up on the farm, I don't think either of us realized exactly how much could be produced out of one of these things. (Future Susie is giving you a hint: A lot.)

In late October, Roy came in one day and told me he was going to have the hoop house built by Thanksgiving. Okey dokey, I smiled to myself.

I started taking pictures, thinking I'd post the progression on the blog, but I barely had time to download them by the time he was done. This is no small feat. If you order a large hoop house as a kit, sometimes the manufacturer will send a crew to assemble it. But most small farmers do the job themselves, albeit with a few friends and helpers. I wasn't surprised to see Roy go at this himself, but I expected he'd at least call me down to help him stretch the plastic over when the time came. He didn't. Show off. ›

ROASTED TOMATO AND GRILLED PEPPER SAUCE

MAKES ABOUT 1¼ CUPS

1 Marinated Grill-Roasted Bell Pepper (4 to 5 lobes), with any marinade, garlic, and basil clinging to it (p. 119)

2 halves Slow-Roasted Beefsteak Tomatoes (p. 213)

This is the bee's knees, I'm telling you. As if a roasted tomato wasn't tasty enough, once you purée one with a marinated grill-roasted bell pepper, you have something that will knock your socks off. Use this sauce on pasta, grilled fish, grilled eggplant, pizza, crostini, whatever you like. Double, triple, quadruple it. Freeze it. Just enjoy it.

Combine the peppers and tomatoes in a blender. Chop, then purée, until the sauce is pretty smooth but still a teensy bit chunky.

› While hoop houses are way more economical than a permanent green house, they still can run to thousands of dollars, depending on the size. After reading up on what it would take to build one, we realized that there were a number of ways to cut costs, so this is what we did to save money:

1. Instead of buying the hoops, we made them. We purchased electrical conduit at a home goods store and a "hoop bender" from Johnny's Selected Seeds. I watched Roy bend the hoops on the picnic table, and this did not look hard (honest).

2. We ordered the film separately after shopping around online for the best price (and the lowest shipping cost!). ›

ROASTED BRUSSELS SPROUTS WITH POMEGRANATE DRESSING, DRIED CHERRIES & TOASTED WALNUTS

SERVES 4

1¼ pounds Brussels sprouts, trimmed and cut into halves lengthwise

3 tablespoons extra-virgin olive oil

Kosher salt

3 tablespoons pomegranate juice

1 tablespoon plus 1 teaspoon balsamic vinegar

1 tablespoon plus 1 teaspoon honey

2 teaspoons fresh lime juice, plus 4 small lime wedges for serving

¼ cup coarsely chopped dried cherries

1 tablespoon cold unsalted butter, cut into 4 pieces

¼ cup toasted chopped walnuts

2 tablespoons very roughly chopped fresh flat-leaf parsley, plus a few sprigs for garnish

2 teaspoons chopped fresh mint

Rustic, festive, yummy. Did I mention easy? Here's a Sunday night side dish for a cold fall night (think pork loin) or a nice addition to the holiday table (double the recipe if you like, but use two pans). It's a recipe that brings out both the nutty and the sweet side of roasted Brussels sprouts and manages to feel warming and bright at the same time.

Heat the oven to 475°F. In a mixing bowl, toss the Brussels sprouts with the oil and ¾ teaspoon salt. Arrange the sprouts in a 9- x 13-inch baking dish (they will be very snug). Roast, stirring once or twice during cooking, until nicely browned and tender, 25 to 27 minutes. Transfer to a mixing bowl.

Combine the pomegranate juice, balsamic vinegar, honey, and lime juice in a small saucepan. Bring the mixture to a simmer over medium-high heat and simmer gently for 2 to 3 minutes, or until the mixture is reduced by about a third. (It will be a bit more viscous but still loose). Remove the pan from the heat, add the dried cherries and the butter, and stir until the butter is just melted and creamy. (Don't reheat the mixture.)

Pour the sauce over the roasted sprouts and stir gently but thoroughly. Add most of the walnuts and herbs and stir well again. Transfer to a serving dish, garnish with the remaining nuts and herbs (and the herb sprigs), and serve right away with lime wedges for seasoning at the table. (A gentle squeeze is enough.)

Roasted Brussels Sprouts with Pomegranate Dressing, Dried Cherries & Toasted Walnuts

› 3. We used as much salvaged lumber and hardware as possible, and we repurposed two old screen doors to use at either end.

4. We repurposed soil and compost from around the property to fill the two raised beds within the hoop house rather than buying expensive top soil. We also repurposed a work table and some damaged screening to make a long potting table down the middle.

5. And, of course, we did the labor "our" selves.

Naturally, as soon as the structure was finished, two storms came along and threatened to blow it down. The first was Hurricane Sandy, and miraculously the hoop house stayed entirely in tact through this event.

The second was a Nor'easter. And if you're a New Englander, you know that these storms can sometimes be worse than hurricanes. This particular one was brutal—the wind blew, and blew hard, for three straight days, pummeling the hoop house (and us, the chickens, ›

THE LAST HURRAH
CHERRY TOMATO GRATIN

SERVES 4

3 tablespoons extra-virgin olive oil, plus more for the dish

1 English muffin

¼ cup grated aged Gouda or Parmigiano-Reggiano

1 teaspoon chopped fresh rosemary

Kosher salt

1½ pounds (about 2½ pints) mixed farm stand or garden cherry tomatoes (red, yellow, orange, or the lemony-green varieties), halved (about 4½ cups)

2 teaspoons honey

1 teaspoon sherry vinegar

1 teaspoon minced fresh garlic

Sometime in late October, our cherry tomatoes begin to fall off the dying vines faster than we can catch them. The chickens get anything that languishes on the ground, but we snag as many as we can, knowing it will be a long winter without fresh tomatoes. Then I make this simple, unctuous gratin to capture the flavor of sun-ripened Sun Golds and Sweet 100s. It's a terrific side, but it doubles as a condiment, too, since it has a saucy texture (great on fish). Cooking times will vary depending on how much moisture your tomatoes release.

Heat the oven to 350°F. Rub a 1½-quart shallow baking dish (I like an oval, ceramic one) with a little olive oil.

Rip the English muffin into chunks and process it in a coffee grinder or small food processor to make loose, coarse breadcrumbs. (You should have a scant 1 cup.) In a small bowl, combine the muffin crumbs, cheese, 1 tablespoon olive oil, ¼ teaspoon of the rosemary, and a big pinch of salt.

Put the tomatoes in a medium bowl. Add the remaining 2 tablespoons olive oil, the honey, sherry vinegar, garlic, remaining ¾ teaspoon rosemary, and a big pinch of salt. Toss well to coat and transfer to the baking dish. Arrange evenly and top with the breadcrumb-cheese mixture.

Bake until the crumbs are a deep golden color and the liquid that the tomatoes give off while cooking is quite reduced, leaving a brown line around the edge of the pan, anywhere from 60 to 70 minutes, depending on how juicy your tomatoes were. (Plenty of leeway here.) Let sit for 10 minutes out of the oven and serve warm.

PEAR STREUSEL COFFEE CAKE

SERVES 12

FOR THE STREUSEL
1 cup toasted finely chopped pecans

⅓ cup plus 2 tablespoons (packed) light brown sugar

3 tablespoons unbleached all-purpose flour

¾ teaspoon ground cinnamon

¼ teaspoon table salt

Baked in a 9- x 13-inch pan, this moist cake serves 12 and is easy to tote along to a potluck. The pan will look very full before baking, but no worries—bake it until there's no jiggling and the top is firm; and let cool for a bit for easiest serving. Studded with diced fresh pears and topped with a deeply flavorful brown sugar–pecan streusel, this is the coffee cake to serve with a brunch of scrambled farm eggs, crisp bacon, and fresh OJ. It freezes well, too.

2 tablespoons unsalted butter, melted

FOR THE CAKE
Baking spray or butter, for the pan

3 cups (13½ ounces) unbleached all-purpose flour, plus more for the pan if needed

1 tablespoon baking powder

½ teaspoon baking soda

1 teaspoon ground cinnamon

¼ teaspoon ground ginger

¾ teaspoon table salt

1 cup (½ pound) unsalted butter, softened at room temperature

1 cup granulated sugar

½ cup light brown sugar

1 tablespoon pure vanilla extract

4 large eggs

1 cup sour cream

2 medium Bartlett pears (about 7 ounces each), peeled, cored, and cut into small dice

MAKE THE STREUSEL

In a small bowl, combine the nuts, brown sugar, flour, cinnamon, and salt. Toss well. Drizzle the melted butter over the mixture and stir until thoroughly combined.

MAKE THE CAKE

Heat the oven to 350°F. Spray a 9- x 13-inch (15-cup) baking dish with baking spray. (Or coat it lightly with butter and flour.)

In a mixing bowl, stir together the flour, baking powder, baking soda, cinnamon, ginger, and salt.

In the bowl of an electric mixer, combine the butter, both sugars, and the vanilla. Mix well on medium-high speed until light and fluffy, 2 to 3 minutes. Add the eggs one at a time and mix well on medium speed, stopping to scrape down the sides and bottom of the bowl after each addition. Add half of the flour mixture and mix on medium-low speed just until incorporated. Add half of the sour cream and mix on medium-low speed just until incorporated. Repeat with the remaining flour and sour cream. Fold in a little more than half of the pears.

Transfer the batter (it will be thick) to the prepared baking pan and spread it out as evenly as possible. Sprinkle with half of the streusel mixture. Sprinkle with the remaining pears and the remainder of the streusel mixture. Drag a paring knife through the batter, across the width and length of the pan to swirl the streusel into the batter a bit.

Bake until the top is puffed and set (firm and no longer jiggly in any places), about 1 hour. Let the cake cool in the pan for at least 30 minutes. Cut out squares and serve warm or at room temperature. Wrap leftovers tightly and keep at room temperature for 24 hours or in the freezer for several weeks.

› and everything else). Slowly the plastic film began to tear and the support struts jiggled around. But when the winds finally abated, the damage fortunately wasn't too bad and Roy was able to patch it up pretty quickly. We'd also bought extra plastic film, so we had backup on hand. (And, yes, the chickens were all fine, though a little tired of being "cooped up" during the storm.)

The first occupants of the new hoop house were the group of 50 chickens, who had fun mowing the grass down and eating bugs. Then we kicked them out.

By February we would have our first crop of lettuce planted ›

*Spiced Butternut and
Cranberry Quick Bread*

SPICED BUTTERNUT AND CRANBERRY QUICK BREAD

MAKES 3 LOAVES

Baking spray or butter, for the pan

3⅓ cups (15 ounces) unbleached all-purpose flour, plus more for pan if needed

1 teaspoon baking powder

1 teaspoon baking soda

1½ teaspoons table salt

1 teaspoon ground ginger

1 teaspoon ground nutmeg

1 teaspoon ground cinnamon

1 teaspoon ground cloves

3 cups sugar

4 large eggs

1 cup vegetable oil

1 teaspoon pure vanilla extract

2 cups (packed; about 1 pound) Slow-Roasted Butternut Squash (p. 162)

3 cups fresh cranberries or fresh blueberries

My mom's famous moist and tender pumpkin bread was a favorite growing up, so I decided to create a variation on her recipe by using roasted butternut squash instead of canned pumpkin and by adding a few fresh cranberries. Wow—lovely! This is just the snack to have around for drop-in visitors during the holidays, and it makes a great gift, too. It freezes well and defrosts quickly. While we make it with fresh cranberries in the fall, in summer, we make it with fresh blueberries, too, which pair beautifully with the spices.

Heat the oven to 325°F. Spray three loaf pans (each about 8 x 4 inches, or a 5- to 6-cup capacity; see Cook's Tip) with baking spray (or lightly coat with butter and flour).

In a medium bowl, combine the flour, baking powder, baking soda, salt, ginger, nutmeg, cinnamon, and cloves. Whisk well.

In the bowl of an electric mixer, combine the sugar, eggs, vegetable oil, and vanilla. Mix on medium speed until creamy and somewhat lightened in color, a full 2 minutes. Add the roasted squash and mix until combined. With the mixer running on low, gradually add the flour mixture until just combined. Remove the bowl from the mixer and stir in the berries by hand. Transfer the mixture to the three loaf pans, dividing evenly.

Bake until a pick inserted into the middle of a loaf comes out with just a few crumbs clinging to it, 55 to 70 minutes, depending on size of the loaf pans.

Let the loaves cool completely on racks and then unmold them. Keep well wrapped at room temperature for up to 2 days or in the freezer for up to 2 months.

› in the hoop house; by March, spinach, chard, and bok choy. Soon after, we would learn how much the hoop house would transform our seedling operation in May and allow us to grow early tomatoes and flawless basil over the summer, to boot.

But for the meantime, I couldn't get over how peaceful and cozy it was down there on a cold and drizzly day. What a neat way to be outside and yet not outside.

A BOOK, A BUSINESS, AND BIG PLANS

As soon as he finished the hoop house, Roy went down to ›

COOK'S TIP

You will need three loaf pans for this recipe. The smaller, narrower loaf pans (closer to 8 x 4 inches rather than 9 x 5 inches) will bake prettier, taller loaves, but you can use the bigger pans, too. Shallow loaves can be cut into squares, rather than slices, if you like. You could certainly use mini loaf pans, too (with a shorter baking time).

› the new back four acres and started building chicken coops, digging fence posts, and tying up deer fencing for a big chicken yard. We had 200 laying hens (pullets, to be accurate) arriving in only a couple weeks.

It always happens this way. You decide to do something, and then things unfold a little too quickly. When we made the decision to go into the egg business for real, our first phone call was to a farm in Connecticut that raises pullets. Pullets are 16-week-old female chickens who will begin to lay eggs in just a few weeks after you get them. Buying pullets is more economical and easier than raising (and feeding) hundreds ›

LITTLE PEAR CROSTATAS WITH HAZELNUT CRISP TOPPING

MAKES 4 CROSTATAS; SERVES 8

FOR THE DOUGH
2 cups (9 ounces) unbleached all-purposed flour

3 tablespoons granulated sugar

½ teaspoon table salt

1 cup (½ pound) cold unsalted butter, cut into cubes (keep cold if working ahead)

4 tablespoons ice water

FOR THE CRISP TOPPING
¼ cup unbleached all-purpose flour

¼ cup very finely chopped, toasted, skinned hazelnuts (see Cook's Tip, p. 226)

3 tablespoons light brown sugar

⅛ teaspoon ground cinnamon

Table salt

2 tablespoons unsalted butter, diced

FOR THE FILLING
3 ripe but firm pears (about 6 ounces each), peeled, cored, and thinly sliced

1 teaspoon fresh lemon juice

2 tablespoons granulated sugar

3 tablespoons unbleached all-purpose flour

⅛ teaspoon ground cinnamon

continued on p. 226

I learned to make these rustic free-form tarts at my first restaurant job more than 20 years ago, and they are still my go-to dessert when friends are coming over. (Great for breakfast, too!) The buttery crust is amazing, and this pear and hazelnut filling is one of my favorites. I make these in a small size that's perfect for sharing with your sweetie. (Vanilla ice cream optional.) The dough keeps well in the fridge or freezer, so make it in advance. Remember to take it out of the fridge 30 minutes or so before assembling. (Move frozen dough to the fridge the night before baking.) You can make the topping ahead, too, and refrigerate or freeze it.

MAKE THE DOUGH

In the bowl of a food processor, combine the flour, sugar, and salt. Pulse briefly to combine. Add the cubes of butter and use your fingers to toss them carefully with some of the flour. Pulse about 20 times, or until the butter particles are quite small. With the motor running, add the ice water in a stream. Process until the dough is beginning to come together (but it will still be loose—if you pinch some together it should form a clump). Don't overprocess. Turn the loose dough out into a big mixing bowl and knead it briefly to finish bringing it together. Use a scale to weigh the dough and portion into 4 equal pieces (about 5 ounces each). Shape each piece into a disk about ¾ inch thick, wrap in plastic, and refrigerate or freeze.

continued on p. 226 ›

Little Pear Crostatas with Hazelnut Crisp Topping

› of chicks, so we knew this was the way to go. Plus, the nice folks in Connecticut were willing to deliver the birds to the Island for a very small fee. The only catch, as we discovered when we called them, was that they were only heading our way one last time before winter. And that date was November 10—right around the corner. It was that or wait until spring. We had a little money in the bank from the profitable farm stand season, so we said, "We're in."

Meanwhile, I had happily signed on over the summer to write my third book. A cookbook, inspired by the farm. A cookbook, with stories and recipes. ›

COOK'S TIP

To get the best flavor from hazelnuts, buy them whole and toast on a baking sheet in a 350°F oven until the skins darken and crack. Rub the nuts in a clean dishtowel until most of the skins come off. If you've got time, pop them back on the baking sheet and toast until golden all over. To chop them very finely, use a small coffee grinder. Just remember to stop before you make hazelnut butter!

⅛ teaspoon ground nutmeg

⅛ teaspoon ground ginger

Table salt

TO ASSEMBLE
1 egg yolk

2 tablespoons heavy cream

3 tablespoons very finely chopped toasted hazelnuts (see Cook's Tip)

MAKE THE TOPPING

Combine the flour, hazelnuts, brown sugar, cinnamon, and a pinch of salt in a small mixing bowl. Add the diced butter and rub it in completely with your fingers until a fine, crumbly topping forms. Refrigerate until ready to use.

FILL AND ASSEMBLE THE TARTS

Remove the dough disks from the refrigerator and let them sit at room temperature for 30 to 40 minutes. Heat the oven to 400°F. Line two heavy-duty rimmed baking sheets with parchment.

When you are ready to assemble the tarts, put the sliced pears in a mixing bowl. Sprinkle with lemon juice and sugar, and then add the flour, cinnamon, nutmeg, ginger, and a pinch of salt. Toss until thoroughly mixed.

In a small bowl, whisk together the egg yolk and heavy cream and set aside.

Sprinkle a light dusting of flour on a rolling surface. Roll out a disk of dough into a round about 7½ to 8 inches in diameter, sprinkling flour as necessary to prevent sticking. Transfer the dough to one of the parchment-lined sheet pans. Repeat with the remaining three disks of dough, so that you have two rounds on each sheet pan.

Sprinkle about 2 teaspoons of the hazelnuts over the middle of each round (in a rough circle, leaving a 2-inch border). Portion the pear mixture evenly among the 4 rounds, arranging it in the center of the dough over the hazelnuts and leaving a 2-inch border of dough around the fruit. Pleat and fold the edge of the dough up and over the outer edge of the pear filling. Brush the top of the dough (and under the folds) with the egg mixture. Arrange a quarter of the crisp topping over the fruit in the center of each tart, letting little pieces of crisp topping spill over onto the dough as well.

Bake for 32 to 36 minutes, rotating the sheet pans halfway through until the crostatas are nicely golden all over and crisp and brown on the bottom. Let cool on the baking sheets and eat warm or at room temperature. Store, covered with plastic, at room temperature for a day or so, or wrap well and freeze.

GRILLED BREAD WITH STILTON AND ROSEMARY-MAPLE DRIZZLE

SERVES 6

Six ½- to ¾-inch-thick slices ciabatta or other crusty, airy artisan bread

2½ tablespoons olive oil

Kosher salt or coarse sea salt

2 teaspoons fresh rosemary leaves, finely chopped

2 tablespoons pure maple syrup

½ teaspoon sherry vinegar

2 to 2½ ounces Stilton cheese, at room temperature and lightly crumbled

Grilled bread is so flavorful and satisfying that I've devised a number of excuses for serving it all year long (thanks to the gas grill!). This savory topping combination of Stilton, rosemary, and maple highlights my favorite fall garden herb (and a favorite cheese) and makes a great starter or side dish for warm salads or hearty soups. If you're not a blue cheese fan, try camembert or another aged creamy cheese instead. My favorite bread for grilling is ciabatta.

Heat a gas grill on medium heat. Generously brush both sides of each piece of bread with olive oil and sprinkle with salt and ½ teaspoon of the rosemary.

In a small saucepan over medium-low heat, combine the maple syrup, vinegar, and the remaining rosemary. Gently heat until fragrant and quite warm, 3 to 5 minutes. (It's okay if the syrup bubbles, but try not to let it boil or it will start reducing.) Remove from the heat.

Put the bread slices directly on the grill grate, cover, and cook until golden, 1 to 2 minutes. Flip each piece of bread with tongs and cook again, covered, until the bottom is golden, about 1 more minute.

With a sandwich spreading knife or small spatula, lightly smear about a sixth of the Stilton on each of the bread pieces. (It will soften up when it contacts the hot bread.) Using a small spoon, drizzle the bread slices with the maple-rosemary mixture. Serve warm.

› A cookbook to be called *Fresh from the Farm*, no less—so exciting! But of course, there would be no cookbook if I didn't meet the last of my deadlines. I'd already developed many of the recipes for the photo shoot earlier in the fall, but I had at least 75 or so left to create—and to send off to my testers Eliza and Jessica, for cross-testing. So I was pretty much snuggled into my (warm) kitchen while Roy worked in the (cold) outdoors.

At least there was good food waiting for Roy whenever he came in. Plenty of sweets to snack on, from molasses cookies (p. 234) and sweet crêpes (p. 229) to Pear Streusel Coffee Cake (p. 220). I'd try to time my main-dish testing for dinner, so he could look forward to Autumn Pot Roast with Roasted Root ›

› Veggie Garnish (p. 183), Spicy Shrimp, Kale, Chorizo & White Bean Ragoût, (p. 186), or Roasted Butternut Squash Risotto with Thyme, Parmigiano & Toasted Pine Nuts (p. 179).

But as any recipe developer will tell you, some days are pretty strange and you might wind up with three desserts for dinner and a soup at 10 o'clock in the morning. And some days (not many, fortunately) are so disappointing that you want to throw in the towel and go out to eat. Except that there is hardly a restaurant open this time of year at our end of the Island. (And certainly no take-out. Subsequently, potlucks are big in the winter!)

But there were always eggs. And the pullets hadn't been here a fortnight when they started dropping the smallest, cutest eggs (it takes a month or so for the eggs to get up to full size). And pretty soon we were washing a couple of hundred eggs a day in the kitchen. That was an interesting dance— weaving the egg washing into ›

SWEET CRÊPES WITH CINNAMON CARAMELIZED PEARS AND VANILLA ICE CREAM

SERVES 6

1 tablespoon unsalted butter, plus more for the pan

Kosher salt

1½ tablespoons granulated sugar

½ teaspoon ground cinnamon

6 Sweet Crêpes (facing page)

Cinnamon Caramelized Pears (p. 230)

Softened vanilla ice cream (about ¾ pint)

This dessert tastes just like pie-in-a-bowl. Really good pie. It's homey and rustic (cinnamon sugar all over the place!), so think of it as a casual, not fancy, dessert. Make the crêpes and the pears ahead and the dessert will come together easily. You can even assemble the filled crepes, put them in the baking dish, and top and bake them right after dinner for a nice warm dessert with melty vanilla ice cream. Kids love this!

Heat the oven to 350°F. Lightly butter a glass pie dish or medium oval baking dish. Melt the 1 tablespoon butter in a saucepan or the microwave and stir in a big pinch of salt. In a small bowl, stir together the sugar and cinnamon.

Arrange the six crêpes on a large cutting board or other surface. Divide the pears into six equal portions. (Don't worry if the portions look small; they will be plenty.) Arrange one portion of pears on one half of each crêpe and fold the unfilled side over to form a half-moon shape. Fold the half-moon over to form a triangle. Arrange the filled crêpes, slightly over-lapping, in a circle in the pie pan or in two rows in the baking dish. Brush the melted butter over the crêpes and sprinkle them with all of the cinna-mon sugar.

Heat in the oven for 15 minutes. The crêpes will be heated through, and the cinnamon sugar will be crisp on the top. Put one small scoop of vanilla ice cream in each of six shallow dishes. Using a spatula, transfer one filled crêpe to each dish. Serve right away with both a fork and a spoon.

MAKES 10 TO 12 CRÊPES

1¼ cups whole milk

2 large eggs

1 tablespoon granulated sugar

½ teaspoon pure vanilla extract

¼ teaspoon table salt

1 cup (4½ ounces) unbleached all-purpose flour

3 tablespoons unsalted butter, melted and cooled slightly, plus more for the pan

SWEET CRÊPES

I'd forgotten how much fun it is to make crêpes until I got a hold of my friend Martha Holmberg's new crêpe cookbook last year. All of a sudden I fell in love again. The batter whips up quickly in a blender (make it ahead to let it rest), and swirling it around in a skillet is a kick. I bought a steel crêpe pan (they're not expensive) and am glad I did. A nonstick skillet works fine, too, but the crêpes cooked in it have a slightly firmer, less lacy texture.

In a blender, combine the milk, eggs, sugar, vanilla, and salt. Blend on high until well mixed. Spoon in the flour, cover, and blend again until the batter is very smooth. Add the melted butter and blend again until well combined. Transfer the batter to a 1-quart liquid measure or a small mixing bowl, cover with plastic, and refrigerate for at least 30 minutes and up to 4 hours.

Heat an 8- or 9-inch crêpe pan or small nonstick skillet over medium heat. When the pan is hot, add ½ teaspoon butter (even a little less if using a nonstick skillet) and swirl to coat the pan. Ladle a scant ¼ cup of the batter into the center of the pan, lift the pan off the heat, and swirl it around to coat the bottom of the pan evenly. Cook until the edges of the crêpe are dry

continued on p. 230 ›

› our tiny space, and in between recipe tests as well.

Thanksgiving Day arrived and we sat down to dinner in the late afternoon sun and marveled at all the food on our plate that we had raised ourselves. (Not the turkey, of course, though if we'd wanted something wild and chewy there were plenty of noisy candidates parading through our yard every day—though it is only legal to shoot them during one week in the year. As it happens, we did get a local turkey that had been pastured in the field across the street only the week before.) The prettiest thing on the table was a bowl of Roasted Beet "Jewels" with Cranberries, Toasted Pecans & Balsamic Butter (p. 205), a recipe I had developed earlier in the fall but now got a chance to make with the last of some little red and golden beets we had planted under the pole beans.

We talked about all the good stuff from the year—our regular customers who'd become so loyal, the crops that did well, the fun at the Fair. And we talked about our business plan, ›

and the bottom is lightly browned (in a lacy pattern, if using a steel pan), 1 to 1½ minutes. Lift an edge of the crêpe with a small silicone spatula, an offset spatula, or a table knife and quickly flip it over (use your fingers!). Cook until the center of the crêpe is firm, about 30 seconds. Slide the crêpe out of the skillet onto a plate. (The top side will be the pretty side; the bottom will be a bit spotty.) Let the pan rest off the heat to cool a bit.

Repeat with remaining batter, buttering the pan as necessary and adjusting the heat as necessary. Stack the crêpes on the plate as you make them. Serve warm, or let cool and refrigerate or freeze.

CINNAMON CARAMELIZED PEARS

MAKES 1¼ CUPS

2 tablespoons granulated sugar

½ teaspoon ground cinnamon

2 large firm-ripe pears (about 9 ounces each) or 3 smaller firm-ripe pears (6 ounces each)

1½ tablespoons unsalted butter

¼ teaspoon kosher salt

These easy sautéed pears are the very color of autumn itself, thanks to a generous sprinkling of cinnamon sugar and the heat of the sauté pan. Not just pretty, they taste awesome, too. Use these as a crêpe filling (p. 228), serve them alongside a crisp waffle, or just eat them straight from a bowl with a little bit of vanilla ice cream or crème fraîche.

In a small bowl, stir together the sugar and cinnamon.

Peel, halve, and core the pears. Put them cut side down on a cutting board and slice lengthwise at ¼-inch intervals. Then cut all the slices crosswise into thirds so that you have slices 1 to 1½ inches long. (You should have about 3 generous cups.)

Heat the butter in a large (12-inch) nonstick skillet over medium-high heat. Add the pear slices and the salt and cook, without stirring or flipping, for 2 minutes. Stir once (or flip gently with a spatula) and cook again for 1 to 2 minutes without stirring. Sprinkle the cinnamon sugar over all and cook, stirring occasionally, until the pear pieces are deeply colored and tender but not falling apart, 3 to 5 minutes. (The sugar will melt first and then begin to reduce and bubble, adding color and flavor to the pears.)

Remove the skillet from the heat. If making ahead, let cool and refrigerate. If using soon, leave the pears in the skillet.

Molasses Crinkles with
Honey–Vanilla Roasted Pears
and Mascarpone Cream

MOLASSES CRINKLES WITH HONEY–VANILLA ROASTED PEARS AND MASCARPONE CREAM

SERVES 6

6 Big Molasses Crinkle Cookies (p. 234)

1 cup (about ½ recipe) Whipped Ginger Mascarpone Cream (p. 64)

2 to 3 tablespoons heavy cream, if necessary

1 recipe Honey–Vanilla Roasted Pears (p. 236), at room temperature

2 to 3 teaspoons very thinly sliced (tiny matchsticks) or finely chopped crystallized ginger (optional)

Here's everything you could want in a delicious, comforting, and handsome fall dessert—a chewy cookie topped with a pillow of cream and garnished with a sublime roasted pear. These "open-faced" cookie sandwiches are fun to put together for a party—make all the components ahead, rewarm the cookies, and assemble when dessert time comes around. But you could also enjoy the cookies or the roasted pears on their own any time. So this recipe really gives you options for three or four different fall desserts.

Heat the oven to 350°F. Place the cookies on a parchment-lined baking sheet and heat for 2 to 4 minutes, or until warm and soft. Carefully transfer the cookies (a slotted spatula works well) to six dessert plates. (If they are very hot when they come out of the oven, let them cool down just a bit so that they don't rip or tear when moving. You can serve them at room temperature, too, but they will be a bit softer warmed up.)

Loosen the mascarpone cream by whisking it for a few seconds. If it is very stiff, add a little heavy cream to loosen it up a bit and to give it a billowy consistency. Using a palette knife or sandwich spreader, lightly spread about 2 tablespoons of the cream on each of the cookies, taking care not to spread all the way to the edges of the cookie, leaving a bit of a border around. (You may have extra cream.)

Arrange the pear halves on a cutting board, cut side down. Leaving the stem end intact, slice each pear lengthwise with about five cuts. Fan the pear slices out slightly, slide your knife underneath the pear, and lift each onto a cookie, gently centering the pear on top of the cream.

Garnish each dessert with a sprinkle of crystallized ginger, if desired. Serve right away with a fork.

continued on p. 234 ›

› about getting our insurance and forming our LLC, about building a new farm stand. And planning a new space for washing and packing eggs and maybe handling the vegetables, too. And how about 300 more chickens in the spring? And a separate cutting garden for flowers? Did we want to try raising meat chickens? Or get a few piglets?

Dreams kept tumbling out as we dug our forks into the flaky crust of Little Pear Crostatas (p. 224), gave Farmer a little plate of Thanksgiving goodies, and then threw on our fleecy lined jackets and mud boots to go lock up the chickens for the night. ›

The days were getting darker earlier, and we knew the long generous Indian summer was finally expiring. Soon we'd be huddled back on the couch under warm blankets, reading seed catalogues and looking at sketches of Roy's new farm stand/processing shed design. I was already envisioning a pretty little herb garden to plant in front of it.

Somewhere along the way, those questions about where we were going had been answered, without us hardly knowing it. (Though of course there were, and are, always new questions to consider.) We didn't wake up one morning and declare that we absolutely had to be farmers. We just kept doggedly pursuing something we both enjoyed and found tremendously satisfying as a ›

BIG MOLASSES CRINKLE COOKIES

MAKES 16 FOUR-INCH COOKIES

2¼ cups (10½ ounces) unbleached all-purpose flour

2 teaspoons baking soda

1 teaspoon ground cinnamon

1 teaspoon ground ginger

½ teaspoon ground cloves

Table salt

¾ cup (6 ounces 1½ sticks) unsalted butter, at room temperature

1 cup dark brown sugar

6 tablespoons granulated sugar

1 large egg

¼ cup unsulphured molasses

1 tablespoon vegetable oil

Sorry Mom, but once again I've taken liberties with one of your recipes, another childhood treat, Molasses Crinkles. I've made this version especially soft and chewy. And, well, it's grown a bit in size, too! Of course you could make a smaller-size cookie from this recipe (and you will, I guarantee you—they're that good), but for the cookie desserts (p. 233), a 4-inch cookie works best. You can make the dough 24 hours ahead (it needs to chill a bit anyway) and keep it well wrapped in the fridge. The cookies also keep well for weeks in the freezer. (You will only need 6 cookies for the pear dessert.)

In a small mixing bowl, whisk together the flour, baking soda, cinnamon, ginger, cloves, and ¼ teaspoon salt.

In the bowl of a stand mixer, combine the butter, brown sugar, 2 tablespoons of the granulated sugar, and a pinch of salt. Beat on medium speed until light and fluffy, about 1 minute. Stop the motor and scrape down the sides. Add the egg and beat on medium speed until combined. With the motor running, slowly add the molasses and the vegetable oil and beat on medium-low speed until well combined. Stop the motor and scrape down the sides. With the motor running on low, spoon in the dry ingredients gradually and mix until just combined (you'll still see some flour). Remove the bowl from the mixer and use a silicone spatula to finish gently mixing the last bits of flour into the dough. Chill the dough in the refrigerator for at least 1 hour.

Heat the oven to 375°F. Line two rimmed baking sheets with parchment. Put the remaining 4 tablespoons granulated sugar in a shallow bowl. Put out a small bowl of water. Roll the dough into big balls that are about 1½ inches (or a smidge bigger) in diameter. (To be really consistent, use a scale—each dough ball should weigh 1¾ ounces.) Dip each ball in the sugar and roll around to coat. Put each on the baking sheet. Sprinkle each dough ball with a little water. Repeat, spacing dough balls 4 to 5 inches apart on the baking sheets. (You'll get 4 to 5 cookies on a sheet pan.)

Bake until the cookies are set around the edges, slightly puffed (they will collapse as they cool), and crackled on the top, 11 to 13 minutes, rotating the baking sheets to opposite racks halfway through baking. (Smaller cookies will bake in about 10 minutes.) Let cool on the baking sheets. Repeat with the remaining dough, putting new parchment on the baking sheets.

Keep the cookies well wrapped in plastic in a zip-top bag in the freezer or well wrapped at room temperature for a day or two. To warm cookies, place on a parchment-lined baking sheet in a 350°F oven for 2 to 4 minutes.

› way of life. We never got too far ahead of ourselves, staying mostly focused on the road just up ahead. But we stayed open to the possibilities and opportunities of, well, traveling to a more exotic destination (if you can call the business of farming that!).

And now, who knows where it all will lead? All I know is that as I look out my window while I'm writing today, I see a newly plowed quarter-acre in our lower fields, and I see Roy pulling down the driveway with three piglets in the back of his truck. And our friend Joannie just dropped by with a gift of a beautiful oil painting of eggs that she would like us to hang on the new farm stand. To see us bring this old place alive gives her a lot of joy. Us, too.

HONEY–VANILLA ROASTED PEARS

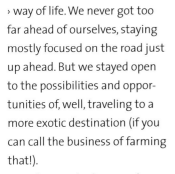

MAKES 6 ROASTED PEAR HALVES

2 tablespoons unsalted butter, plus more for baking dish

3 small firm-ripe pears (6 to 7 ounces each), peeled, halved, and cored

Kosher salt

2 tablespoons honey

1 teaspoon pure vanilla extract

Yum. These are a fall staple at the farm. We use our no-name Bartlett-look-alike pears (very sweet and delicious), but an iconic Bosc makes a lovely shape when roasted, too. I like to use pears on the smaller side for this; you'll need to extend the baking time a bit for bigger pears. Keep these on hand to serve with vanilla ice cream, or, of course, to crown the cookie dessert (p. 233). You can add a pinch of ground cardamom or other spice to the butter if you like.

Heat the oven to 450°F. Choose a 1½- to 2-quart shallow baking dish (oval is nice) that fits the pear halves comfortably but does not leave too much room around them. Butter it lightly. Arrange the pear halves, cut side up, in the baking dish. Sprinkle each with just a pinch of salt.

Melt the 2 tablespoons butter in a small saucepan over medium-low heat. Add the honey, vanilla, and a big pinch of salt. Cook, stirring, until the honey has loosened and the mixture is warm. Use a small basting brush to brush the tops of the pears with some of the honey butter.

Bake the pears for 10 minutes, baste again with some of the honey-butter (rewarmed to loosen if necessary), and bake for 10 minutes more. (If your pears are on the larger size, bake for 5 to 10 additional minutes on this side.) Gently turn the pears over, baste with some of the butter and some of the pan drippings, and cook for 15 to 20 minutes longer, basting after 5 minutes and again every couple of minutes. (When you baste, be sure to "wash" the bottom and edges of the pan with the pastry brush to prevent burning. If the pan is getting too dark, add 1 to 2 tablespoons of hot water and "wash" the pan juices again.) Cook until the pears are nicely browned all over and caramelized around the edges (you can peek underneath with a very thin spatula). Let them cool for 5 to 10 minutes in the pan and then transfer to a plate. (If you let them cool completely in the pan, the sugar will begin to harden and they may stick.) Keep well covered in the fridge for up to several days.

IF YOU'RE INTERESTED IN STARTING YOUR OWN MARKET garden—or just doing your own twist on backyard farming—there are a few structures that can make life easier. The nature of small-scale growing invites smart thinking and efficient use of materials, so you might find yourself tackling any number of projects. We've chosen four that have been particularly useful to us along the way and hope that they'll inspire you.

To make the projects most cost-effective, Roy recycles as many parts as possible from found materials (you know the saying, "one man's trash..."). There are no home centers on Martha's Vineyard, so Roy barters with the foreman at our local lumberyard, trading fresh eggs for what are called "culls": pieces of lumber that are rejected due to poor quality—though they are perfectly fine to use in our homemade structures. The cost is minimal to Roy, plus it saves the lumberyard the cost of getting them to the dump and the disposal fees.

Roy's designs are pretty straightforward, and anyone with basic skills and a few common tools can build these projects.

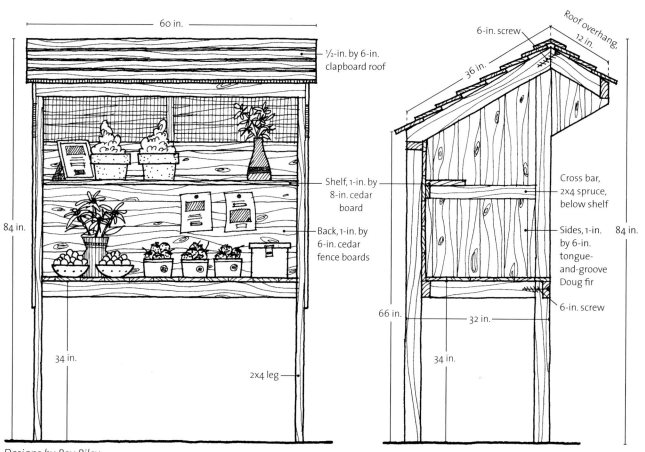

60 in.

½-in. by 6-in. clapboard roof

6-in. screw

Roof overhang, 12 in.

36 in.

Shelf, 1-in. by 8-in. cedar board

Back, 1-in. by 6-in. cedar fence boards

Cross bar, 2x4 spruce, below shelf

Sides, 1-in. by 6-in. tongue-and-groove Doug fir

6-in. screw

84 in.

84 in.

66 in.

32 in.

34 in.

34 in.

2x4 leg

Designs by Roy Riley

FRONT VIEW

CUTAWAY SIDE VIEW

FARM STAND

The materials for the original farm stand were all recycled. Roy used old clapboards for the roof (fourteen ½ in. by 6 in. by 6 ft.) and tongue-and-groove Doug fir decking for the sides and base (seven 1 in. by 6 in. by 6 ft.). He used old 1-in. by 6-in. cedar fence boards for the back, but any similar lumber would work. Everything was screwed together.

Our farm stand ended up 5 ft. wide, but depending on materials available, it could have been anywhere from 4 ft. to 6 ft. wide.

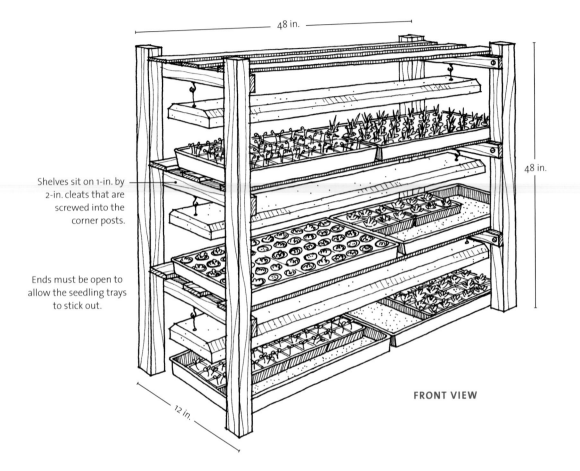

48 in.

48 in.

12 in.

Shelves sit on 1-in. by 2-in. cleats that are screwed into the corner posts.

Ends must be open to allow the seedling trays to stick out.

FRONT VIEW

SEED-STARTING SHELVING RACK

A vertical light rack saves space when you have more than a couple flats of seedlings to start. (You gain a lot of square footage by going up rather than spreading out!) This seedling light rack is made from four 2-in. by 2-in. by 4-ft. corner posts with ⅝-in. by 2-in. by 4-ft. slats. Hooks attached to the underside of the shelves allow for a shop light to hang down. The slats were predrilled with countersunk holes and screwed to the corner posts. When the seedlings move out to the garden, the unit knocks down and is stowed away until it's needed the following year.

RAISED BED WITH HOOPS

Small raised beds with a hoop frame are incredibly versatile. In the summer, covering the hoops with fabric row cover keeps greens and other veggies protected from beetles and other pests. In the shoulder seasons, the fabric adds a degree of warmth and some frost protection. The fabric can be replaced with greenhouse film in the coldest months to make a cold frame. Predrilled holes for plastic piping is a great way to keep the hoops in place.

Roy built these raised beds from 2×8 spruce. (Don't use treated lumber, as that has chemicals that will leach into the ground and your plants.) Three holes, 1¼ in. by 6 in. deep, drilled on each side, hold 1-in. plastic water line (each piece is 42 in. long) that is bent for the hoops. This bed is 24 in. wide and 8 ft. long, but you can make yours as long as you need it. We stretch the row cover over the top of the hoops and pin it down with anchor pins or hold the sides on the ground with bricks.

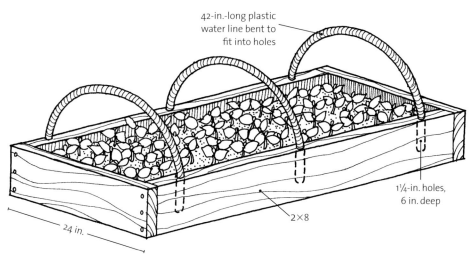

42-in.-long plastic water line bent to fit into holes

1¼-in. holes, 6 in. deep

2×8

24 in.

FRONT VIEW

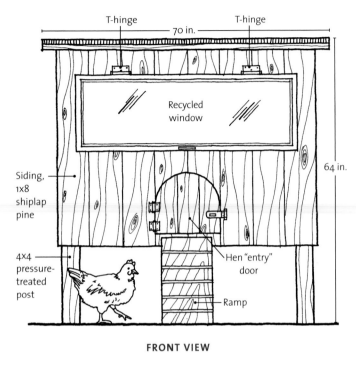

FRONT VIEW

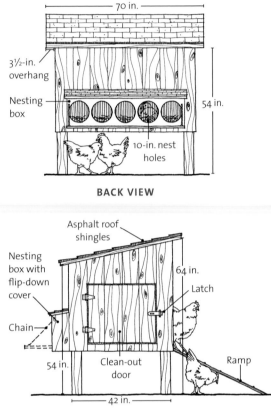

BACK VIEW

SIDE VIEW

CHICKEN COOP

Roy designed this chicken coop to hold between 8 and 12 hens, but the design can be adapted for fewer or more hens. Don't forget to include an outdoor pen located adjacent to the coop, for the ladies to wander around. Be sure the fencing around the pen is tall and strong for security reasons.

Roy built the design with 4×4 pressure-treated posts on the front and back corners. A 2×4 frame was built, with the boards used for the bottom and top plates on the front and back as well as for floor joists and rafters. A piece of ⅝-in. plywood acts as roof sheathing, which was covered with asphalt roof shingles. The exterior of the coop is 1×8 shiplap pine, which weathers to a lovely gray color. Hardware cloth is used as the "floor" of the coop.

A nest box, with individual holes, is attached to the back of the coop; a flip-down door covers the nest holes, allowing easy access to the nests when it's time to collect eggs. An old window on the front of the coop, a clean-out door attached with T-hinges on the side, and a hen "entry" door with ramp finish off the coop.

LIQUID/DRY MEASURES

U.S.	METRIC
¼ teaspoon	1.25 milliliters
½ teaspoon	2.5 milliliters
1 teaspoon	5 milliliters
1 tablespoon (3 teaspoons)	15 milliliters
1 fluid ounce (2 tablespoons)	30 milliliters
¼ cup	60 milliliters
⅓ cup	80 milliliters
½ cup	120 milliliters
1 cup	240 milliliters
1 pint (2 cups)	480 milliliters
1 quart (4 cups; 32 ounces)	960 milliliters
1 gallon (4 quarts)	3.84 liters
1 ounce (by weight)	28 grams
1 pound	454 grams
2.2 pounds	1 kilogram

OVEN TEMPERATURES

°F	GAS MARK	°C
250	½	120
275	1	140
300	2	150
325	3	165
350	4	180
375	5	190
400	6	200
425	7	220
450	8	230
475	9	240
500	10	260
550	Broil	290

RECIPE INDEX